AN EDUCATION

AN EDUCATION

HOW I CHANGED MY MIND ABOUT SCHOOLS AND ALMOST EVERYTHING ELSE

BY DIANE RAVITCH

Columbia University Press
New York

Columbia University Press
Publishers Since 1893
New York   Chichester, West Sussex
cup.columbia.edu

Copyright © 2025 Diane Ravitch
All rights reserved

Library of Congress Cataloging-in-Publication Data
Names: Ravitch, Diane, author
Title: An education : how I changed my mind about schools
and almost everything else / by Diane Ravitch.
Description: New York : Columbia University Press, [2025]
Identifiers: LCCN 2025012944 | ISBN 9780231220293 hardback |
ISBN 9780231563161 ebook
Subjects: LCSH: Ravitch, Diane | Educators—United States—Biography |
Education and state—United States | Educational change—United States |
LCGFT: Autobiographies
Classification: LCC LA2317.R295 A3 2025 | DDC 353.8092
[B]—dc23/eng/20250613
LC record available at https://lccn.loc.gov/2025012944

Printed in the United States of America

Cover design: Noah Arlow
Cover image: Shutterstock

GPSR Authorized Representative: Easy Access System Europe,
Mustamäe tee 50, 10621 Tallinn, Estonia, gpsr.requests@easproject.com

I DEDICATE THIS BOOK TO THOSE
I LOVE AND HAVE LOVED:

MY WIFE MARY

MY SONS JOE, MICHAEL, AND STEVEN

MY GRANDSONS NICO, AIDAN,
ELIJAH, AND ASHER

MY EX-HUSBAND RICHARD

A foolish consistency is the hobgoblin of little minds, adored by little statesmen and philosophers and divines.

—RALPH WALDO EMERSON, "SELF-RELIANCE"

CONTENTS

INTRODUCTION
1

1 CHILDHOOD
8

2 FAMILY
16

3 SCHOOL IN HOUSTON
39

4 WELLESLEY
48

5 MARRIAGE
62

6 *THE NEW LEADER*
69

CONTENTS

7 DOMESTICITY AND TRAGEDY
75

8 IN SEARCH OF A CAREER
85

9 MOTHERHOOD AND CAREER
92

10 SCHOLARSHIP AND A SHOCKING DEVELOPMENT
103

11 A NEW LIFE
120

12 INSIDE THE GEORGE H. W. BUSH ADMINISTRATION
130

13 BACK TO NEW YORK CITY
143

14 DISILLUSIONMENT SETS IN
159

15 REFORMING MY VIEWS
177

16 ACTIVISM
206

FINAL WORDS
218

Acknowledgments 225

AN EDUCATION

INTRODUCTION

This is a book about my life, about admitting "I was wrong," and about how important it is to say it out loud. For many years, I advocated strongly for certain ideas in the field of education based on competition, standardization, and accountability. I felt sure such policies would produce higher test scores. But when I saw what happened after they were put into practice, I discovered that they didn't work and had bad consequences for students, teachers, and communities. I was wrong. I admitted I was wrong. I said it in writing and in public. In our opinionated and polarized world, people don't do that. But I realized the importance of admitting error, of keeping an open mind and regularly looking at evidence, of listening to people with whom I disagreed. I not only changed my mind and admitted that I was wrong, but I also revised my outlook on education, politics, and social issues. My thinking evolved into a different political and social philosophy. To use current parlance, I went from being a staunch conservative to being "woke." There are many people who are far more "woke" than I am, for sure. I am still a traditionalist in many spheres of life, such as decorum, public behavior, and respect for most norms. I oppose violence and hatred. I don't approve of hiring people solely because of their race, gender, ethnicity, or sexual orientation. I do believe that workplaces and educational institutions should seek qualified, diverse staff and students.

If they seek, they will find. There are many ways to be successful at the work you choose. When I saw Michael Phelps racking up gold medals at the Olympics, I wondered (but not seriously), "What were his SAT scores?" I had the same reaction to the incredible feats of Simone Biles and to the brilliant accomplishments of artists, musicians, actors, and many others who achieved success in fields that had no connection to the ability to find the right answer to a multiple-choice question. I expect that even geniuses like Albert Einstein would have produced low test scores because of their wild, unconventional, and unpredictable ways of thinking. I still believe in standards, but not so much in standardized testing, which has built-in biases and is best at measuring family income, family education, and the ability to answer questions on standardized tests. I believe in judging people by their experience, their integrity, their capability, and their character. What would it mean to be "not woke"? Uncaring, heartless, indifferent to the suffering and needs of others? That's not me. That's not who I want to be.

I believe in telling the truth to the best of one's ability and pursuing justice. I wish to see our society eliminate poverty and ensure that everyone has a decent life. A good nation would not permit people to die on the street because they can't afford food or housing or medical care. I am puzzled by people who say they are Christians yet rail against those who are "woke." I believe that the Jesus of the New Testament was woke. Although I am a Jew, my views are aligned with his: feed the hungry, tend to the sick, comfort the afflicted, clothe the naked, give drink to the thirsty, welcome the stranger. Help the most vulnerable among us. That's my definition of woke.

The changes in my worldview are real and deep. Old friends wonder what happened to me. New friends have asked me repeatedly, "How did this happen?" In this book, I try to explain. I try to recapture my childhood in Houston, before air-conditioning, before television, before the Internet, a time when I was a barefoot girl in a big family, shaped by family, schools, and circumstances. This is also the story of how I became a public intellectual, an actor on the national stage. I hope it can be helpful to others, especially to young people seeking to find their way in a world of masks and artifice.

I began life in Houston as part of a large, rambunctious, and disorganized family that was struggling to maintain a secure middle-class status or at least the appearance of one. I was third of eight children, five boys and three girls. Early on, I was taught that boys would grow up to have a job or a business or a career to support their family, and that girls would grow up to marry and have children. I wanted to marry and have children, but I also wanted to do something more.

I sought to find a path to a different life. I didn't know what it would be, but somehow I knew it would rely on words, on reading, writing, and thinking. I counted on using my brain to get ahead, excelled in my local public schools, and was eventually accepted by an outstanding eastern women's college, one that no one in my family had ever heard of. Education was my path to a new life with new opportunities. I was raised in a racist, conservative milieu, but I considered myself a liberal, a true-blue Democrat. My parents always voted for the Democratic candidate; they loved Franklin Delano Roosevelt and credited him with ending the Depression. My parents were less racist than most white people in Houston back then; we children were never allowed to say the N word. But they were racist. Racism and segregation were deeply embedded in the culture around them. They expected that Black people would never enter the house through the front door, and they were never disturbed by the fact that Black people were not allowed to go to the same movie theaters, schools, or restaurants as white people. Is it "woke" to look back on that era with a sense of shame? I do.

Immediately after college, I married a man from a prestigious family in New York City who was successful in business and civic affairs. I began to write about education in newspapers and small magazines. I championed the values that I had grown up with and believed in: meritocracy, standardized testing, color blindness, and high academic standards. Those, I thought, represented fairness, in contrast to the racism that I had seen. I believed in traditional marriage and family values and tried to live accordingly. My sons attended an elite private school in New York City. I opposed as divisive such policies as affirmative action, bilingual education, and special studies for racial and ethnic groups. I believed in teaching everyone the common culture to which we all belonged, which in my youth did not include anyone but Great White Men. I opposed the Equal Rights Amendment as unnecessary and scorned the women's movement as shrill. I did not smoke marijuana or use any other illegal drugs. I did not like hippies, especially men with long hair. I was appalled by the Weather Underground and the Students for a Democratic Society, for both their radicalism and their political violence. I applauded the civil rights movement and attended the March on Washington in 1963, but I abhorred the Black Panthers and the radicalism of Stokely Carmichael and SNCC. I admired Dr. Martin Luther King Jr. but was concerned that Malcolm X would provoke violence. I opposed the war in Vietnam but never joined any protests. I thought of myself as an old-fashioned Democrat, the kind who supported Franklin Delano Roosevelt and Lyndon B. Johnson. I believed that American society was making steady progress and that in time we would work out all our social and economic problems, step by step, day by day. I was a patriot who never questioned my country and its leaders. My complacency was a reflection of my comfort and affluence; radicalism had no appeal to me. If I were to meet that version of myself today, we would have a vigorous argument over everything related to education, race, and politics, although I still abhor violence. Today I want change, demonstrable change that narrows the gap between rich and poor; that provides equal opportunity to all; and that ensures health care and good education as a matter of right, not income. I am still not a radical. I don't want to overthrow the government. I want it to work on behalf of its ideals to benefit everyone.

My life took a sharp turn in the mid-1980s. After a quarter century of marriage, during which I raised two sons, lost one son to leukemia, and launched a career as a historian and writer, I left my marriage and took a plunge into a new world as the partner of the woman I loved. I continued to be a prominent conservative writer and scholar of education, though I no longer spoke out on behalf of traditional family values.

For decades, I wrote many articles expressing conservative views in *The New York Times, The Wall Street Journal, Commentary, The American Scholar*, and many other publications. I published books about education policy and received honorary degrees. I was a founding member of the board of the Thomas B. Fordham Foundation, which grew into one of the nation's most influential conservative think tanks. I was an advocate for school choice, accountability, and standardized testing. I served in the administration of President George H. W. Bush, where I supported academic standards, accountability, and standardized testing. While serving in the Bush administration, surrounded by proponents of school choice, I decided that government aid to private and religious colleges—as in the GI Bill—set a precedent for government aid to private and religious schools; I occasionally advocated for vouchers. At one point, I wrote an article in *The Washington Post* (with William Galston) endorsing vouchers on a trial basis, but only to be used in Catholic schools (how silly we were, as vouchers cannot be restricted to one faith but must be available on an equal basis to the schools of all religions). After the Bush administration ended, I was invited to work at the Brookings Institution, where I wrote a book about national standards and a stirring appeal for vouchers called "Somebody's Children," asserting that vouchers would rescue the poorest children from the lowest-performing schools. Following my stint in government, I resumed my board membership at the Thomas B. Fordham Foundation and joined other conservative think tanks, including the Koret Task Force at the Hoover Institution and the Manhattan Institute, where I was allied with like-minded supporters of school choice and high-stakes testing.

By the 1990s, I was well-entrenched in right-wing circles, though I never was invited into the inner sanctums of right-wing billionaires like the Koch brothers, the DeVos family, and the other powerful people promoting privatization of all things public. At the time, I was unaware of them or of the American Legislative Exchange Council (ALEC), which developed model laws for state legislators to advance the same goals.

Despite my decades of immersion in conservative circles, I experienced an intellectual and emotional epiphany when I was in my late sixties, certainly late in life for such a transformation. I struggled with my beliefs and ultimately moved philosophically and politically from right to left. Whereas once I championed test-based meritocracy as a just reward for intellect, I became a critic of the underlying social structures and educational practices that had made me (and others like me) privileged. I became acutely conscious of and outraged by racism, sexism, homophobia, and xenophobia. Whereas I was once repelled by the term *white privilege*, I began to understand that I benefited from it. Whereas I was for many years a vocal defender of standardized testing, I became an outspoken critic of it. Despite years of arguing on behalf of school choice, I became a fervent advocate for public schools and an equally fervent opponent of public funding of privately managed charter schools, as well as public funding of private and religious schools. I reaffirmed my belief in separation of church and state in K-12 schools. Whereas I had previously supported charter schools and even testified on their behalf before an education committee of the New York State legislature in 1998, I now saw them as a step toward the privatization of public schools and a prelude to vouchers. I adopted a straightforward principle: public funding for public schools, not for privately managed schools and certainly not for religious schools. Ironically, in 2023, Christina Pushaw, the communications director for Florida governor Ron DeSantis, launched a Twitter attack on me because I had sent my own children to private school half a century earlier; the story was treated as hot news by Rupert Murdoch's *New York Post*, FOX News, and even the *Daily Mail* in England. "Hypocrite," Pushaw cried, and the media echoed her scolding. My response: "Well, Christine, it was sixty years ago, and I went along with family tradition. We paid for it. People have a right to make a choice, but they don't have the right to expect government to pay for their private choices."

My conservative friends were baffled when I switched sides. Some who did not know me speculated that I had moved from right to left because I had been bought off (by the teachers' unions, of course). That was ridiculous; my views are not for sale. In this book, I retrace my unusual journey. Perhaps my experience is sui generis. I was certainly not part of a wave of defections from conservativism to liberalism. I became "woke," and I wear the label with pride. To me, it means that I awakened to the inequity and injustice that deprives millions of people of a good life, the life that everyone wants and deserves. I wish everyone would embrace these values. Perhaps the lesson I offer is to keep thinking and learning, to anticipate the possibility of uncertainty based on new facts, new insights, to be willing to change as facts change, and to cling ferociously to your integrity, but not your opinions. In 1977, when the eminent educator Robert Hutchins died, the obituary in *The New York Times* ended with this admonition by him: "We have to learn to live with those whose opinions differ from our own. After all, they may turn out to be right." I kept that clipping in my wallet for many years, but for three decades I didn't realize that it was intended for me.

1

CHILDHOOD

I was born on July 1, 1938, at 12:01 a.m. at St. Joseph's Hospital in Houston, Texas. That night, my father was at the professional boxing matches. He loved sports, and he loved to watch boxers beating each other up. When my mother went into labor, her younger sister Rosalie took her to the hospital; their parents lived in Houston but neither of them knew how to drive a car. I was the third child in the family, which over sixteen years grew to include eight children. My older brother David was born in 1932. Then came Adele (1934), me (1938), Jules (1941), Robert (1942), Sylvia (1944), Sandy (1946), and the youngest, Michael Moses (called M. M.), born in 1949.

The name on my birth certificate was Diane Rose Silverstein, but by the time I entered kindergarten five years later, my name was Diane Rose Silvers. Apparently, my parents changed our name to sound less Jewish, although they never denied being Jewish. My father often told us that no matter what you call yourself, the rest of the world will always call you a Jew.

We lived in a small white frame house at 2109 Huldy Street. I know this house only from photographs of me and my older sister and brother. In one of them, I was about four years old, and we were holding little American flags; our nation was at war, and our family was patriotic. In another, I am looking at the camera intently, seriously; directly behind me is my sister Adele, hanging upside down on a trapeze, shirtless. In those days, not all families had cameras. There are very few surviving photographs of my earliest years. When I was a teenager, one of my prized possessions was a boxy Brownie Hawkeye, but I don't have any photographs that I took. Our entire family sat for an annual picture, in which a professional photographer took a portrait of all of us, dressed in our best clothes and smiling. In one of them, I had a cut on my chin, a barrette was in my straight hair to keep it off my face, and my legs were crossed, like a boy. Although I was wearing a dress for the family portrait, I usually wore blue jeans. I was a tomboy, and I never cared much about clothes or looks. I grew taller than my older sister Adele, and I always felt awkward and ungainly.

During World War II, we moved to a two-story brick house at 1314 Richmond Road, a big step up from the little frame house on Huldy Street. My earliest memories are associated with living in that house. The family was growing, and we needed space.

The house on Richmond Road had a screened-in porch on the side, where we sat on hot evenings to get an occasional breeze. During the summer in Houston, it was always hot and oppressively humid. There was no air-conditioning, not in houses or cars or stores. One very hot night, I fell asleep on the outdoor sofa. When I awakened in the middle of the night, the doors were locked, leaving me outside alone. As one of eight children, I was always afraid that I would be forgotten because there were so many of us: that I would be locked out, and no one would notice; that I would not be picked up after school, because no one remembered me. It happened more than once. Strangely, today I enjoy being alone because it gives me time to think, to read, to write. But as a child, I had both the fear of being neglected and a desperate need to carve out time and space that belonged to me, not the collective family.

Being one of eight and third in line was an important factor in my development. We competed with one another. We teased each other. Each of us tried to find something to make us stand out from the crowd. Sometimes I felt that we were eight strangers who happened to live in the same house. I didn't really know my older brother David. My older sister Adele was obsessed with clothes, an obsession I did not share. I was the only one who loved books. Of my seven siblings, I was closest to my youngest brothers: Robert (Bobby), Sandy, and M. M., probably because I was expected to take care of them. Jules was closest to me in age, but he enjoyed playing dumb, talking like a hillbilly, and saying "ain't." I think he did it to annoy me. In my large family, I often felt lonely. When I read a book and liked it, there was no one to talk to about it. My father liked to read "true crime" magazines and news about sports; my mother didn't have time to read anything. My siblings had their own interests. Most of the time, I was on my own.

The house on Richmond Road was a child's paradise. The backyard had a large pecan tree that dropped hundreds and hundreds of pecans each year. We would collect them, pull the husks off, shell them, and eat them. There were never more delicious pecans than those we picked up in the backyard. Behind the backyard was a stand of bamboo, and behind the bamboo was an orchard where my father planted fig trees and other fruit trees. We kids would sometimes cut a piece of bamboo and smoke it; the bamboo was hollow and made a good replica of a cigarette, albeit with no flavor. To one side of the orchard was a pergola, an open wooden structure covered with wisteria vines so strong and thick that we kids could climb up the vines and sit on top, surrounded and hidden by the beautiful purple blooms. No one could see us, but they could surely hear us as we sang songs and gave our best Tarzan yells. People would call from blocks away to complain to our parents about our imitations of Johnny Weissmuller's yodel.

To the side of the pergola was a chicken house, a flimsy wooden structure about 12 feet by 12 feet. It contained tall chicken coops (cages) where the chickens hatched their eggs. I have no idea how anyone knew which chickens were pregnant and about to lay eggs. The glass windows on each side of the building were hinged at the bottom. When I was nine years old, my younger brother Jules and I went into the chicken house to run around, stamp our feet, and generally make as much noise as we could. One of the hinged windows came loose and crashed over my head. The blood came streaming down my face, and I couldn't see. Jules, who was six years old, started crying; he was crying so hard that he couldn't run for help. When I got to the house, my mother picked the pieces of glass out of my head and my hair, then took me to the hospital to get stitches. I still have the scar, under my hair, just above my forehead.

There was yet another yard behind the one with the orchard, the pergola, and the chicken house. The last yard was fenced in, and it contained chickens and a wooden shack for my father's hobby, his homing pigeons. I never understood what he liked about pigeons and saw nothing endearing about them. He loved his pigeons, just like the guys in the film *On the Waterfront* who kept homing pigeons on the roofs of their tenement apartments. I understood the reason for the chickens. They were a ready supply of fresh eggs and food for our large family. But the pigeons just flew around and came back.

Once my daddy kept someone's horse in the fenced area for a few weeks. Now, that was exciting! I loved the horse. I loved grooming it and stroking it. I longed to have a horse of my own. Somewhere I found a wooden bookend in the shape of a horse's head, and I clung to that bookend. I slept with the bookend. I read the classified ads in the morning *Houston Post* and the evening *Houston Press* and *Houston Chronicle*, scanning the "horses for sale" ads. I would run to my father and say, "Daddy, look, there is a horse for sale for only $300! Please, please, can I have a horse?" My daddy would laugh and say no, but I didn't give up, not until we moved to a different house with a regular backyard where there was no possibility of keeping a horse.

We always had dogs, usually more than one at a time. They lived in the house with us. At different times, we had dalmatians, cocker spaniels, bulldogs, terriers, and mutts. My father's favorite dog was a bulldog named Mike who was his constant companion. One day, Mike went under the house on Richmond Road and ate rat poison and died a terrible death. My father grieved as if Mike were a child. He stayed in bed for three days crying over Mike's death. Many years later, I realized that Mike had swallowed warfarin, a rat poison also known as Coumadin that was prescribed to me as a blood thinner many years later, when I had a blood clot. If you take too much, your internal organs burst, which is what happened to Mike. To this day, like the rest of my family, I love, love, love dogs and have never been without one.

To one side of the house on Richmond Road was the main office of the telephone company, which had a large parking lot where we learned to ride our bicycles on weekends, when the lot was empty. To the other side, behind a thick hedge, was the Convent of the Good Shepherd, where nuns took care of pregnant girls. Sometimes we would peer through the hedges and spy on the girls, who played games like ring-around-a-rosy as if they were small children.

Other than when we went to school or shopping, we went barefoot. When we were home, there was no need for shoes. Until I was ten or eleven, I usually went shirtless at home because it was so hot. One day one of my father's bossy older sisters was visiting from Georgia, and she saw me barefoot and shirtless, and she said sharply, in her loud, guttural voice, "Put a halter on that girl! That's disgraceful!" And that ended my shirtless days.

One of my greatest regrets was that I never learned to play a musical instrument. It wasn't my mother's fault. She sent me to the neighborhood piano teacher, Mrs. Colish, for lessons. The lessons were no fun at all. I started skipping piano lessons so I could join the boys after school and play baseball, hardball or softball. A proud tomboy, I could dive headfirst into any base, and I could climb trees higher than my siblings. Mrs. Colish complained to my mother that I was skipping lessons, but it was useless. I wouldn't go, and I have paid for my obstinance for the rest of my life. My mother never gave up on her efforts to turn me into a lady. She sent me to ballet school, but that didn't last long. In high school, she enrolled me in modeling school, which was a waste of my time and her money. My mother wanted me to have the opportunities that she never had as a girl in Bessarabia or as a teenager in Houston. Her father was a tailor, and her parents never had spare money for any sort of lessons.

On Saturdays, the biggest event of the week was going to the Delman Theater on Main Street for the Saturday morning kiddie movies. Admission was 9 cents. There were cartoons, followed by a short "March of Time" feature where we learned about what was happening in the rest of the world. It was like seeing CNN for 10 minutes, but only once a week. Every week, the news was followed by a serial about a character like Superman or Dick Tracy, each new episode bringing new thrills and adventures and leaving viewers eager to learn what happened next, which would not be revealed until the next week. And then came a feature film, perhaps an Abbott and Costello or Tarzan or Superman movie. Quite a bargain for 9 cents. During intermissions, there was usually a contest; I remember winning a Duncan yo-yo contest, after spending hours waxing my yo-yo string.

Many years later, I was lying in bed with my eight-year-old grandson Elijah when he asked me what was the most embarrassing thing that had ever happened to me. I told him about a time when I was his age and I was waiting to go into the Delman. I arrived too early to enter, so I went to the toy store next door and looked at the items in the display case. The woman behind the counter began asking me questions and showing me things, thinking I was a real customer. I suddenly realized I had to pee, but I was too embarrassed to tell her. Suddenly, I felt hot pee going down my legs, and I was humiliated. I had to run home and change clothes. Elijah thought that was one of the funniest stories he had ever heard. He called me "Grandma Pee-Pee Pants."

I have vivid memories of the Second World War, which ended in 1945, when I was seven. In Houston, we had frequent blackouts, when everyone all over the city turned off their lights and stayed as quiet as possible while the air raid sirens blared. Houston never experienced an actual air raid, but we were prepared. Everyone knew that the military needed all the metal it could get to make bombs and bullets and airplanes and tanks, so we saved metal, even the metal foil wrapping paper on every stick of spearmint gum, and donated it to the war effort. The most prized possession at that time for children was Fleer's Double Bubble Gum, even though it was wrapped in paper. From time to time, an aunt or uncle would turn up with a box of fifty pieces, and that was unimaginable good fortune, to be shared with friends. The ability to blow a very large bubble and to suck it in before it exploded on your face was a much-admired skill. At school, we sang patriotic songs, and it seemed that everyone in the country was united in the war against the Nazis and Japanese. My uncle Herman (married to my mother's sister Rosalie) served in the South Pacific in the army; my father was too old (thirty-eight) and had too many children to be drafted.

It was so hot in Houston in the summer that my parents sometimes rented a house near the Gulf of Mexico in Galveston, an hour's drive away. Galveston had a busy amusement park with a Ferris wheel and many other rides and attractions. It had sandy beaches and long, covered piers that stretched far into the water, where you could buy souvenirs—like a conch shell that had the sound of the sea when you put it up to your ear—or rent a bathing suit and a locker for your clothes. My grandparents did not own bathing suits; they rented them and changed in the dressing rooms on the pier when they came to visit. When you went into the salty water of the Gulf of Mexico, there were big waves, in which you could bodysurf or get knocked over by the waves, hit the hard, sandy bottom, and come up gasping for air. Invariably, when you left the water, you had tar on your feet because of discharges from tankers. The lifeguards kept a jug of solvent to remove the tar. I assumed that every beach in the world had tar in the water and on the beach. Jellyfish were ever-present in the Gulf waters, and my worst Galveston memory was being up to my neck in the water and seeing a big blue jellyfish with long tentacles just a few feet away from me. I tried to get away from it, but I couldn't move fast enough. I seemed to have lead blocks on my feet. Soon the jellyfish was wrapping its tentacles around my legs, and I suffered severe stings. That was a genuine waking-life nightmare, and for years I experienced that nightmare again and again, that sense of helplessness in the face of inescapable danger.

One of the long piers had a nightclub at the end, called the Balinese Club, where there was gambling, dancing, and drinking. Gambling was illegal, and the Texas Rangers would arrive periodically in search of criminal activity. By the time the Rangers reached the end of the pier, where the casino was located, all evidence of gambling would have disappeared into the floor or walls. My parents liked to go there for a night on the town. The house on the corner of our block was owned by the Maceo family, which owned the Balinese Club. The scuttlebutt was that Mr. Maceo was a big wheel in the Mafia. The Maceo house had air-conditioning when no one else did. Recently I searched online for Sam Maceo (aka Salvatore Maceo), and lo and behold, he was described as "a businessman, community leader, and organized crime boss in Galveston." He had as much power and influence as elected officials, maybe more, and helped develop the Las Vegas Strip. He and his brother turned Galveston into a resort town with its own red-light district. I never met the Maceos, nor did I ever enter their palatial home. We had no air-conditioning, just the breezes from the Gulf of Mexico.

We spent the summer of 1945 in Galveston. There was a prisoner of war camp not far from the house we rented. The prisoners were German boys, mostly blond and blue-eyed, probably young kids of eighteen or nineteen. We would stand at the fence and jeer, calling them names and spitting at them. I'm not proud of that, but at the time it seemed like the right thing to do. We were in Galveston on V-J Day, and the streets were filled with people celebrating. Many sailors were in town on leave, and everyone was in the streets, laughing, cheering, dancing, hugging, kissing, and setting off firecrackers.

After the Second World War, there was a great demand for new houses and plenty of government financing for homes for veterans. My father built tract houses on the empty land behind our chicken yard. One day, I took my younger brothers Jules and Bobby exploring, and we prowled around the construction site. We poked into unfinished houses and probed every mysterious container. By the time we came home, my brothers were covered in tar. My mother wanted to give me a good whipping. I climbed a tree and hid out until the storm was over. Usually, when I misbehaved, she hit me on my legs with the back of a hairbrush or a switch cut from the hedges; it stung a lot. My father often threatened, "I'm going to take my belt off" when one of us got into trouble, but he never did.

I learned about honesty as a child. My mother never tired of reminding us that our most important possession was our good name, and we must never, never, never compromise it (I can't say that every one of us followed her advice). I had a life lesson at a young age. One Mother's Day, I wanted to get my mother something special. I didn't have any money. I went to the local drugstore, where the owner knew each one of us. When I thought no one was looking, I picked up a bottle of my mother's favorite cologne, stuck it in my pocket, sauntered out, and went home, about two blocks away. By the time I got there, a few minutes later, my mother was waiting, and she was fuming. The pharmacist had seen me and called her at once. Although she was generally soft-spoken, she yelled at me and told me to never steal, never lie, ever again! She made me take the bottle of cologne right back and apologize. I probably did get a good whipping. And I learned an unforgettable lesson about the importance of honesty.

2

FAMILY

We never learned about our family history before the lives of our grandparents. My parents' attitude was that what happened in Europe was left behind in Europe. My mother had no nostalgia for the old country, and my father had never been there. Europe to them meant anti-Semitism, pogroms, and the Holocaust. No matter what problems they faced here, they loved America. When I asked my father about his family history, he would say, "My family was in iron and steel. My mother took in ironing and my father stole." That was the kind of corny humor he specialized in.

This much I knew. My father's father and mother were born in Lomza, Poland. Nearly half the population of this town was Jewish in the mid-nineteenth century; although the Jewish community was an important part of the local economy, anti-Semitism flourished; Jews were periodically expelled, then allowed to return. My grandparents were lucky to get out in the mid-nineteenth century. The entire Jewish community of Lomza was later murdered by the Nazis. My grandfather left Lomza for America as a boy in the late 1850s. Many years later, I visited Poland and met a teacher from Lomza. When she learned that my family had ties to her home, she took my address and sent me photographs of the Jewish cemetery. All the headstones were broken and overturned. Some of them must have belonged to my family.

I never knew my father's parents, who died long before I was born. I don't know anything at all about my paternal grandmother, other than that she too came from Lomza. My father's father immigrated to America at the age of fourteen or fifteen and settled in Savannah, Georgia. He went to work for a grocery store owned by a man named Silverstein, and he took on the owner's name. Thus my name at birth (Silverstein) was not my real name.

Two years after my grandfather arrived in Savannah, the Civil War broke out, and young David Silverstein was recruited into the Confederate Army. From the few surviving photographs I have seen of him, he must have been a small, skinny boy, not much of a soldier. As an immigrant who barely spoke English, he likely wondered whether it was such a great idea to leave Poland for a country about to go to war. Nonetheless, he survived the war, was duly discharged, and my older sister has a certificate showing that he qualified for benefits as an indigent veteran of the Confederate Army. Very few people can say, as I can, that their grandfather served in the Civil War. But it is true.

After the Civil War, he returned to Lomza to find his bride, Annie Cooley, and brought her back to America. My grandparents in Savannah had eight daughters and, at long last, a son, my father. My father was born in 1903, when his father was in his late fifties. I was told that my paternal grandfather worked as a butcher at the commissary on Henry Ford's plantation in Georgia and that Ford fired him when he learned he was Jewish. Ford, of course, was notorious for his anti-Semitism. He had famously distributed the virulently anti-Semitic *Protocols of the Elders of Zion*. However, after I did some research, I became convinced that my grandfather never ran the commissary on Ford's plantation. This was a family myth. One website said that Henry Ford's personal butcher was Jewish—and I thought, aha!—that must have been David Silverstein! But Ford purchased the land for his Georgia plantation in the 1920s, and my grandfather died in 1920. By the time the commissary was open, my grandfather was dead.

What I do know about my grandfather is that he owned a kosher butcher shop located in Savannah's historic City Market Square. My cousin Alice Gerber took me there when I visited Savannah in the 1990s.

It was not a business in which one could get rich, but it gave him a living to support his large family of many daughters and one very spoiled son.

When I visited Savannah, Cousin Alice took me to the modern-day descendant of the synagogue my father's family had attended in the early twentieth century. There was a class picture, in which I recognized my father, a skinny kid of thirteen. He had a reputation as a scamp, a kid who was always getting into trouble. He didn't finish high school. In his era, that was not unusual. He would have been sixteen in 1919, the year that my mother got off the boat from Europe as a ten-year-old. What my father remembered most vividly about his childhood was what he heard about the lynching of Leo Frank.

Leo Frank was born in Texas to a Jewish family. He earned a degree in mechanical engineering at Cornell University. At age thirty-one, he became the superintendent of a pencil factory in Atlanta. When a thirteen-year-old girl, Mary Phagan, was found strangled and murdered in the basement of the factory in 1913, Frank was arrested and eventually convicted of her murder based on the testimony of a man who was also a suspect. Frank was sentenced to die. The governor of Georgia concluded that the evidence was insufficient to convict Frank and commuted his sentence. A mob in Marietta, Georgia, the hometown of the girl, decided to take justice into their own hands, and they took Leo Frank from his jail cell and lynched him. That was 1915. My daddy was then twelve. He said that every Jew in Georgia knew about the Leo Frank case. It attracted national attention. Leo Frank was wrongly convicted and lynched because he was a Jew. A month after Leo Frank was lynched, the Ku Klux Klan reassembled after years of inactivity and burned a cross on Stone Mountain, near Atlanta, to announce their revival of terrorism on behalf of white supremacy.

My father remembered the virulent anti-Semitism and the constant undercurrent of menace during his youth. He was also keenly aware of white hatred toward Blacks in Georgia, where fear and violence were always simmering below the surface and often right out in the open. Decades later, when I was growing up in Houston, Blacks in the South were expected to be deferential toward whites, even poor whites. If a white person approached a Black person while walking, the Black person was expected to step off the sidewalk and onto the street. Blacks never addressed a white person by his or her first name, and whites addressed Blacks only by their first name. They never entered a white person's house through the front door. Racial segregation was rigidly enforced by law and by custom throughout the South. In the grocery stores, the water fountains were labeled "white" and "colored." In the public buses, there was a little movable tag that said "colored," and it would be moved depending on how many white people were on the bus. Blacks had to go to the back of the bus, behind the marker, so that every white person got a seat, even if Blacks were standing. Schools, movie houses, hotels, restaurants—all public and private facilities—were racially segregated.

My daddy told me about postcards that he had seen when he was a boy, showing pictures of Blacks who had been lynched, hanging from a tree. No matter how brutal, the lynchings often attracted a crowd of hundreds or thousands of spectators who came to be entertained by the violence. These obscene visuals contained an implicit warning about the danger of disrupting the racist social order.

The lesson he drew from the violence was that Jews should not express their views on political subjects. The best way to stay out of trouble was to stay silent, to keep your head down. He was not immune to the racism in which he had grown up. He was a racist. He liked the Black people he knew, but he never considered them his equals. He knew that there was a racial and religious hierarchy, and that Jews and Catholics were just one notch above Blacks. Speak up too much, and you would put yourself in danger, like Leo Frank, although Leo Frank seems never to have said anything at all to anger the mob. It was just dangerous to be Jewish.

My father was nicknamed "Cracker" because he came from Georgia and considered himself a Georgia cracker. He spoke with a Geechee accent, also known as Gullah. He had a gravelly voice with a southern accent. Ironically, his language and manner of speaking were derived from that of the African Americans who lived on the Sea Islands near the Georgia–South Carolina coastline. But he did not know this. Everyone in his family in Savannah spoke that way.

He wasn't interested in school. He wanted to be a performer in vaudeville. He and a school friend named Lily Wise teamed up to create an act called "The Wise Crackers." He sang, danced soft shoe, and told jokes. She played Gracie Allen to his George Burns. It must have been a flop because he soon became a traveling salesman. When I was twelve, my parents brought their three oldest children to visit New York City, and I met Lily Wise. She was running a business, manufacturing ladies' blouses, with her name on the label. She gave me a blouse. I remember the two of them reminiscing about their efforts to break into vaudeville. From him, I learned to love Beatrice Kay, Eddie Cantor, Al Jolson, and other entertainers of his era. We had their records and played them often. Beatrice Kaye's rendition of "Mention My Name" is still one of my favorite songs.

My parents met when he was a traveling salesman. On his travels, he passed through Houston, where he met Anna Celia Katz. He was twenty-six. She was twenty. My mother was a stunning blue-eyed blonde, working as an usher in a movie house. She was petite, soft-spoken, and shy. She was meticulous about the way she dressed and aimed to look her best on her meager earnings. My dad was a handsome rogue with a tiny moustache and slicked-down black hair. They fell in love and were married in 1930.

My mother was born in Bessarabia. Bessarabia no longer exists. It is now part of Moldova, a tiny country between Romania and Ukraine. From my mother's accounts, Bessarabia was an awful place for Jews. The countries on either side took turns trampling little Bessarabia, and Jews were often a target of marauding gangs. My mother was born in 1909 in Balti. She had a younger brother Isadore (Itzy) and a younger sister Edith. Itzy died of diphtheria at a young age. Her grandfather owned a bakery. When Cossacks on horseback came rampaging through Balti, my mother told me, the women and children of the family hid under the floorboards of the bakery. Her family and the Jewish community lived in fear of the next raid.

She told me that as a little girl, she went walking in the countryside near Balti and found a little hut that "the Christians" had set up. She wanted to see what was inside. She knocked over the unlit candles. Fifty years later, she told the story to me in a whisper. She was embarrassed and ashamed of what she had done. Maybe she was still afraid. I sensed a certain satisfaction at this small act of rebellion.

Her father Gerson Katz left for America in 1913 and arrived at Ellis Island. He eventually wound up in Houston, Texas, sent there by a New York–based Jewish philanthropic society that resettled Jews away from the Northeast to prevent the creation of new ghettos. When he got to Houston, he set about learning English and worked as a tailor.

Gerson Katz, my zadie, saved up enough money to send for his family to join him in Houston. In 1914, he sent them tickets to travel to New York City on the German-American shipping line. My grandmother Brana (who later Americanized her name to Bertha) spoke only Yiddish; she and her two daughters set out on the journey to America. From Balti, they traveled to a town on the Black Sea, where they boarded a ship to Constantinople. There they changed ships and sailed on to Marseille. When they got to Marseille, they learned that their tickets on the German-American line were no good. France was at war with Germany, and they were stranded in Marseille. My grandmother was on her own, with two little girls, very little money, and no language skills other than Yiddish. When the money ran out, my grandmother put the children in a Jewish orphanage and found work as a scrubwoman, cleaning stoops, doing any menial work she could to survive. My mother didn't like to talk about those years. When asked, she would say, "I'm an American. That's what matters now."

The war ended in November 1918. Eventually my grandparents made contact with one another, and my grandfather sent new tickets. The Katz family was on its way to America again, this time on a French ship, after terrible years of poverty and isolation in Marseille. They boarded a ship called *La Savoie* in Le Havre. My mother recalled that many of the ship's passengers were American soldiers heading home after the war. The ship arrived at Ellis Island on December 30, 1919. I found the details on the Ellis Island website with a copy of the ship's manifest. My grandmother was thirty-one; my mother was ten; her little sister was eight. The manifest incorrectly said that they were Hungarians from Romania.

When they finally arrived in Houston in 1920, they must have been thrilled by the temperate climate and by the very fact of being in America, at last, far from pogroms and war. My mother and her sister, Edith, were enrolled in the neighborhood public school. My grandfather continued to work as a tailor, and my grandmother stayed home to take care of their modest home and the children. I recall that she scrubbed the floors of her little house until they were spotless. She cooked the best chicken soup I ever ate and made scrumptious blintzes, stuffed with cheese.

My grandmother died in 1967. In her forty-seven years in Houston, she never learned to speak English. She spoke only Yiddish, and her grandchildren could not communicate with her, because we didn't understand more than a few words of Yiddish. I never had a conversation with her. Our parents knew how to speak it, but they used it as a secret language to say things that none of their children could understand. My grandfather learned to speak excellent English. He joined the Knights of Pythias and faithfully attended its meetings, going a long distance by bus since he didn't know how to drive a car. I once went with him and my grandmother, and she sat by, watching, listening, and smiling, not understanding a word. When my zadie died, members of his Knights of Pythias Lodge—none of whom was Jewish—were the pallbearers.

In 1927, when my mother graduated from public high school in Houston, it was the proudest day of her young life. With much determination, she had taught herself to speak flawless English. She did not have a trace of a European accent. She was a true American!

When she met the dapper and irrepressible Cracker Silvers, her life changed forever. They married in 1930, in the early days of the Great Depression.

Cracker and Ann set out on the road and headed for California. My father landed a sales job in San Diego, which didn't last long. According to family lore, his boss refused to pay him his monthly wages, and my father exploded, as he was wont to do. He pulled out his handgun—he always owned a handgun—and shot his boss in the foot. Cracker and Ann left San Diego in a hurry. Moral of the story: Don't mess with Cracker Silvers. He has a hot temper, and he might be armed.

The young couple drove back to Savannah to rejoin my father's family. They opened a beauty salon, and my mother was the beautician. My father probably spent his days with his friends, playing cards, gambling, fishing, and telling jokes. His sisters ruled the roost, their own and everyone else's. My mother was not happy nestled in the bosom of my father's large and very outspoken family, so they packed up again and drove to Houston, where her parents lived. When Prohibition ended in 1933, they opened a liquor store and named it Jack & Jill. Following the pattern established in Savannah, my mother worked behind the counter, ringing up sales on the cash register, while my father went fishing, played poker with his buddies, or hung out in the back of the store shooting the breeze with liquor salesmen. On several occasions, a man would come into the store, point a gun at my mother, and say, "Give me the money in the cash register." My mother did what she was told; she gave them the money. Sometimes they told her to lie down on the floor while they emptied the cash register. No point disagreeing with an armed robber. Just another day at work.

After my parents returned to Houston, my mother surely thought she had escaped my father's bossy sisters, but some of them moved to Texas, probably after hearing from him about the opportunities there. My parents sincerely believed that there was no place on earth that was better than Texas. We owned a popular graphic book called *Texas Brags*, which gave all the reasons why Texas was the biggest and the best of everything, which is what most Texans believed. It began: "Texas occupies all of the continent of North America except a small part set aside for the United States, Canada and Mexico. . . . Texas is both in the South and in the West. But Texans are neither Southerners nor Westerners. They are TEXANS, which is a God's plenty in itself." An exaggerated "map" showed Texas as the biggest state, dwarfing the rest of North America, and pointing out that Texas was 1 and 1/2 times larger than California and 224 times larger than Rhode Island. The rest of the book consisted of all the ways in which Texas was remarkable, with humor. "The West Texas sand fleas are acknowledged to be the most active and intelligent in the world. They are sought after by the world's largest flea circuses." And "If all the cotton grown in Texas were baled and made into a stairway, it would reach to the pearly gates." And "Texas has MORE GOATS than Missouri has people and MORE SHEEP than there are Pennsylvanians."

Well, of course, the aunts and uncles wanted to move to Texas! Aunt Frieda and Uncle Phil owned the only pharmacy in Kilgore, Texas. When I visited them, I was amazed to see oil wells all over town, pumping oil in backyards, front yards, and empty lots. Another sister, Aunt Lizzie—the sharpest tongue of all—moved to Houston, married, and opened a toy store (no free toys for us). Aunt Sophie and Uncle Al moved to San Antonio, where they opened a shoe store (Uncle Al, to the family's shame, was arrested for passing a "hot check" and spent time in prison.)

My parents were unabashed Democrats. They credited Franklin D. Roosevelt with ending the Depression, winning the Second World War, and enabling them to support their family. They never voted for a Republican. Years later, when I told my mother that FDR's State Department had closed the doors to Jews fleeing Europe during the war, my mother refused to believe it. Despite his devotion to Roosevelt, my father did not like unions. He thought they might encroach on his right to pay workers as little as he wanted. My parents had a strong class consciousness, and they were very sensitive and fearful about their own status. They felt that they were not good enough. They were never good enough. They were not even nouveau riche, although they wanted to be. My mother didn't learn to drive until she was forty; my father bought her a Cadillac, the ultimate status symbol. They knew that the gentiles would never accept them. Certain neighborhoods were "restricted," meaning Jews were not allowed to buy property. Every country club in town was restricted, except for one that was entirely Jewish (a "country club" was a private association with a swimming pool, tennis courts, and a restaurant and bar, where people socialized). Not only did my parents feel rejected by the gentiles, but they felt spurned by the established and prosperous Jewish community leaders. The members of the Jewish country club were wealthy merchants and professionals, not owners of small liquor stores whose wives stood on their feet and worked behind the counter. And then there was Jewish snobbery based on family origins; the German Jews looked down on the Eastern European Jews, that is, Jews from places like Poland, Bessarabia, and Russia. They were outsiders, and they knew that they would never be accepted either by the goyim or the highfalutin' German Jews. I longed to go to the all-Jewish Westwood

Country Club, to which many of my school friends belonged, but my family would never have been accepted.

Being in the liquor business didn't help their social status, but it was a living. Neither of my parents drank alcohol, neither wine nor liquor. They said that liquor and wine were for the goyim. They looked down on the stuff they were selling. I felt that they were more than a wee bit ashamed of being in the liquor business because it had an unsavory reputation, having been banned during Prohibition and associated with mobsters. My father hung out with liquor salesmen and distributors, many of whom were Italian, and they played poker together. In retrospect, I think he did know some mobsters, though it didn't occur to me at the time. He often said that a Jew is a Catholic turned inside out, which was his way of expressing his kinship with his fellow outsiders.

My mother was a hard worker; my father was not. My mother worried about tomorrow; my father went fishing. His friends loved that he might break into a song-and-dance routine at any moment. They enjoyed his corny jokes and his camaraderie. He loved getting up at 4:00 in the morning to go fishing in the Gulf of Mexico with his buddies. He packed a lunch of hard-boiled eggs and a can of "Vienna sausages" and off he went, before anyone else was awake. He sometimes took his children to Galveston for the day to go swimming and crabbing in the Gulf. We would pile into the family station wagon—the kind with the wooden sides—stop at a gasoline station to go to the bathroom and play a one-arm bandit, then arrive in Galveston ready for a day of intense sun. We would bring raw horsemeat with us, tie chunks of it with strong twine to a jetty, wait for the crabs to cluster on the horsemeat, then shake them into a big burlap bag called a croaker sack. We would come home sun-burned and carrying a croaker sack full of live crabs, which Mama would boil, and everyone would eat. We didn't have sunscreen, and we usually came home with sun blisters and peeling skin.

Sometimes my parents had one liquor store; sometimes they owned two or three. They were always in debt because they had to lay out money to keep the stores stocked with merchandise and needed to make enough to pay off their debts to the liquor wholesalers, pay their employees, and support a large family. They were always paying off loans to Irvin M. Shlenker, the banker. Mr. Shlenker was one of those German Jews who looked down his nose at them. Years later, I got a good laugh when I learned that the daughter of the Shlenkers was an artist named Gay, who was gay and had taken a picture of her impeccably dressed mother, wearing a hat and jewels, but naked from the waist up. Eventually, I met Gay in Santa Fe, New Mexico, where she was living, and I was giving a lecture. We struck up a brief but wonderful friendship, and I told her that her father was greatly respected and feared in my household. She gave me a gift of one of her books of photographs, the one that had the infamous photograph of her elegant, partially nude mother.

Mama worked all day, counted the money, and made up the bank deposit. Every morning, Daddy took the money to the bank. We managed because Mama watched every penny. For as long as I could remember, we had domestic help in the house. We had to, because someone had to be home while Daddy was playing and Mama was working. When we lived on Richmond Road, a Black couple worked for us, Leonard and Mary. Mary cooked and took care of the house. Leonard tended the yard and did odd jobs. He taught me how to drive a stick-shift automobile. He called me " 'gyptian" because I had dark skin, always tanned from the sun; not until I moved north did I discover that I was not dark-complexioned.

My older brother David and sister Adele went to the local public school, Montrose Elementary School, about six blocks from our house. When I was five, my parents tried to enroll me in the private school directly across the street on Richmond Road, called the Kinkaid School (it still exists but in a different location). Mrs. Kinkaid interviewed me and rejected me. My parents said it was because Mrs. Kinkaid did not like Jews.

Having been turned down by the snooty private school, I too went to Montrose Elementary School, walking to school each day with my older siblings.

We were one of the very few Jewish families at Montrose Elementary School. Usually I didn't think about it, but once in a while someone would yell "kike" at me. It should have hurt my feelings, but it didn't.

I wasn't quite sure what a "kike" was, but I knew it was not a compliment. I could always fall back on the saying that "sticks and stones may break my bones, but words will never hurt me."

The biggest problem I had in school was that I was left-handed, and my teachers did not want anyone to be left-handed. The wooden classroom chairs had extensions for right-handed students, not for left-handed students. When I started school, we used quill pens, which we dipped in ink. I was an ink-stained wretch. When ballpoint pens were invented, that changed everything. No more inkwells, no more quill pens! But ballpoint pens were even worse for a left-handed person; as I held the pen, my hand curled around the pen and smudged whatever I had written, leaving ink smudges all over my hand. At one point, the teachers tried to force me to write with my right hand, but that was a total failure.

After I learned to write, I faced another ordeal. At the beginning of every school year, the teacher handed out a form for everyone to fill out. The form asked you to list your name, address, birthdate, parents' names, where they were born, and the names of your siblings and their birthdates. It took a long time to fill in the names of my seven siblings. But there was another problem. Mama kept changing her mind about where she was born. Some years, she admitted she was born in Bessarabia. Other years, she insisted that she was an American, and that was all they needed to know.

I had very kind teachers in elementary school. Miss Christie (behind her back, we said, "Miss Christie, Miss Christie, a bottle of whiskey!" because it rhymed). Mrs. Murphy. Mrs. Wise. Our principal, Mrs. Doty, was also kind. Many years later, I heard that she was injured in a terrible event. She had become the principal of an elementary school in another part of Houston. A man came to the school and wanted to enroll his son. Mrs. Doty asked for the boy's birth certificate and proof of vaccinations. The man did not have the documents, left with his son, and went to the playground, carrying a suitcase. One of the teachers alerted Mrs. Doty. She went out to speak to him. As she approached him, he exploded the dynamite in his suitcase, which killed him, his son, two other children, and two members of the staff. Mrs. Doty lost a leg but survived.

Montrose Elementary School was a one-story building arranged in a square around an open courtyard (it is now the Houston High School for the Performing Arts, and nothing remains of the original school). There was an ample playground behind the school. I liked school. I loved to read. I often checked books out of the school library. When I had my tonsils removed, I opened my eyes in the hospital to find my mother reading a book about Mickey Mouse to me. Funny, I still remember the sensation of losing consciousness, because I remember seeing green, red, and black plaid, then waking up to the pleasant sound of my mother's voice. Aside from this experience, I don't remember my mother ever reading to me, so this was a special treat. Worth the surgery.

I have two other vivid memories of my mother from this period of my life. Sometimes she invited me to go with her to the ice locker. At home, we had an icebox, like other families, which was replenished every few days when the iceman came around and carried a big block of ice into the house with his tongs and put it into the tightly insulated icebox in the kitchen. We kids would go running after his truck, hoping to catch a few ice chips when they fell off. Once a week, our mother would go to a large facility called the ice locker, where she rented a storage space that was the size of a modern refrigerator. The entire facility was kept at below freezing temperatures. Mother would buy large quantities of meat and put them in the freezer at the ice locker, then bring them home as needed. It was a great thrill in a town as unbearably hot as Houston to walk into the ice locker and feel the cold air, especially in the summertime. The other special memory I shared with my Mama was going with her to Weingarten's, the neighborhood grocery store. When she invited me to go along, we would sit at the counter of the store's coffee shop and have a cup of coffee. It was the only private time I ever spent with her.

There were two activities we did as a family that I especially enjoyed. On Sundays, we would go to ride the ponies. There was a place on Main Street where you paid a few cents to ride a pony around a small ring, possibly 50 yards in length. The ponies were trained to walk very slowly. The older children paid a little more to ride on horses that trotted. The other fun thing was when Daddy took all of us on Friday nights to an outdoor joint near Rice University that sold ice-cold slices of watermelon. We put salt on the slices, which somehow made them even sweeter. I have never tasted watermelon as delicious as those slices. Neither of those places of childhood delight exists anymore.

It was also a family tradition to go to the rodeo when it came to town once a year. When I was nine, the stars of the rodeo were Roy Rogers and Dale Evans. At the end of their musical performance, they rode around the gigantic ring and slapped the hands that were outstretched. Mine was one of them. Roy Rogers slapped my hand! I determined on the spot that I would never wash my hand again! Could anyone ever be that lucky?

When I was in the middle of fifth grade, my parents decided to move to a house in another part of town, a block away from the bayou, on a quiet residential street. We had Jewish neighbors on each side. The house—at 3922 Roseneath Drive—was bigger than our brick house on Richmond Road. It had four bedrooms upstairs and a master bedroom downstairs. We eight children all doubled up, and our parents slept downstairs. The house also had a detached bedroom and bath unit for "live-in" help, usually a Black woman who stayed with us five days a week, made breakfast and dinner, and cleaned the house. In the years before I left for college, Ludie lived in and was a kind and loving substitute mother who could whip up any kind of pie on short notice. Ludie's real home was in the segregated Fifth Ward of Houston, where home ownership was low and poverty levels were high.

We played baseball in the front yard, and occasionally broke a plate glass window in the house. My father planted his fruit trees and kept his homing pigeons in the backyard. Each pigeon wore an identifying band. He would let them out, and they would always come home. My father said that they got pregnant by eating the little white balls that were part of the pigeon feed. I believed him.

Now, instead of having a convent and a telephone company for neighbors, we had people living next door. On one side was the Proler family, who were in the scrap metal business; they had a swimming pool, which was unusual in those days. My younger sister Sylvia was friends with their daughter, Joy. Sylvia had her strange ways. One day, she went into Mrs. Proler's bedroom with a scissors and cut up the evening dress that Mrs. Proler had left on her bed, planning to wear it that night. Another day she set fire to the closet that we both shared, and all our clothes went up in smoke. Sylvia and I were never close, and we had no common interests. I was a nerd who loved school and books. She loved neither. She was always getting into trouble, breaking things, disobeying our parents. Our father used to shake his head at her latest mishap and say in a low but audible voice, "She is hell on wheels, hell on wheels." I think if she were a child today, she might be diagnosed on the autism spectrum.

To the other side of us was the Roberts family. They were wealthy and sophisticated. My younger brother Bobby was best friends with their son, George. George had the best of everything. He had the fancy baseball equipment I longed for—the catchers' mitt, the leather leg coverings, the face mask. He allowed me to put them on one afternoon, and Mr. and Mrs. Roberts and their guests had a good laugh at my expense. I was so pleased to wear this wonderful outfit that I didn't care that they were laughing. Mrs. Roberts was an elegant, well-coiffed woman; unlike my mother, she never worked. They entertained celebrities who were passing through Houston, like the great cabaret singer Sophie Tucker, whom I was thrilled to meet (we had her records). George Roberts grew up to become a billionaire as one of the founders of a company called KKR. He and my brother Bobby both went to Culver Military Academy, and they remained close friends. (My parents sent Bobby to military school to "straighten him out.")

Although I was not happy to leave our idyllic home on Richmond Road, with its fruit trees and pergola and animals, I quickly adjusted to the new home on Roseneath. We had a lot of freedom. I could ride my bicycle everywhere. It was fun to explore the bayou, although I had to watch out for dangerous snakes like cottonmouths and rattlesnakes.

There was an empty lot next door (between us and the Robertses) with a large tree lying on its side, just perfect for climbing, building a tree house, and devising adventures. Across the street was another large empty lot with high grass; I would sometimes go there to lie in the grass where no one could see me, watch the clouds roll by, and wonder where I would go in life, who I would be, what was in store for me. I imagined myself as Lois Lane, girl journalist. Whatever I imagined, I was a writer. Whenever I needed privacy, just to get away from the constant hubbub in my house, I would go either to the high grass across the street or climb a tall tree in front of our house and nestle into a flat space about 7 feet off the ground. No one could bother me there. High up in the tree's branches, I would read a book in peace and quiet. In our raucous house, it was difficult to get time alone.

When we moved, I left Montrose Elementary School and enrolled at Sutton Elementary School in midyear of the fifth grade. My teacher was Mrs. Rose; she was warm and welcoming. A girl named Rae Nelkin offered me a pencil. Isn't it funny how you remember a small act of kindness like that seventy-five years later? My first boyfriend was Bobby Sakowitz. His family owned a big department store. They lived in a beautiful home a block away from us on South McGregor, on the other side of that empty lot where I daydreamed. He gave me a Tom Mix whistle ring that came in a box of Ralston cereal. That was a sign of true love. I should have known it wouldn't last, but at the time I was not aware of the social distinctions that separated our families. His parents were part of the city's Jewish elite, who were often featured on the society pages of the newspapers. His older sister Lynn eventually married an oil magnate, Oscar Wyatt, and became a global fashion icon. Bobby left public school at the end of elementary school and went to St. John's, an elite private school.

One of the advantages of the new house was that, for the first time, we had our own telephone. On Richmond Road, we had a party line. Four families shared the same telephone, and we didn't know the other three families. When someone was on the phone, you had to wait until they got off. When I was six or seven, I imagined that God was a telephone operator, sitting somewhere in the clouds deciding who would get to use the telephone. I must have thought that God was a woman, because only women operated the switchboards at the telephone company.

What made the new house on Roseneath livable was that David, our oldest brother, left for college. Adele, my older sister, had her own room. Little sister Sylvia and I shared a room. Jules and Bobby shared a room. Sandy and M. M. shared a room. Sylvia was annoyed at me almost every night because I kept the light on while I was reading or doing homework. Maybe setting our closet on fire was her revenge.

I wasn't happy about having all my clothes get burned up, but I wasn't unhappy either. I didn't care about clothes, other than knowing that it was necessary to wear them. I had no sense of fashion, and I still don't. Left to my own choices, then and now, I would wear jeans and a T-shirt (or turtleneck) all the time. By contrast, my older sister Adele was always well dressed. She had cashmere sweaters, which was a sign of great affluence and taste. When she got a new one, she might deign to hand down a used one to me. I thought she was a fashion queen. Adele and my mother cared about clothes. I didn't. At school, we wore jeans every day, so dressing for school was no problem. It was only at Sunday school and special events when jeans would not do. My mother would take me shopping at one of the downtown department stores (Foley's or Levy's or Sakowitz's), and she would say, "This is what they are wearing this year." And I would ask, "Mama, who are 'they'? How do you know what 'they' are wearing? Why should I want to wear what 'they' are wearing anyway?" Somehow, she managed to keep me clothed, but—to her despair—I never developed an interest in "keeping up with the Joneses" or "the Cohens" or anyone else.

My mother tried hard to make me ladylike, but it was a losing battle. Whatever I wore didn't look right. My hair was straight, and Mama would take me to the beauty shop to get a permanent wave (which was not really permanent, but that's what it was called). Girls were supposed to have curls, she said. The beautician would take a handful of my hair and wrap it in a thin piece of paper, which I handed her one at a time, coat my hair with some awful-smelling chemical, then put a heavy metal clamp on the paper. By the time they were done, I had about 10 pounds of metal on my head, maybe more. It felt like 50 pounds. After 20 minutes, the beautician would unroll one of them and say, "Not done yet." After about 40 minutes, she would decide I had a curl, and my hair would be washed and set, and I would sit under a hair dryer for another 30 minutes. At the end of this torture, I would have curls and a hairdo! But, of course, it wasn't me. Despite my mother's best efforts, I did my best to resist the pressure to run with the crowd.

All the personal freedom we had as children was, I think, in direct proportion to the lack of television and computers, and the cell phones that are now ubiquitous. We had a big wooden Stromberg-Carlson radio console in the living room. Most of us kids would lie on the carpet on our stomachs and listen to weekly shows like *The Lone Ranger, The Shadow, The Green Hornet,* and *Sergeant Preston of the Yukon,* as well as quiz shows and comedy shows. We imagined the action. We heard the clatter of the horses' hooves, the thunder of storms, and gunfire. But we didn't see them. We imagined them, and they were vivid. My daddy loved baseball, especially the Houston Buffaloes, and he listened to their games when they were playing out of town. It was always a delayed broadcast, meaning that the announcer was not actually at the game but was reading from a wire, and the sound of the crowd was added. "He got a hit, the crowd roars, it is going, going, gone, it's a home run!" And in the background, there was canned cheering.

We got our first television set when I was twelve, but we could only watch reruns because there was no direct connection to any of the networks. There was great excitement two years later, in 1952, when we learned that Houston would be connected to the television cable on the first of July. That happened to be my birthday. The local television stations incessantly played the jingle "the cable is coming the first of July, the cable is coming the first of July." We sang it too. We were very excited. When the cable finally arrived, the family gathered to watch shows like Milton Berle's *Texaco Hour* and *The Ed Sullivan Show.*

None of us kids ever had much spending money. Depending on our age, our weekly allowance might be a dime or a quarter. But we had another source of money. Every night, my father put his pocket change on his dresser. Whichever child got there first swiped the nickels and dimes and quarters that he left out, and when he asked who took his change, no one ever confessed.

Being part of a family of eight children could be fun, but it was also a burden. Everyone else was part of a family that had one or two or three children. Being part of such a large family was a source of merriment—for other people. I had to endure the same stale jokes about my parents being ignorant of birth control. When we went to Sunday school at the synagogue, someone would always say, "Here come the Silvers kids." I hated that. I wanted to be an individual, not part of a traveling team.

Our religious training was not at all pious. We belonged to a reform synagogue, where very little Hebrew was spoken. The only Sunday school teacher I remember was a strapping guy who discussed Bible stories and the Jewish religion with us. He told us that when he was our age he had run away with the circus.

Our superficial religious instruction was a slight counterweight to the daily religious training we received in public school. Every school day began with a Bible reading over the loudspeaker that went into every classroom. The reading might be from the Old Testament or the New Testament. We also said a daily prayer, the Lord's Prayer, which we memorized by daily repetition.

Our reform synagogue, Emanu El, had religious services on Saturday mornings, and we regularly attended. On one occasion, when I was twelve years old, the rabbi invited me (without warning) to step up to the pulpit and offer a prayer. I got up and recited the Lord's Prayer. When I was done, the rabbi looked stricken. There was a palpable gasp from the congregants. I didn't understand why. Only later did I discover that the Lord's Prayer came from the New Testament and that I had just recited the Anglican version of the Lord's Prayer in synagogue. I wasn't invited to speak from the pulpit again.

At public school, we learned Christmas carols, and every year there was a Christmas pageant. Sometimes I hummed the words instead of saying them. That was just the way things were, and Christian practices were taken for granted as part of the routine of public school. My schools were only about 3 percent Jewish, maybe less. The references to Christianity didn't bother me at all. I enjoyed the Christmas carols, and when I go to midnight mass on Christmas Eve now, I am glad I know the words.

The eight of us were a spectacle, and my father enjoyed creating a spectacle. He had an elderly lady friend who died and left him her prized 1927 Rolls-Royce. It was a large convertible with a wide front seat, a large back seat, and two jump seats in the middle. There was a glass divider between the front seat and the rear seats that was both a windbreaker and a glass class divide between the chauffeur and the owner in the rear. Daddy was the chauffeur, and on Sundays we all piled in. The car had a loud, old-fashioned horn (it went "a-ruga, a-ruga"), and he liked to drive around the neighborhood to show off the car full of his children. He had it painted a beautiful shade of yellow. When Franklin D. Roosevelt visited Houston in 1936, he rode in that very car. We had photographs of the historic event. When I was married in 1960, the same car took my new husband and me from the synagogue to our hotel to change from our wedding clothes to our travel attire.

When I turned fourteen, I was old enough to get a driver's license. I can tell you from experience that allowing fourteen-year-olds to drive is a very bad idea. I am lucky to be alive. I had several accidents between the ages of fourteen and sixteen—the result of drag racing with friends on the highway or on rain-slicked neighborhood streets—and have had none since then.

After school and on weekends, the kids my age liked to go to local drive-in restaurants. One of them was a drive-in called Prince's that had the world's best hamburgers; girls on roller skates delivered the food to the cars. Another was a seafood restaurant called Bill Williams, where I had oysters for the first time. On my inaugural oyster tasting, I found a large round pearl and showed it to the other girls. We decided to drive downtown to the *Houston Press*, a tabloid that we were sure would be interested in our story. At the *Press*, we found a reporter and a photographer who indeed thought this was a marvelous story. The photographer took my picture holding up the pearl. All of us were fourteen, and all of us were wearing short shorts, as was the custom in Houston in the summer. As soon as he took the picture, I accidentally dropped the pearl into a very tall trash can, and that was the end of it.

That night, I was deathly ill and began vomiting nonstop. Maybe oysters with pearls are sick oysters? The next day, after the newspaper appeared with a photograph of me in short shorts, identified by name, strange men began calling the house, asking for me and saying impudent things. That went on for days, along with the vomiting. My mother was not amused.

When I became a teenager, it was time to get a summer job and make some spending money. The first job I had was as the receptionist at the local beauty salon, called the Town & Country Beauty Salon. It was owned by an Italian couple named Vera and Lewis. I answered the phone and booked appointments. Both Vera and Lewis worked very hard for long hours. He was often angry, and she was often depressed. One day, when I arrived at work, the shop was closed. I learned that Lewis got angry at Vera's younger brother Tommy, who lived with them, and shot him dead. They closed the shop for a week but then were back to work. Vera, of course, was more depressed than ever.

The next summer, I got a job working as a filing clerk at the Houston National Bank, Mr. Shlenker's bank. Each day, I would sort personal checks into their proper places in the customers' files. I was paid every week and had some spending money of my own. What did I spend it on? Not clothing, for sure. Books and my own typewriter.

I did not have an idyllic adolescence. No one ever does. Mine was destroyed by my father abusing me. Like my siblings, I thought my father was a funny and endearing rogue who liked to tell jokes, play poker, go fishing, dance a little soft-shoe routine for everyone's amusement, and watch sports events. Sometimes he took me with him to the professional baseball games, and we sat in the stands cheering the Houston Buffaloes. If a player from the opposing team hit a high fly ball, he would shout, "Can of corn, can of corn," which meant that it was an easy catch. He taught us not to smoke by offering us a puff from the big nasty cigar that he always had in his mouth, chewing and smoking at the same time. One puff and you never wanted to smoke again. I never did, nor did any of my siblings.

But when I was about thirteen or fourteen, he came into my bedroom one night when I was alone. Most of the family was away; the few that were home were watching television downstairs. He pushed the dresser against the door so that no one would enter unannounced, and he got into bed with me. He undressed me, touched my private parts, and rubbed his penis against me. After a few minutes, he ran to the bathroom, I wasn't sure why but now I know, to ejaculate. This happened several times. I knew it was wrong, but I didn't say anything to anyone. Like others who are molested by someone they trust, I felt embarrassed and guilty. I felt that I was somehow complicit, that perhaps it was my fault. I thought that if I told anyone, they would blame me or they wouldn't believe me. I didn't want to make trouble. I knew it would hurt my mother, and I had to protect her, so I kept quiet and began to hate him.

I tried to keep my distance from him. I tried never to be alone in the house with him. I never again snuggled up to him for a hug for fear that he would understand it as an invitation for intimacy. I knew I could never trust him again. He had introduced a deep shame into my life, and I had done nothing to invite it. I kept our relationship literally at arms' length. I never confronted him about what happened. Later, much later, I learned that he had done the same thing to my little sister Sylvia. I didn't confess to her until she was older, long after she had married, and I realized that I should have spoken up. Unlike me, she told, and no one believed her. People thought she was lying. I knew she wasn't. But I couldn't talk about it. Even now, I have trouble talking about it. I never told my mother; she adored my father, and I didn't want her to know. The few people with whom I shared my secret many years later asked me how it was possible that my mother didn't know and why I was not angry at her. I was not angry at her. She suffered a lot in her lifetime, and I never wanted to hurt her.

On the surface, nothing had changed. But inside me, everything had changed because I had a secret shame, one that I expected never to share with anyone. And I was very angry at my once-beloved father. I no longer saw him as a fun-loving guy but as a selfish, spoiled manchild, concerned about no one but himself. I could never again have a conversation with him, other than the most perfunctory. My father died when he was sixty-nine. I was living in New York City and heard about it from my siblings. He was walking to the car one morning, heading for the bank with the cash receipts from the previous day. He always carried a handgun, but he didn't have a holster. He tripped, the gun went off, and the bullet just missed his heart. When he got out of the hospital, he was weak and depressed. He didn't want to see any of his old friends. He had a stroke, and he died in 1972. I had barely spoken to him for twenty years.

When I was an adolescent, my most prized possession was the Royal portable typewriter I bought with my earnings from the summer job at the bank. It was mine and mine alone. It was my passport to becoming a writer. I wrote stories about the local teens for the neighborhood newspaper, which paid me $10 a week. I spent that $10 buying books from a club I read about on the back page of a comic book, called the Classics Book Club of Roslyn, Long Island, New York. I began to have my own collection of books, my own little library. I am not sure anyone else in the house had any books. I devoured books as other people devoured candy. One day, my father came to my room and asked if I would type a business letter for him. I was perpetually angry at him, and I told him I was busy, which was very impertinent of me. He grabbed my typewriter, my precious typewriter, and threw it down the stairs. That was the most hostile thing he could do. The typewriter represented my aspirations; it symbolized what I hoped to be. Aside from my small library, it was the only thing I owned, the only thing that was mine. I got it repaired, but I never forgot.

3

SCHOOL IN HOUSTON

I started Albert Sidney Johnston Junior High in seventh grade. Albert Sidney Johnston was a Confederate hero. Like every other school in Houston, public and private, this one was racially segregated. Nowhere in Houston did white and Black youth meet or share the same experiences. I still remember the school's marching song (we never marched, but we had a marching song):

> Albert Sidney Johnston Junior High
> Now our voices rise to thee in song.
> Southern hero's name we proudly bear
> We pledge our love and loyalty,
> Our hearts to thee belong.
> Fall in line,
> O may we ever stand for the right!
> Ready to fight!
> For Victory!
> Fall in line and give a cheer
> With all of your might,
> Forever praise his glorious name,
> We sing now to thee!

We sang our marching song at assemblies and athletic events. The school no longer exists. No one is pledging their hearts, their lives, or their loyalty to Albert Sidney Johnston anymore.

Johnston Junior High was never challenging for me. The hardest thing was that I followed in the footsteps of my older brother and sister, neither of whom was interested in academic pursuits. All my teachers knew them, so they had low expectations for me. Unlike my older brother and sister, I loved school and got high marks, which created problems for the siblings who followed me. There were few electives to supplement the basic studies of English, math, social studies, and science; there was shop for the boys, home economics for the girls, typing for whoever signed up. I took typing and was active in many sports. I wanted to be a good typist to overcome my left-handed penmanship, which was almost illegible, and to prepare myself to be a writer someday. I lettered in several girls' sports, including basketball, volleyball, and bowling. My favorite refuge was the school library. In home economics, the girls were supposed to learn basic cooking and sewing skills. I learned how to scramble and boil eggs; however, my effort to sew a skirt was a failure. I never completed the skirt.

I had responsibilities at home. When Mama was working, I took care of my younger brothers. I taught them how to tie a Windsor knot. I helped them with their schoolwork. When my brother Bobby was in second grade, he failed in spelling, and I worked with him every night. We went over his vocabulary words, and I taught him how to spell. In six weeks, he brought his grade from an F to an A. He never struggled in spelling again. My mother called me "the little mama" because of my devotion to my younger brothers Bobby, Sandy, and M. M.

In 1952, I started tenth grade at San Jacinto High School. Understand that the Jewish enrollment at the public schools I attended was very small, 3 percent, maybe less. But Johnston Junior High was derisively called "Jewstown" by non-Jews, and San Jacinto was referred to as "San Jew Center." I carpooled to school with kids from my neighborhood. One of my neighbors, a beautiful girl named Marlene Cohen, lost her little sister Natalie to leukemia. Natalie's face was all puffed up because of the prednisone she took. It was very sad. I didn't dream that one day I would lose a child to the same terrible disease.

San Jacinto High School enrolled some twelve hundred students. The school dated back to 1926 and had a few distinguished alumni, such as the broadcaster Walter Cronkite, the heart surgeon Dr. Denton Cooley, and the once-famous actress Gale Storm. Football season was the pinnacle of the school year. If a boy invited you to the Friday night game, he sent you a large pom-pom, a beautiful chrysanthemum that was either white or gold. Girls wore them on their chests like combat medals. I had lots of boys who were friends, but no boyfriends. I never got a pom-pom. I didn't feel badly about it because there was no boy that I was interested in. I wanted to fit in, but I didn't care for any of the boys I knew. I was known as "a brain," which was both a compliment and a put-down, mostly the latter.

Like all the other teens I knew, I idolized James Dean and Elvis Presley. Like everyone else, I knew the lyrics to every song that Elvis sang. I also loved the bebop and doo-wop music of my generation, songs like "Earth Angel" and "The Great Pretender," groups like Bill Haley and the Comets, the Four Aces, the Ink Spots, the Platters, the Everly Brothers, and singers like Johnnie Ray, Doris Day, Nat King Cole, Fats Domino, the Big Bopper, Buddy Holly, Little Richard, Bing Crosby, Frank Sinatra, and many of the songs that are now considered classics in the Great American Songbook. I knew the lyrics to all the songs I loved.

I wanted to go to college, an ambition not shared by most of my fellow students. Most girls got married right after they finished high school. Bound for marriage or work, most students did not take academics seriously. I did. High school life was dominated by social life and athletics, not academics, just as the sociologist James Coleman described in his book *The Adolescent Society*. Cheating was rampant, and I often let friends copy my answers. That's what friends were for.

When I entered high school, I crossed my fingers and hoped that I would be invited to join a secret Jewish sorority called STP (Sigma Theta Pi). Sororities were theoretically banned, but school officials ignored their existence. However, I was passed over at the beginning of the year, and I was crushed. Not being invited to join STP was a social stigma. In midyear, the members of STP voted in three new members, and I was one of them. Oh, joy! The pledges were supposed to act as obedient servants of the full-fledged members, who thought up useless, often demeaning tasks for us to perform, say, driving a long distance to pick up a package or shining their shoes. One night I stayed over at the home of one of the other new members, a girl named Pat Richter, and we took our small revenge. Pat had a dog who barked on command. The really snooty girls in the sorority had private telephone numbers, and we called several of them about two in the morning. When they sleepily answered, Pat's dog barked at them. Pretty silly, but we felt that we had one-upped the grandes dames of STP.

STP had no purpose other than to sort out the girls based on their social status and to provide access to social networks. I am not sure why the snobs agreed to accept me, but my older sister, who was a student at the University of Alabama, told me that she threatened to blackball them and so keep them from getting into the most prestigious Jewish sorority (Alpha Epsilon Phi) when they went to college. I have no idea how she got in. She was pretty and vivacious, and far from home, so no one knew that her parents worked in and owned a liquor store.

My closest friend in high school was Marilyn Oshman. She shared my irreverent view of the secret sorority. Marilyn's father, Jake Oshman, was a Russian immigrant who had lived in an orphanage. As a young man in Houston, he founded a very successful chain of sporting goods stores, and the family became wealthy. Her home was very proper and well-ordered; mine was not. She loved to visit with me because she loved the spontaneity and absurdity that was likely to break out at any moment. I recall one night when she was sleeping over. We went to bed; shortly after we turned off the lights, my brothers Jules and Bobby popped up from under our beds. That would never happen in the Oshman household! Marilyn was a lifelong friend. She drove a pink Ford Thunderbird convertible, the only one I ever saw in the city. As an adult, she became an iconic figure in Houston because of her passion for cutting-edge art. She collected the works of Mexican artists like Frida Kahlo, Diego Rivera, and David Siqueiros when they were little-known here. She discovered and launched the Orange Show, which showcased the work of self-taught folk artists. She created the Art Car Parade, which attracts car enthusiasts from across the nation who decorate their cars and show them off to large audiences who line the streets. She hired a group of offbeat architects called the Ant Farm Collective to design a vacation home for her; they located a pink Ford Thunderbird convertible at her request and buried it halfway in the ground to serve as a huge flower bed. Marilyn served on the board of every major museum in Houston. She died in December 2024. She was one of a kind.

I had some wonderful teachers at San Jacinto. My homeroom teacher, Mrs. Ruby Ratliff, instilled in me a love of literature. In her English class we read Byron, Keats, Shelley, Melville, and many of the other greats of British and American literature. Many years later, I tracked her down at a nursing home in South Carolina and thanked her for being such an inspirational teacher. She confessed that she was teaching out of license; she was really a social studies teacher, but she loved literature.

I had some wacky teachers too. My high school history teacher, Anastasia Doyle, was a great admirer of Senator Joseph McCarthy, who was then at the peak of his power. She often told us that he was the greatest American of our era. My biology teacher, Miss Bell, was the butt of the boys' dumb humor. She was an innocent, a perfect foil for their mean tricks. On one occasion, they filled up a prophylactic rubber with water and put it on her desk before she arrived. On another, the class pretended that the bell for the end of class had rung 10 minutes early, and we all stood up on cue and walked out of the room, leaving her puzzled. I think we were truly horrible, and we only respected the teachers who won our respect. Mrs. Ruby Ratliff was one of them. No one dared to cross her or challenge her. She was considered a "hard" teacher, a teacher who demanded lots of work and was a tough grader. And students stood in line to gain admission to her classes.

I was in junior high school and high school during the McCarthy years. Every two years, the school board stood for election, and sometimes the sane faction would win, while other times the extremist Minute Women would win. The Minute Women were the female version of the John Birch Society. They were certain that some of our teachers were Communists and that their eternal vigilance was needed to protect us. When the sane people were in charge, our schools had an assembly to watch a film of Frank Sinatra singing "The House I Live In," a beautiful song about racial and religious tolerance. But then the right-wing nutcases took over, and our schoolwide assembly featured a speaker who talked about his life as an undercover spy in the Communist Party. Message: The Communists are everywhere. When the crazies took charge, Minute Women would sit in the back of classrooms to watch for any hint of subversive activity. When my dear world history teacher Miss Nelda Davis applied for permission to attend the annual conference of the National Council of Social Studies, the school board turned her down because they thought the NCSS was controlled by Communists. They canceled student participation in an essay contest about the United Nations because they believed the UN was part of a Communist plot to undermine our national sovereignty. They considered civil rights groups like the NAACP and the Urban League to be "pinko." At one point, during a search for a new superintendent, a well-qualified candidate from the West Coast was eliminated because he belonged to the Urban League. When I went to college, the first paper I wrote in my freshman-year political science class was a study of the politics of the Houston school board.

This adult political madness didn't touch students much, although it surely prevented us from learning anything about current events. During my free period, I worked in the high school library, and I noticed that all the books about Russia had been removed from the shelves. They were stashed under the circulation desk, so I spent my free time reading the forbidden books. One that I recall was Walter Duranty's book *I Write as I Please*. I didn't know at the time that Duranty was obsequious to Stalin (he should have called his book *I Write as Stalin Pleases*). Duranty had been the *New York Times* correspondent in Moscow from 1922 to 1936, and he used his important platform to cover up Stalin's crimes, the show trials and the Stalin-created mass famine in Ukraine. He won a Pulitzer Prize in 1932, which has shamefully never been revoked, for the propaganda he wrote on Stalin's behalf. It would have been enlightening to read Duranty and critiques of his views; but we were denied access to both. How foolish it was to ban the study of Russia. We really needed to learn more about its history and the nature of Stalinism. The school board's censorship guaranteed that we would be uninformed.

In May 1954, at the end of my sophomore year in high school, the US Supreme Court issued the *Brown v. Board of Education* decision, declaring de jure racial segregation unconstitutional. Our schools, of course, were segregated. The Houston school board was determined to preserve segregation, and it fought the decision. The Court's decision was never discussed in our classes, but we had access to newspapers, radio, and television news. I went to see the principal of San Jacinto, Mr. W. S. Brandenburger, and asked him why we were not obeying the Supreme Court decision. He was a kindly old gentleman, and he said that if the schools were desegregated, most Negro principals and teachers would lose their jobs in the consolidation of schools. I couldn't argue with him because, frankly, I didn't know whether he was right. I just didn't think the school board should ignore a Supreme Court decision. And I didn't feel right about racial segregation. I didn't know any Black students my age. I didn't have any Black friends until I was an adult. I learned only recently that Mr. Brandenburger was making an excuse for doing nothing but that he was right. My friend Leslie T. Fenwick, the dean emeritus at Howard University's School of Education, recently wrote a book called *Jim Crow's Pink Slip*, in which she documented that about one hundred thousand Black principals and teachers were fired across the South when schools desegregated; they were replaced by white principals and teachers who were often less qualified.

We never took any standardized tests in junior high school or high school except for some ridiculous multiple-choice tests that allegedly determined our "aptitudes" and predicted our future occupations. I don't remember what I was supposed to be. Our teachers wrote their own classroom tests, based on what they had taught. The only other standardized test I took was the Scholastic Aptitude Test, because I wanted to qualify to go to an eastern college. I graduated high school in 1956, and at the time, the College Board revealed the scores only to guidance counselors, not to the students who took the tests. Since they knew our SAT scores, the guidance counselors would tell us which colleges to apply to. This policy of secrecy changed in 1958. I didn't learn my scores until many years later, when I had lunch at a professional conference and sat next to someone in charge of the testing program at the College Board; I told him that I had never seen my scores. Not long after, he sent me a faded copy of the microfilm with my scores. I was stunned to discover that they were nearly identical to those of my two grown sons and equally stunned to learn that I had high scores in math. I never took a math class in college because I didn't think I was any good at math.

When I was in tenth grade, I discovered a mentor. He was my rabbi, Dr. Hyman Judah Schachtel of Beth Israel Synagogue. Dr. Schachtel was a highly literate man who loved books and classical music. He was the chief rabbi at Beth Israel from 1943 to 1975 and was a greatly admired figure in Houston because he was learned. Beth Israel was the synagogue of the well-established German Jews. It was also across the street from San Jacinto High School, which made it easy for me to drop by in the afternoon for spontaneous conversations with Dr. Schachtel. My family had switched temples because my father had a falling-out with the Brotherhood at Emanu El, the other reform synagogue (I don't recall why, but he had a bad temper and was easily provoked). At that time, Jewish boys prepared for their bar mitzvah, but girls were not eligible for bat mitzvah. However, we were all "confirmed" at the end of tenth grade. Confirmation was a public ceremony in which we gave short speeches about our commitment to our faith. Dr. Schachtel saw something in me that he liked, a mind that wanted to grow, and he adopted me as his mentee. Born in London, Dr. Schachtel had a British accent, and he was something of an intellectual snob. I sometimes wondered if he felt trapped in Houston, where the pursuit of money was far more admired than the pursuit of knowledge. I would visit his book-filled office, where he encouraged my intellectual life. He lent me recordings of classical music and books that he thought I should read. After I was confirmed, I continued to meet with him to be inspired by his love of learning. When I entered my senior year in high school, Rabbi Schachtel's wife, Barbara, who had attended Wellesley College, invited me to attend a reception to meet representatives from the Seven Sisters, the elite Eastern women's colleges. Without her, I would never have heard of these colleges. At the reception, representatives of Radcliffe, Barnard, Wellesley, Smith, Mount Holyoke, Vassar, and Bryn Mawr met with about a dozen girls from Houston schools. I never visited any of the campuses; I studied their catalogues. I applied to Wellesley, Smith, and Vassar, and selected Vanderbilt as my safety school. Mrs. Schachtel said to me, "You must promise me that if you are accepted to Wellesley that you won't waste your time." And I solemnly promised. Many years later, I asked the college alumnae office when Barbara Schachtel had graduated and learned, to my great surprise, that she had dropped out of college to marry.

When I graduated from high school, my English teacher, Mrs. Ratliff, gave me two lines of poetry as a gift. The lines she gave me were "Among them, but not of them," from "Childe Harold's Pilgrimage," and the last line of "Ulysses" by Alfred, Lord Tennyson: "To strive, to seek, to find, and not to yield." I can't remember any other graduation gift I received. She reached my heart with those lines.

In early May of 1956, shortly before graduation, the envelopes arrived on the same day: I was accepted at Wellesley, Smith, and Vassar but rejected by Vanderbilt, my safety school! Many years later, I lectured at Vanderbilt and shared that story, to the great mirth of my audience in Nashville.

4

WELLESLEY

When I entered Wellesley, my life and fortunes began afresh. I had never seen the campus, never been to Massachusetts. My parents drove me there in September of 1956, a long trip from Texas. The huge trees on campus were beginning to change colors. I had never seen that before. In Houston, we had only two seasons: summer and not-summer. But at Wellesley there was a season called fall, when the tree leaves turned yellow, orange, and red; yet another called winter, when there was snow, something I had seen only once for a few minutes in Houston, and a season called spring, when everything bloomed again. There was surely summer, too, but I was not there when it happened. I was assigned to Severance Hall, a beautiful Gothic building in the center of campus. A huge maple tree stood next to the entrance to the dormitory, covered in bright yellow leaves. My room was in the basement overlooking Lake Waban. I didn't realize at the time what a privilege it was to have a room with a view of the serene lake. I had a Jewish roommate, in keeping with the college's policy of matching people with others of the same religion. My roommate, Rachel Friedman, was from Baltimore. We disagreed about music. She played "shew" tunes (the Baltimore pronunciation for "show"), while I played pop songs and country music. It must have been very hard on her to be exposed to my hokey Texas tastes.

Coming from the Houston public schools to Wellesley College was a culture shock. Wellesley was nothing like San Jacinto High School, and Massachusetts was nothing like Houston. The campus was startlingly beautiful: five hundred acres of rolling lawns and hills, historic buildings with turrets and towers, with beautiful Lake Waban in the center, surrounded by rustic walking trails. And all was steeped in beloved traditions that dated back to the nineteenth century (Wellesley was founded in 1870 as a female seminary and opened as a college in 1875).

The student body at Wellesley was all female, as it still is. This was a novelty, since I had spent all my years of schooling in coeducational settings. This meant that students focused on their studies and friendships, not on how they were perceived by boys. It meant that no one won any points for their clothing or makeup. It meant that girls could express their thoughts without being called, derisively, a "brain." It was okay to excel. It was encouraged, rather than repressed. It was okay to be competitive in the classroom. For the first time in my school life, I was no longer the smartest girl in the class. There were many, many students who had a far better high school education, many who had attended the best private schools, many who came from educated and cultured families, and many who were brilliant and talented, far more than I.

Many aspects of the Wellesley experience were novel. Whereas I could count the number of truly outstanding teachers I had known in K-12 on my fingers and toes, almost every one of my professors was outstanding. Each was an expert in his or her field. My freshman-year English teacher was Philip Booth, who was later recognized as one of the nation's best poets. He was very handsome, and almost everyone in the class—including me—was in love with him. Many of my teachers had taught at Wellesley for decades and were legendary as teachers and/or scholars.

One of the hardiest and, in retrospect, most bizarre traditions at Wellesley was the posture portrait that all freshmen were required to pose for, completely nude. We were told that the purpose of the picture was to study our posture, but we suspected it had to do with lascivious gym teachers. Later, I discovered that the posture pictures had nothing to do with gym teachers; it was part of a vast, pseudoscientific study of body types launched by a quack scientist intent on divining links between a person's body type and his or her intelligence, temperament, and future achievement. Many colleges participated in this purported "study," as I learned later from an article by Ron Rosenbaum that appeared in *The New York Times Magazine* on January 15, 1995, called "The Great Ivy League Nude Posture Photo Scandal." As the study of body types disappeared along with other eugenic theories, the tradition ended, and many of the portraits were burned, although some boxes of these portraits are stored at the National Anthropological Archives at the Smithsonian Museum. Each negative is labeled by height, weight, date, and age, but thankfully, not by name.

As incoming freshmen, we were also required to stand in front of a group of professors and answer their questions to see if we needed speech lessons to correct our regional accents. I had a fairly strong Texas twang. When I pronounced the word *I* to sound like an elongated *eye*, I could see them scribbling furiously. Then one of them asked me where I came from. I said "Houston," or "you-stun." She said, "That is not the proper way to pronounce *Houston*. You should say 'Hee-youston.'" She said it with a whistling sound. And I replied, "If I said that in Houston, everyone would laugh at me." Somehow, I talked myself out of having to take speech lessons. I later learned that if I came from New York City, I might have pronounced it "House-ton," because there is a street in Manhattan with that name.

In my freshman year, I was deeply interested in the 1956 presidential election. Although I was too young to vote (the voting age was then twenty-one), I was an ardent Democrat. So was my roommate Rachel. Of course, we supported Adlai Stevenson and Estes Kefauver, who were running against Dwight D. Eisenhower and Richard Nixon. Rachel and I had enormous posters of Stevenson and Kefauver hanging over our beds in our dorm room. One night that fall, before the election, we went to a concert in Boston. When we came home late that night, we were in for a shock. Other girls had moved our beds into the large common bathroom, and on each bed was propped our posters of Stevenson and Kefauver. That was pretty hostile, but we decided to laugh and overlook it. We moved our beds and posters back to our room without complaint.

We were disappointed but not surprised when our candidates lost, but Eisenhower was a good man and we did not despair.

While I was living in Severance as a freshman, I wrote and produced my own newspaper, which I called *The South Basement Bugle*. I posted it on the bulletin board so that everyone could read the news in our corner of the basement. The housemother, a kindly older woman, took me aside and suggested that I try out for the newspaper, which I did. I joined the staff of *The Wellesley News* in my sophomore year, and it became an important part of my life at Wellesley.

Wellesley was the opposite of everything I knew about school. In addition to its traditions, there was an honor code, high academic standards, and a wonderful stuffiness that I loved to make fun of. I was in the class of 1960. My classmates came from across the country. We were tasked with writing a class cheer and a class song. Every class had its color, and ours was red. Whereas cheating was commonplace in high school, it was unheard of at Wellesley. I jumped enthusiastically into my new life: I soon learned the class song and the traditional college songs that we all sang enthusiastically every week at "Step Singing" outside the chapel.

One of the songs was a tribute to evolution:

Oh, Evolu, Oh, Evolu!
There is nothing in this world you cannot do.
You took a monkey and you turned him to a man, long since,
  'tis true.
But now you've brought a greater phenomenon to pass.
You've taken 1960, an embryonic mass.
And turned it by a miracle, into a freshman class.
There is nothing in this world you cannot do!

I majored in political science because I had an intense interest in politics. But the courses in political science were largely disconnected from reality (for example, we studied the politics of the Hoover Dam, which did not interest me). Sixty-five years later, what I remember better than the courses in my major was an introductory course in psychology, in which the professor, Claire Zimmerman, taught me an unforgettable lesson. She said that when you write, you must always have an audience in mind. Are you writing a newspaper article for the general public? Are you writing a letter to your family? Are you writing for specialists? She was teaching psychology, not giving advice, but it was one of the most powerful writing lessons I learned: know your audience. That piece of advice enabled me later in life to write opinion pieces for mass-circulation newspapers, even tabloids, and scholarly articles for scholars. Different audiences, different voices, different tone, different vocabulary. I read Professor Zimmerman's obituary in the college magazine. She was ten years older than I was, Wellesley class of 1950. She taught psychology at the college for fifty-seven years. Her obit said, "Claire's introductory psychology course was wildly popular with generations of Wellesley students. Her syllabus, which included *Goodbye, Columbus* and *Franny and Zooey*, introduced students to psychology in a way that made the subject personal for them." She did that for me and taught me many valuable lifelong lessons.

The course that I loved most at Wellesley was far removed from my major and my immediate interests. It was a course in Greek drama, taught in English by Barbara McCarthy, a professor of Greek. Rumor had it that Professor McCarthy had recited the Lewis Carroll poem "You Are Old, Father William" in Greek while standing on her head. True or false, it was indicative of her reputation for blending humor and learning. We read plays by Aeschylus, Sophocles, Euripides, and Aristophanes. I had never heard of them in high school. What a wonderful course that was! More lifelong lessons and a newfound love for ancient Greece.

Wellesley was formal, but its traditions were democratic. Every girl had to take her turn waiting tables at dinner, delivering food to the table, and clearing it after the meal, no matter who her parents were or where she went to high school (and yes, we referred to ourselves as "girls," not women). Every girl had to take her turn at the front door of the dormitory on a shift called "bells," where you received guests and used the sound system to summon any girl who had a visitor or a phone call on the house phone (there were no private phones). I heard that there were once maids who worked in the dorms, but when I was there, everyone did her part to clean her own room and carry out her regular assignment in the dining room and at the front door.

As at all my previous schools, my classmates were all white. There was one Black student in the class of 1958, who later became a federal judge, and one in each of the other classes, but none in ours. There were a few Asian-American students, and a few Hispanic students (one was the daughter of the governor of Puerto Rico). Half the students in my class had attended private prep schools, and half had graduated from public schools. Although Wellesley had distribution requirements (meaning that everyone had to take a certain number of credits in each field of study), I never took a math class. I took freshman chemistry to dispose of my science requirement. I memorized the periodic table, using mnemonics as my strategy for each element, line by line; but no knowledge of chemistry remains with me today. I saturated myself with classes in literature, history, political science, philosophy, history of music, and Greek literature. In high school, I had taken two years of Latin and two years of Spanish. At Wellesley, I had two years of French. This was an unintentional combination that ensured that I would not be literate in any language but English.

As a freshman, I joined the crew and became a cockswain. I had never been in a crew shell in my life, and there I was barking out commands and telling the other girls to "feather their oars" and "stroke, 2, 3, 4." I also learned to play squash. Squash was wonderful fun. It was fast, furious, competitive, and very physical. After college, it was a shock to learn that there were no squash courts in New York City that allowed women to play (that has since changed).

In sophomore year, everyone received a new dormitory assignment, chosen by lottery, and I landed in Beebe Hall on the Quadrangle with three other dorms. I made lifelong friends in my three years at Beebe. Almost all my Beebe friends were Protestant. There were probably fewer Catholics than Jews at Wellesley. None of us was passionate about religion in terms of our daily life, so it didn't matter, and we could joke about our differences and enjoy them.

Wellesley had many taboos, and I took great pleasure in breaking them or making fun of them. Our dorms had a weekly high tea during which we were supposed to practice the correct behavior and protocol for such occasions. I went with a small group of Beebe buddies to a thrift shop in the town of Wellesley where we bought old-fashioned hats and outfits and dressed very properly for high tea as if it were 1900 instead of 1958. I also found another way to pierce the veil of propriety. All our dormitory rooms had rope ladders in the event of fire, and I tried mine out during a formal dinner, when I swung back and forth outside the dining hall windows while everyone was trying to be well-behaved.

Then there was the time-honored tradition of "calendar days." A calendar day was the day before a major vacation. Under no circumstance was any student allowed to be absent on a calendar day; this rule prevented students from leaving early for extended vacations. On the day before a calendar day, I went with a few friends to New Haven to visit Yale boys we had dated. To be unusually audacious, we wore our gym suits (which were bloomers) on the train to New Haven. Once at Yale, we drank and partied. We left New Haven about midnight and staggered to the train station. We boarded our train, which unfortunately broke down in Providence, Rhode Island. We had to hire a taxi to bring us to Wellesley, and we barely made it to the first period class at 8:40 a.m., looking bedraggled and hungover. We had succeeded in what we set out to do. We defied the tradition, we flaunted our independence, but we ultimately broke no rules. We were in class for all of calendar day. Very childish, I know, but fun at the time and unforgettable.

My involvement with the *Wellesley News* opened many doors for me. I was able to go to plays in Boston and review tryouts before they reached Broadway. I attended a lecture that Fidel Castro gave to a large audience at Harvard in 1959, soon after he seized power in Cuba. I made new friends who did not live in my dormitory. One of those was Emily Cohen, who was a year ahead of me, class of 1959. She was brilliant and beautiful; she came from the Bronx. I visited her and her family and stayed in their apartment on the Grand Concourse in the Bronx, the first time I had ever been to New York City other than a tourist visit when I was twelve. Sleeping in her apartment, I heard the traffic and subway trains at night and wondered how anyone ever got to sleep. Little did I know that one day I too would live in the great city. I had a huge crush on

Emily. I wanted to be just like her. After college, Emily went to London, where she was a journalist for *The Economist* and wrote about China and South Asia. As was then the custom at that magazine, she never had a byline. Had she stayed in the United States, she would have been a celebrated writer for a major journal like *The New Yorker* or *The Atlantic*. She married a handsome, erudite Brit named Rodney MacFarquhar, who was a China scholar; he served briefly as a Liberal in Parliament, then lost his seat. The family moved to the United States, and Rod joined the faculty at Harvard. While they were still in London, my husband Richard and I joined them for opera at Glyndebourne, a famous venue where patrons dress in formal attire and bring a meal to eat while sitting on a blanket outdoors on the well-tended grounds. Rod and Emily surprised us by bringing a bucket of Kentucky Fried Chicken to remind us of home (ugh! ugh! ugh!). My beloved friend died far too young of a brain tumor, at the age of sixty-two. She was working on a biography of the Pakistani leader Benazir Bhutto when she died.

Emily gave me a unique gift when we both worked on the *Wellesley News* staff. She wrote on a card: "Shall I compare thee to a Wellesley rose? Thou art more lovely in being less temperate. . . . Call it your own shade of red, kiddo. Wellesley's been waiting a long time for you. *Bonne chance*, Em." I framed it and have kept it on my desk for more than six decades. I admired her more than anyone else I knew.

Three other members of the *News* staff achieved fame after college. One was Madeline Korbel, class of 1959. I knew her as Maddy, a smart and friendly girl whose parents came from Czechoslovakia and settled in Colorado. She told me that her father was a member of the government when the Communists took charge in Czechoslovakia, and the family escaped. Her father became a professor of international politics at the University of Denver. After college and graduate school, she married a newspaper scion named Joseph Albright (his family owned *Newsday* on Long Island). They had twin girls, and our young children played together a few times. She later divorced, but was ever after known as Madeleine Albright, and she eventually became secretary of state. Another staff member was Nora Ephron, class of 1962. She was as witty in college as she was after graduation, when she achieved fame as a journalist, humorist, and writer of movies and essays. The cartoonist for the *News* was a beautiful and talented girl named Ali McGraw, a member of the class of 1960. A few years after graduation from Wellesley, Ali became a movie star when she appeared in a movie version of *Goodbye, Columbus* in 1969 and *Love Story* in 1970.

Now I must confess my most embarrassing moment at Wellesley, which happened in my senior year. There was a tradition in which sophomores in each dorm performed skits, roasting the seniors. I am the kind of person who is always on the lookout for a new gadget. I had read in a magazine about a little rubber cup to use during one's menstrual period to collect blood, thus replacing tampons and sanitary pads. It was the latest thing. I bought one by mail and showed it to my friends. It didn't work all that well, because if you bent the wrong way, the contents might spill and make a mess. When it was time for the sophomore roast, the girl impersonating me walked across the room carrying this little bag without saying what it was. Everyone roared, and I was mortified, because they clearly assumed that it was a diaphragm to prevent pregnancy. I couldn't very well jump up and say, "It is not what you think! It is a blood catcher for my period!"

I worked very hard at Wellesley. I studied long hours, conducted research on political and historical issues, wrote essays, and spent days in the library, enjoying easy access to the college's open shelves and great collections. I even found a book about Jewish life in the ghettos of Europe that described the one my mother lived in and learned for the first time that Jews in Bessarabia were not allowed to own property, go to school, or engage in many other activities.

Wellesley was very different from high school, which was a breeze. I was challenged and intellectually stimulated. I took long walks around Lake Waban, often reciting out loud my new favorite poem by Gerard Manley Hopkins, "Spring and Fall: To a Young Child," which I had read in freshman English class. ("Margaret, are you grieving / Over Goldengrove unleaving? / Leaves like the things of man, you / With your fresh thoughts care for, can you? / Ah! as the heart grows older / It will come to such sights colder / By and by, nor spare a sigh / Though worlds of wanwood leafmeal lie . . ."). Wellesley was the right place for me and shaped the person I became. I had to stretch intellectually, and I learned that I could do whatever was expected and more. Many of my classmates were surely better prepared than I, but I never felt at a disadvantage. I could not only keep up, I could excel if I put my mind to it.

The best of times was Junior Show. This was another Wellesley tradition (which has since disappeared, unfortunately). Every year, volunteers from the incoming junior class would gather in a rented house on Cape Cod to write a musical in a week's time, before classes began, that would be staged for the entire college in the fall of junior year. The theme of the show had to be connected to the class color. Our show was titled *Call It Red*. About thirty members of our class assembled at an old house in Chatham, Massachusetts, to write the play and the music. Several of my Junior Show colleagues became friends forever. The chair of the script committee was Linda Salzman, who became an important part of my life. Later in life, with the married name of Linda Gottlieb, she wrote daytime soaps and was the producer of several films, most notably, the classic film *Dirty Dancing*.

On the Cape, we wrote a play that reflected our times. By today's standards, it was thoroughly sexist. It was about a cosmetics company modeled on Revlon (we called it Redlon) that was in dire financial straits. It recruited several ordinary women for total makeovers, using Redlon products and the company's experts. The girls had a physical education coach, a psychiatrist, makeup artists, beauticians, and the elegant Aunt Jean, the Redlon representative who would teach the drab women how to be glamorous and poised. The owner of Redlon was known as B. S. Redlon.

The songs and lyrics were splendid. Our director was Ali McGraw. Aunt Jean was played by Barbara Babcock, who later became a successful performer on television and in the movies. I had a small part as the public relations guy Jim (and dressed in drag in a man's suit from the town thrift shop). The show was so beloved by our class that we performed it again at our fortieth and our fiftieth reunions. The highlight was the theme song, "Call It Red." It referred to the shade of lipstick that turned every homely housewife and lonely girl into a beauty. At the end, the totally made-over women emerged with identical red lipstick and red wigs, dressed in identical red outfits, looking like Stepford Wives and singing, "Oh, we could have called it scarlet or burgundy instead, but for the benefit of the public, we think we'll call it red." The show was not about the color red but about the 1950s ideal of feminine beauty to which all women supposedly aspired in hopes of pleasing their men. Little did we know! At least two of us turned out to be gay, and another later married a transgender woman.

A few events stand out in my memory. One was the time in 1958 when the senator from Massachusetts, John F. Kennedy, came to campus to meet with the political science majors. There were twelve of us. We talked to the handsome, charming Senator Kennedy for two hours about state and national politics. None of us imagined that he would be elected president two years later. Senator Kennedy brought with him a strange fellow named Langdon P. Marvin Jr., who had briefly roomed with JFK at Harvard. Kennedy left us but Langdon P. Marvin Jr. didn't. He came back to campus several times to regale us with stories of his adventures and his many romances. I suppose he enjoyed having an audience of pretty young things. I later learned that Marvin was a bit of a whacko who was barred from the Kennedy administration.

Another event involved a then-famous Indian writer named Santha Rama Rau. The daughter of a distinguished Indian family, she had graduated from Wellesley in 1944 and went on to write numerous books about India. She delivered a public lecture at the college when I was a sophomore. She said this (I paraphrase): "You are not a writer unless you publish. You cannot write and put your work in a drawer. A writer writes." Why do I still remember those lines (or the gist of them) more than sixty years later? Why did they make such a large impact on my then-forming sense of identity? Santha Rama Rau spoke to me directly. She told me what I must do. A writer writes. A writer must publish.

The epochal event of my four years at Wellesley occurred in the spring of my junior year. The political science department had a tradition of sending its majors to Washington, D.C., to intern in government offices for the summer. Everyone lived together at the Meridian Hill Hotel. When the time came for me to decide which federal agency I wanted to work for, I realized that I didn't want to work in a government office.

I wanted to work for a daily newspaper. I wrote a letter to the editor of every major newspaper on the East Coast from Washington to Boston. I said I would do anything, including sweeping floors, for the opportunity to work in the newsroom for the summer. I got a polite turndown from James Wechsler of the then-liberal, now Murdoch-owned *New York Post*. Then silence. One night when I was at dinner, someone working the front desk came to tell me that I had a very important telephone call. I ran to the phone, and the voice on the other end said, "Hello, this is Ben Gilbert. I am the managing editor of *The Washington Post*. When can you report for work as a copyboy?"

Wow! My heart was thumping, and I was shaking. This was what I wanted most in the world at that moment in my life. I was going to work for *The Washington Post*, and I would room with my college buddies at the Meridian Hill Hotel. They would work in government agencies, and I would be a copyboy for *The Washington Post*. I reported to the *Post* as soon as school ended and learned that I would be paid $33 a week, enough to cover the cost of the hotel and at least a few meals. This was heaven!

At the *Post*, I reported to Ben Gilbert. As a copyboy, I did whatever any reporter or editor asked of me. A reporter would shout "Boy!" and I ran to do whatever he or she wanted. I sharpened pencils. I ran errands. Being the lowest copyboy on the totem pole, I often worked from 3:00 p.m. to midnight, a shift that no one else wanted. I did "copy runs" and picked up stories at the Associated Press offices or anywhere else I was told to go and brought them back to the reporters (there were no faxes or computers or cell phones at that time). The society editor once asked me to cover a wedding in the suburbs, and I wrote a couple of paragraphs. My copy must have been a stinker because she never asked again. I got to know the legendary Meg Greenfield, who was only a few years older than I was but was already a member of the editorial board.

I became friendly with a quiet young reporter named Tom Wolfe, who would later become one of the nation's most celebrated novelists and essayists. That summer of 1959, he carried out a very impressive assignment when President Eisenhower dispatched Vice President Richard Nixon to tour the nations of Eastern Europe. Evidently the *Post* did not have a budget to send a reporter, so Wolfe was assigned to write about each of the places that Nixon visited without leaving Washington. He wrote so vividly about each stop that readers assumed he was accompanying Nixon and his entourage. I invited Tom over to have brunch with me and my roommates. I thought he might connect with one of them, but he didn't. We thought he might be gay, but he wasn't. He just wasn't interested in any of us. Years later, I ran into Tom at some event, and he said, "Oh, yes, you were the copyboy who was armed with a scimitar because you were afraid of going out to pick up copy at night." I never had a scimitar. I never was afraid. He had a vivid imagination.

One of my great adventures while working at the *Post* occurred when one of the foreign affairs journalists received an invitation to attend a reception at the Soviet embassy in honor of Vice President Nixon. The reporter had no interest in going. His name was Carroll Kirkpatrick. I asked him if I might go in his place and use his name. He said sure. I called to RSVP as Carroll Kirkpatrick and wore his name badge. I saw Nixon arrive in his big black limousine. I ate a few hors d'oeuvre. A *Post* photographer took a picture of me standing under a gigantic portrait of Stalin. There I was, Carroll Kirkpatrick, enjoying a night at the Soviet embassy under the malign gaze of the world's worst dictator. It is a picture I treasure.

And then there was the event that changed my life forever. My classmate Linda Salzman told me that she was dating a New Yorker who was working in D.C., and she asked him to find dates for me. Meanwhile, she was off to the World Youth Festival in Moscow. Her boyfriend's name was Richard (Dick) Ravitch. Dick was working for California congressman Chet Holifield, who was involved in issues of nuclear arms and atomic energy. Dick invited me to meet him at the congressional lunchroom. I happily accepted. Living as I was on a Spartan budget, I loaded up my tray with several dishes. He was amazed. He realized I wasn't eating regularly. Dick is a person who likes to take care of people, and he decided to take care of me.

First, he set me up on a date with one of his best friends. His friend was both bald and boring. Then he set me up with someone else, who was not bald but was boring. Then he called one night and said he had just gotten tickets to hear Ella Fitzgerald perform at Rock Creek Park in D.C., where she would be accompanied by the Oscar Peterson Trio and Nelson Riddle. Was I available? Of course. He drove a snappy Ford convertible. He was very handsome, very dynamic, highly intelligent, and had a commanding presence. The rest is history, as they say. That Christmas 1959, he proposed marriage, and I accepted his proposal. We were married two weeks after I graduated college, on June 26, 1960.

When my friend Linda came home from Moscow at the end of the summer of 1959, I felt sure she would not be happy that I was dating her boyfriend. But she had met a wonderful American guy at the World Youth Festival in Moscow, Paul Gottlieb, and they too got engaged and married. Paul eventually became the publisher of Harry N. Abrams, which published gorgeous art books. They had two sons; we had two sons. Eventually, we all divorced and remarried. Linda and I remain close friends. To this day, my best friends are women I got to know during my years at Wellesley: Linda, Susan Krieger Jonas, Marilyn Claster Nissenson, Patsy Fogarty Elliott, Vicky Garriques Fay, and Joan Brownstein Leibovich, all accomplished professionals. Much to the consternation of the young women of today, we still refer to each other as "girls."

5

MARRIAGE

On June 26, 1960, Dick and I were married in Houston at Congregation Beth Israel by Rabbi Hyman Judah Schachtel, the mentor whose wife had steered me to Wellesley. The morning of the wedding it rained buckets and boatloads, as it can only in Houston; fortunately, the sun broke through by the time the ceremony started. That seemed to be a good omen. His aunts from New York City were there, dressed in black as they almost always were, even for weddings. We flew to Dallas that night to get away from family, then set off for a long honeymoon in Europe. I had never been to Europe. Dick planned the trip meticulously, and we visited the great hotels in London, Paris, Rome, the Riviera, and Athens. We took a cruise to Mykonos, Crete, Santorini, and other Greek islands. It was a dream honeymoon. As I look back at the pictures in my scrapbook, I see that I was very young (twenty-two), surprisingly pretty (surprising to me since I never thought of myself as pretty), and extremely innocent, even naïve. I thought he was incredibly handsome. I felt he was destined for greatness; I didn't have a clue what I was destined for. Dick must have felt he was Henry Higgins to my Eliza Doolittle. I was madly in love with him and excited about our new life together.

Having never been to Europe, having never stayed in grand hotels, my eyes must have been popping. I have a vivid memory of the fruit served at the hotel in San Remo on the Riviera. The cherries seemed to be twice as large as any I had ever seen and twice as luscious. Every place we visited was a revelation. I marveled at the Parthenon and was thrilled by the donkey ride up a mountain in Santorini. I was mortified and embarrassed by a live sex show in Amsterdam.

But I felt the first hint of a problem in our relationship. When I wrote notes to his family, thanking them for their wedding gifts, Dick insisted on reading them before I mailed them. Sometimes he didn't like the wording, and he made me write them again. He was definitely the man of the house, and I was the little lady who was expected to follow his orders. Before our marriage, he took me to the elegant Bonwit Teller department store to buy some appropriate clothing for me. Nothing I owned was worth keeping; out it went. He determined which dresses I would buy.

When we were engaged, I had dinner at his mother's elegant apartment at 15 West Eighty-First Street in Manhattan, which his father's construction company had built in the 1920s. She had a Black couple who had worked for her for many years, Letha and Dixon. Letha was an expert cook, and Dixon was both a butler and a chauffeur. The more I learned about Dick's family, the more I realized that I had married into a dynasty. His grandfather Joseph and Joseph's brother had come from Russia in the 1880s as penniless boys. They lived on the Lower East Side of Manhattan in what was virtually a Jewish ghetto. As young men, they started the Ravitch Brothers Company, an iron-making business that made a variety of products, including steel gratings and manhole covers for the streets. By the 1920s, the company had grown into a full-fledged construction business, and the brothers became very wealthy, building grand apartment buildings in Manhattan, like the Beresford on West Eighty-First Street, overlooking Central Park.

Joseph Ravitch, Dick's grandfather, was the family patriarch. Joseph had one son, Saul, and two daughters, Miriam and Sylvia. Dick's father, Saul Ravitch, became a partner in the family business, as did Saul Horowitz, who married Miriam, Dick's aunt. The new generation renamed the business HRH Construction Company. Joseph's other daughter, Sylvia, married a lawyer, Irving Lipkowitz. When I met Dick, his paternal grandparents were no longer living, and all three families—the Ravitches (Saul and Sylvia), the Horowitzes (Saul and Miriam), and the Lipkowitzes (Irving and Sylvia)—lived in identical apartments on different floors at 15 West 81 Street, built by the family business. (Among the three related families—descendants of Joseph Ravitch—there were two Sauls and two Sylvias!).

Dick's father, Saul Ravitch, was a graduate of Tufts College, and was devoted to his family, his business, and golf. Dick's mother Sylvia graduated from Hunter College and earned a master's degree at Cornell (her master's dissertation was about Chaucer). Her closest friend at Hunter College was Dick's aunt Sylvia. They were then known as the two Sylvias. Dick had home movies of his parents skiing in the 1930s at a time when my parents were struggling to make a living, reminding me of the great social distance between his family and mine. Dick's father died before I met him. He was forty-nine when he died of leukemia; Dick left Oberlin to return home and finished college at Columbia University.

My mother-in-law Sylvia Ravitch was probably the most fascinating and most difficult person I ever met. She was well-read and cultured. She was charming, elegant, beautiful, and always perfectly dressed. She had friends in the arts—classical pianists, playwrights, and Broadway composers. She played the piano, she sculpted, she painted, she wrote short stories. She entertained regally. She missed her late husband; she kept a portrait of him on her Steinway grand piano in the living room. Though she dated, she never married again. If you met her, you would never know that she had been brought up in Flatbush and had gone to public schools. Her father Samuel Lerner was a postal worker (after she married into the Ravitch family, he became a stockbroker, undoubtedly through family connections), and her mother Ida was a homemaker. And yet this daughter of Flatbush became a grande dame, a woman whom everyone fell in love with, a woman to whom taxi drivers poured out their hearts, a woman who was revered and feared. I admired her for her beauty and talents, but I was also afraid of her. When she walked into a store where she was known, the salespeople became obsequious because they knew how sharp-tongued she could be. She got the "yes, your majesty, no, your majesty" treatment everywhere.

When Dick and I were engaged, he took me to meet his mother. At the time, she was living in a charming private cottage at the Austen Riggs Center in Stockbridge, Massachusetts, then known as a residential facility for neurotic people. She was in psychoanalytic therapy for most of her adult life; she checked herself in to Riggs whenever she needed extra support. She had very high spirits and very intense rages, and it was impossible to know which to anticipate. When I first met her, she was warm and welcoming. She took pictures of me and sculpted a beautiful head of me in clay, which I still have.

When Dick and I returned from our honeymoon and began to create a new life together, my relationship with my quixotic mother-in-law became stormy. Sometimes she would call early in the morning in a rage. I never knew what set her off. Dick told me to ignore her rages. I was glad for his support, but I never felt equal to her expectations. I had no interest in going to the latest fashion show at Saks or Loehmann's or wherever it was. Despite my Wellesley education, I was still a Texas rube. She arranged for me to have my hair cut at a famous salon owned by Julius Caruso, and the great man cut my hair. Thank God, no more permanents! He was a celebrity hairstylist whose clients included Marilyn Monroe, Joan Rivers, and members of the Ford, Rockefeller, and Vanderbilt families. I knew nothing about these famous clients. In his obituary in *The New York Times*, his daughter said that her father would spend hours styling Marilyn Monroe's hair, "and then she would put her hands in her hair and just mess it up as much as she could. My father would say, 'I just spent two hours trying to get her to look like a lady.'"

My beautiful, accomplished mother-in-law had a circle of remarkable friends. I knew that they were very rich and polished, like she was, but I did not realize that they were at the pinnacle of high society in New York City. They were the crème de la crème. It was not until I searched for their names on the Internet (not possible in the 1960s and 1970s!) that I felt retroactively awed by her close circle.

There was Marietta Tree, one of Sylvia's best friends. I later learned that she was Marietta Peabody Tree, the mother of the historian Frances Fitzgerald and the model Penelope Tree. Wikipedia says she had an affair with John Huston and married Ronald Tree, a member of the British Parliament. They moved to New York City, where Marietta became active in Democratic politics and began a long relationship with Adlai Stevenson. President Kennedy appointed her to be the US representative to the UN Commission on Human Rights, where she reported to Ambassador Stevenson. She was walking with him in London when he had a heart attack and later died. John Huston cast Marietta in a role in his 1960 film *The Misfits*.

Another of Sylvia's close friends was Dorothy Hirshon (Dorothy Hart Hearst Paley Hirshon, to be exact). She too had a remarkable background, not only because she was gorgeous but also because she married powerful men. When she was nineteen, in 1927, she married one of the sons of William Randolph Hearst while sailing on a yacht off Santa Barbara. The couple went to live in New York, where she began to build a magnificent art collection. Since her husband drank too much and was not fond of work, she divorced him and, in 1932, married William S. Paley, the founder of CBS. Dorothy was named one of the best-dressed women in the world. She was sketched by Matisse, photographed by Cecil Beaton, and often featured in *Vogue* and *Harper's Bazaar*. She and Paley lived on an 85-acre estate in Manhasset on Long Island that was tended by twenty-two servants. Dorothy was a member of the famous Algonquin set, the writers and intellectuals who lunched weekly at the then-celebrated hotel in Manhattan. Dorothy and Paley divorced in 1947. Six years later she married a stockbroker named Walter Hirshon; they divorced in 1961. Dorothy was one of Truman Capote's "swans." My mother-in-law, Sylvia Lerner Ravitch, born in Flatbush, graduate of the New York City public schools and Hunter College, was one of her best friends.

I did not know anything about high society. Should I have been deferential? Should I have learned how to act and dress from these women? I could not, because that potential person was not me. Not being impressed by the circles in which she moved and psychologically unable to be part of it, I continued to find it difficult to establish a close relationship with Sylvia. She expected her daughter-in-law to fit in with her circle; I did not.

Sylvia died of pancreatic cancer in 1974. It was a horrible time. The custom in the family was never to tell the truth to a person with cancer. It was referred to as "C," and no one said it out loud. Sylvia was very proud that Dick's father was never told that he had leukemia; she told him he had mononucleosis. She told me that when he was in the hospital, she went to St. Patrick's Cathedral to cry, where no one would know her. When her own mother, in old age, developed cancer, everyone lied to her, but she confided in me that she knew. She played along with the game to make them happy.

Sylvia knew that she had pancreatic cancer. The doctors opened her up and told her there was nothing they could do. As she bravely faced death, she had only one consolation: she had lived to see Richard Nixon forced out of the White House. She was a passionate Democrat, and she hated Nixon.

When we returned to New York City from our honeymoon, Dick joined the family business, HRH Construction Company. He was proud of his family heritage, but he had mixed feelings about joining his cousins in the business. He always longed to be in politics and public service, but the time had come for him to take his place as a partner at HRH. Dick's cousin, Saul Horowitz Jr. (known as J. R.), was the oldest partner. He was in charge of the construction business. J. R.'s younger brother, Alan, was also a partner, but he was more a playboy than a businessman; when he opened a branch office in Los Angeles, he dated Dinah Shore and other stars but imperiled the company's finances. Dick was in charge of real estate development, scouting out and developing new projects. J. R. was the father of four children, a West Point graduate, and mayor of Scarsdale. He and Dick were both friends and rivals. In 1975, J. R. died in a plane crash at LaGuardia Airport as he was returning from a business conference in New Orleans. His death was a terrible loss to his family and everyone who knew him.

Dick went on to have a successful career as a real estate developer. I was very proud of him, not because of his business success, but because of his idealism, his intellect, and his readiness to help others. Dick had graduated from Columbia College and Yale Law School. He retained close friendships from every part of his life. Whenever any of his friends had a problem, they called him. He would drop everything to go to their side and fix their problems if he could. He cared deeply about the civil rights movement; his law school roommate was Clifford Alexander, Jr., an African American man who later became Lyndon B. Johnson's secretary of the army (and father of Elizabeth Alexander, the poet and president of the Andrew Mellon Foundation). While his peers in the real estate industry built luxury housing and acquired huge fortunes, Dick used his knowledge of federal, state, and local laws to build middle-income and mixed-income housing. He built Waterside, a mixed-income housing project on the East River in Manhattan; Manhattan Plaza, a middle-income housing project for artists on West Forty-Second Street in Manhattan; the first racially integrated housing development in Washington, D.C.; and many other major projects. But his heart was always in politics. He was a true child of the New Deal. Making money was never as important to him as making a difference. He was involved in many Democratic campaigns as an adviser and fundraiser. He advised not only candidates but also labor unions. He wanted to make the world a better place. He was not a leftist, however. He never liked the petty, sectarian infighting on the Left, which usually doomed progressive candidates and damaged the candidacy of centrist Democrats. He despised radicals. He influenced my views; I admired him and helped whenever I could, occasionally writing a speech for him or a brochure for his latest housing project.

When Dick and I returned to New York City after our honeymoon in 1960, we settled into our first home, a modest one-bedroom apartment at 240 East Thirty-Fifth Street. I had never decorated anything before, and I am sure it must have been awful. My favorite colors then were blue and green. Not so bad. But I had never bought furniture by myself. And I had never cooked a meal. Dick was a good sport.

Once the furniture was delivered and the curtains were hung, I went to work in the Kennedy campaign. Its headquarters were at 277 Park Avenue in a stately old building that has since been replaced by a steel-and-glass skyscraper. Just as during my summer as a copyboy at *The Washington Post*, I handled menial chores. I folded letters, stuffed envelopes, ran errands, did everything that volunteers do. I organized a tea party honoring Mrs. Rose Kennedy at the home of a wealthy matriarch, Mrs. Louis Gimbel. John Kennedy was the voice of my generation, I believed. The day he visited the campaign headquarters and shook hands with each of the volunteers was thrilling, just as thrilling as the day I touched Roy Rogers's hand at the rodeo in Houston as a young girl.

6

THE NEW LEADER

When the 1960 campaign ended with Kennedy's narrow victory over Nixon, I was ecstatic, but I still had to figure out what to do with my life. I did not need to make money, but I needed to work. Every day, I read the classified advertisements for women in *The New York Times* (at the time, the ads were separated by gender), and almost every day I went to job interviews. It was discouraging. I could type but otherwise had no skills and no work experience. What could I do? There were many ads for a "gal Friday" (that's what the ads said), but I was not interested. Nor did I want an entry-level job at a publishing house, another choice for educated young women of my generation. That sounded too much like being a copyboy again. Dick did not mind that I was looking for a job since I had nothing else to do.

Then, in early January 1961, in the midst of my job hunt, I happened to read an intriguing editorial in *The New York Times*. It said that Sol Levitas, the founding editor of *The New Leader*, had died. *The New Leader*, the editorial said, was "one of the most stimulating and valuable magazines of our day," a forum "for every variety of democratic opinion." I thought, that's where I want to work. Set aside the fact that I had never heard of Sol Levitas or *The New Leader*. I knew as soon as I read the editorial that it described what I was looking for, a small magazine where I would have a chance to discuss ideas, learn about magazine publishing, perhaps have a chance to write, and interact with people who were fully engaged in the political, cultural, and social issues of the day.

I immediately called the magazine and spoke to the secretary to Mr. Levitas. I told her I was looking for a job as an editorial assistant, and that I would do anything. She said, "We are in chaos right now. But come to the office. Someone will talk to you." That was the best thing I had heard in weeks. I lived on East Thirty-Fifth Street and the magazine's offices were on East Fifteenth Street. Half an hour later I was there.

The offices were located in a stolid, dingy building at 7 East Fifteenth Street, a block from Union Square. On the outside of the brick building was a faded sign announcing the "Rand School for Social Science" (I didn't know it then, but the Rand School was founded by the Socialist Party of America to educate workers). The creaky, manual elevator was a large cage with a door that the passenger opened and closed. I ascended to the fourth floor hoping that this was the place where I would work.

The new editor, Myron "Mike" Kolatch, seemed pretty old to me (he was thirty-two). He was short and slender, with coal-black hair and a thin mustache. He was annoyed that I was asking for a job at such an unpropitious moment. He asked about my previous experience, and I told him that I had graduated from college just eight months earlier and had never held a full-time job. As a cloud passed over his face, I asked him, "How can I ever get any experience unless I get a job?" Then he told me that the magazine could not afford to pay me much. I was so eager to work for him that I quickly assured him that I would work for $10 a week. He told me that I was hired, and we agreed that no one else on the staff would know how much (or how little) I was paid. What Kolatch didn't know was that I would have paid *him* $10 a week just to breathe the air at *The New Leader* and ride that aged elevator!

I started at once and was promptly listed on the masthead of the magazine as an editorial assistant. The regular contributors were William Henry Chamberlin, Leslie A. Fiedler, Sidney Hook, Reinhold Niebuhr, and Theodore Draper, all well-known intellectuals in 1961. They and other writers were never paid, yet they eagerly contributed to a magazine where their copy was carefully edited and treated with respect. Sol

Levitas, the founder of *The New Leader*, was a Menshevik, I learned, and the magazine was democratic, socialist, and anticommunist. I was not a socialist, but I was definitely a Democrat and anticommunist.

When I began work at the magazine, I quickly discovered that only three of us (plus the secretary) were in regular attendance: the editor, Mike Kolatch, the associate editor Joel Blocker, and me. Writers often stopped in, either to drop off their copy (remember, no fax machines, no e-mail, no FedEx) or to meet with Mike Kolatch about future assignments or just to schmooze with whoever was there. I listened eagerly to their talk about "the situation" in every hot spot around the world—to deep discussions about the errors of American foreign and domestic policy, to reports of the latest literary sensation or scandal, to debates about what Khrushchev might do next, to whispered conversations about the latest secret letter from a dissident trapped behind the Iron Curtain. Off and on for five years, I was an editorial assistant, with time taken off for childbirth and my husband's brief stint in the military.

The New Leader introduced me to the kind of political discourse that made me feel both ignorant and exhilarated. There was so much that I did not know, so much I had to learn, and I reveled in the magazine's intellectual vitality. What I knew was defined and limited by the courses I had taken in college. There were huge lacunae in my understanding of the world.

On any given week, I would proofread articles about the economic miracle in Italy, the upheavals in Algeria or Kenya, Kennedy's latest tax proposals, American policy toward Castro, or the civil rights movement. A few months after I started work, the magazine featured a debate about "the bomb" between eminent philosophers Erich Fromm and Sidney Hook. The best thinkers of the day opined on subjects they knew intimately, like Hans J. Morgenthau on Kennedy's foreign policy, Theodore Draper on Castro's revolution, Zbigniew Brzezinski on Germany, Willy Brandt on Berlin, Immanuel Wallerstein on Africa, Ralph Ellison on Irving Howe (and Howe's response to Ellison), Paul Samuelson on the American economy, Michael Harrington on poverty in America, and Walter Z. Laqueur on "the Moscow-Cairo rift." All these intellectual riches in a magazine that didn't pay its writers!

There was wonderful banter in the office. Joel Blocker was succeeded by Joseph (Mike) Epstein, who later became the editor of *The American Scholar* and then a celebrated essayist. Mike has a marvelous sense of humor, and we often played a game of writing imaginary *New Leader* headlines, like "Five Minutes to Midnight in Brazil," or "Showdown in Nigeria," or "What Next for Germany?," or "Agonizing Opportunity in Southeast Asia." You could switch the names of the countries or continents, and the headlines always worked for all of them.

The arrival of the latest issue of the *Partisan Review*, a literary haven for intellectuals like Susan Sontag, set off intense discussion, as did the newly published novels by J. D. Salinger, Bernard Malamud, Shirley Jackson, Saul Bellow, and other literary giants of the day. And of course, there was fierce debate in our office about high culture versus mass culture. There was, I have to say, a certain snobbishness among the tiny editorial staff and its followers against popular culture and against those who abandoned the insular orbit of the impoverished intelligentsia. Writers who moved from the elite realm of the *Partisan Review* to *The New York Times* or some other mass-circulation publication were condemned for "selling out." Since I had never been part of the intelligentsia and had instead been deeply immersed in the popular culture of the 1950s, I was an outsider, with my nose pressed against the glass, picking up cues about who was in, who was out.

Another of my life lessons at *The New Leader* was about the nature of the American Left in the 1930s. I knew nothing about the factional fights within the Left. I learned about the heated debates at the City College of New York in the Depression era, in which one declared one's political identification by choosing to sit at a particular table in the dining hall. Trotskyites were at one table, Stalinists at a different table, and various factions at other tables. Over time, I learned about the Shachtmanites, the Lovestoneites, the Cannonites, and a few other "-ites" as well. I later had the privilege of meeting Max Shachtman (whose wife Yetta was Albert Shanker's private secretary at the United Federation of Teachers in New York City) and Jay Lovestone, both of whom had legendary roles in the history of the Left. Lovestone had been leader of the Communist Party in the United States but had split from the party after

Stalin expelled him in a face-to-face confrontation in Moscow. Eventually he became active in the American Federation of Labor (AFL) and was strongly anticommunist, even spying for the Central Intelligence Agency (CIA). When old socialists gathered in the office, they would speak in hushed tones about the great debate in 1950 between Shachtman, the anti-Stalinist leader of the Independent Socialist League, and Earl Browder, former secretary general of the Communist Party of the United States, about whether Russia was a socialist society.

The New Leader often obtained bootleg statements by dissidents or leaders behind the Iron Curtain. In 1956, the magazine was the first to publish Khrushchev's secret speech to the Twentieth Congress of the Communist Party denouncing Stalin's crimes. On several occasions during my time at the magazine, it published essays that had been smuggled out of Russia or Eastern Europe, such as an exposé of Soviet prison camps by the Serbian dissident Mihajlo Mihajlov, which landed him in prison. I was proud to be on the masthead of *The New Leader* when it was first to publish Martin Luther King Jr.'s "Letter from Birmingham City Jail," a now-classic American essay.

While I was at the magazine, my job was to do anything and everything, including copyediting, writing, soliciting advertising, and running errands. On occasion, I would write a letter to the editor and sign it with a fake name if we needed to fill space. I even sold tickets for a benefit; the magazine bought a large bloc of tickets for the second night of a new musical called *Fiddler on the Roof*, but it was nearly a disaster. No one wanted to buy the tickets, and I unloaded most of them to friends and relatives at face value. When the show opened to rave reviews, everyone was looking for a ticket but the suddenly-valuable second-night tickets were gone. I had gotten rid of all of them.

At one point in 1962 I knocked on a carefully guarded door to pick up a manuscript by Boris Nicolaevsky, a leading figure in Russia and the Soviet Union. His name meant nothing to me at the time. Half a century after knocking on his door, I read about him online and discovered that he was a Marxist, a radical, and a Menshevik who was arrested by the tsarist government several times and repeatedly sent into exile in Siberia. After the Russian Revolution, he became the head of the Marx-Engels Institute in Moscow and a leader of the Menshevik Party. He was arrested by the Soviet secret police, deported, and stripped of his Soviet citizenship. He became a historian and archivist of Soviet communism and wrote several books about the Soviet system. He lived in Berlin and Paris and then immigrated to the United States in 1942. Knowing Leon Trotsky's fate, he was terrified of assassins. I knocked on his triple-locked door twenty years later to pick up a manuscript, with no idea who he was.

Before I left the magazine in 1966, I had a talk with Mike Kolatch about my desire to be a writer. I had written a few pieces in the magazine, mostly book reviews. Mike gave me good advice: he told me to find a subject that I cared deeply about, learn everything I could about it, and make it my own. I never forgot what he said.

As I reflect on what I learned at *The New Leader*, it seems to me that I earned one graduate degree in world and national politics and another in contemporary American literary culture. But I learned something more that indelibly marked my own political and intellectual development. *The New Leader* never had a party line. It was not for or against any ideas or policies, other than having a clear, unwavering commitment to democratic values. It was, as that *New York Times* tribute to Sol Levitas said, a forum "for every variety of democratic opinion." The magazine preferred think pieces that explored issues from differing perspectives, and it relished debates between leading thinkers. If there was a *New Leader* cast of mind, it was skepticism. True believers and zealots would not have found it a congenial environment. I took away something of that same attitude, that same demand for evidence, that same need to look at all sides of a question before coming down on one side or the other, that same distrust of ideologues, zealots, and utopians, and a willingness to admit error and change positions. This was the mindset that I brought to my study of education in the next phase of my life: a persistent skepticism toward panaceas, miracles, and fads.

7

DOMESTICITY AND TRAGEDY

I was not yet able to launch a career because life intervened. In the summer of 1961, the Soviets and the German Democratic Republic built a wall that split Berlin in two. President Kennedy responded by mobilizing 150,000 reservists. One of them was my husband. He was a private in the army reserve, which he joined in hopes of never seeing active duty. But in the fall of 1961, Dick left for his deployment at Fort Gordon in Augusta, Georgia. Dick was assigned to a unit from Buffalo, New York; he didn't know anyone in his unit. The leader of his military unit was a butcher from Buffalo. The men lived in the barracks at Fort Gordon, but we didn't. Before I left to join Dick in Augusta, I placed a person-to-person telephone call to the commanding officer at Fort Gordon. I don't know how I got the nerve to do it; it must have been naivete, not nerve. I told him that my husband would have to live off-base because I was pregnant, and I couldn't live alone. I don't know if he was amused or aghast at my cheekiness, but he agreed to let my husband live with me off-base. We rented a home on Tobacco Road, literally. Dick had his own stroke of luck. Although he was a private, he persuaded the commanding officer to let him act as a lawyer for the men in his unit who got into legal trouble. That became his full-time assignment. It surely beat doing latrine duty.

Our son Joseph was born on February 9, 1962, in Augusta. The baby was named for Dick's grandfather. Dick didn't have a middle name, so neither did Joseph. He quickly became Joey, and he remained Joey until he was an adult. I loved being a mother. I had read a novel by D. H. Lawrence in which he used the phrase "a mother of men," and I wanted to be "a mother of men." I breastfed Joey because I had seen my mother breastfeed the children who came after me. Breastfeeding was a nearly spiritual experience. I locked eyes with baby Joey, who stared intently and lovingly at me. It was beautiful. However, I was not prepared for colic. Joey slept all day and cried all night until he was three months old. The blessed three-month mark!

Living in Augusta was a daily reminder that the Deep South had not changed in the eight years since the *Brown* decision. Everything in Augusta was racially segregated; most Blacks lived in deep poverty. I protested by such lame actions as riding in the back of the bus with Black people. But there was no civil rights movement in Augusta, and the outlook for change was bleak.

The reservists who were pulled away from their civilian lives complained bitterly. They were called up for the Berlin Crisis, but when the authorities began giving them lessons in Vietnamese, they fretted. When the men marched, they chanted, "We're not killers, we're just fillers, why me? Why me?" They complained so loudly that President Kennedy was asked by a reporter at a news conference when he would send the reservists home. He responded with a simple, irrefutable fact: "Life is unfair."

Eventually, the reservists were released, having accomplished nothing more than serving as a grand political gesture. When we got back to New York City with baby Joey, we moved into a two-bedroom co-op at 535 East Eighty-Fifth Street, which we had bought shortly before Dick was called up for active duty. I took Joey for long walks in his large Silver Cross English baby carriage, which was de rigueur for affluent moms on the Upper East Side of Manhattan. And I walked and walked and got to know every part of the Yorkville neighborhood. In time, Joey graduated from the baby carriage to an equally elegant stroller.

I was doing my best to be a dutiful wife, mother, and daughter-in-law. Being a mother was the easy part; I adored my baby and wanted to be sure he was healthy and happy. Being a good daughter-in-law was exceedingly difficult because my mother-in-law was as volatile as ever. Being a good wife was even harder, because I soon realized that my husband was as demanding as his mother. He angered easily, and his anger depressed me. On occasion, Dick would come into the kitchen as I was giving dinner to Joey and want to know why I hadn't baked a potato for the child. Every mother except me, he insisted, knew that children should have a baked potato every day. I didn't know that. What was wrong with me? I broke down in tears and promised to give Joey a baked potato every day. There were many more such confrontations, in which he became enraged over insignificant matters, and I retreated. I can remember many occasions when I slipped out to the balcony of our apartment and wept copious tears, not just because he was angry but because I was incapable of living up to his expectations. All too often, I felt like a failure. When my unhappiness became more than I could bear, someone in the family told me to see a psychoanalyst, which was the family's way of dealing with unhappiness. I went to a famous psychoanalyst, Dr. Gustav Bychowski, who had studied under Freud in Vienna. I saw him for only a few months, and what I took away from our meetings was that I needed to be more understanding of my husband. His criticisms, the doctor assured me, were expressions of love. The lesson I took from these sessions was not that I should stand up for myself, but that I should try harder to satisfy my spouse's demands, no matter how unreasonable they appeared to be.

In the summer of 1963, we went to Washington, D.C., to join the March on Washington, a thrilling experience. There were over a quarter-million people, people of all races, all joined together to demonstrate for "Jobs and Freedom." The largest demonstration in U.S. history, the march brought together civil rights groups and labor unions from across the nation. It was an inspiring day that gave everyone present the hope that American society really might be able to change for the better. Having grown up in the segregated South, I was deeply moved by the speeches, the songs, and the spirit of unity, as well as by the interracial character of the event and the strong bonds between the civil rights movement and the labor movement.

Back home in New York City, I established a routine: a few days each week at *The New Leader*, a few days with baby Joey. I didn't know many people in New York City outside my new family, but Joey was my link to some new friends. The closest park to our home on East Eighty-Fifth Street was Carl Schurz Park on the East River, half a block away, and I often took Joey there to play in the sandbox. One day I spotted another mother, about my age, with a copy of the *Partisan Review* tucked in her stroller bag. Ah-ha. Someone I could talk to. She was educated. She read. Our sons began to play, and I met May Shayne, who became a dear friend.

Soon May and I joined with two other mothers who had little boys about the same age as ours, and we would take turns meeting in our apartments, all within a half-mile radius. May, who graduated from Radcliffe, was a social worker. Dotty Dubin, a graduate of Mount Holyoke, was an interior decorator; Nicky Shefrin was an artist. We came from different parts of the world—May from Nashville, Dotty from Maine, Nicky from the Netherlands. Dotty, Nicky, and I decided that we would go into business together designing board games (May was busy at work). While the little boys played and fought, we created a satirical board game called CLASS. It was a mirror of our lives. The players drew a card that had several contemporary references, and if you answered correctly, you moved up the ladder of social class.

An example:

"Your doctor is chief of staff . . . up 6."
"Your decorator is heterosexual . . . down 2."
"Your lawyer is a congressman . . . up 5."
"Your accountant uses an abacus . . . down 1."
"Your dentist has bad breath . . . down 1."
"Your banker lives next door . . . up 6."

We shared many laughs as we wrote the questions and answers. When we thought we had a full package, we contacted game manufacturers, but no one was interested in our amateur effort. So we decided to produce it ourselves. Our husbands thought our efforts were endearing, and they chipped in $5,000 to fund our little project. Everyone used their talents, and we ended up with a sharp-looking silver box with big black letters, CLASS. We had the question cards printed and found game pieces. Then we began selling retail. We visited every major department store, and several stores bought a few dozen games. We were able to get small notices in a few national publications. We learned that the only way to get featured in a department store catalogue was to pay for the space. When it was time to fill the orders, we put boxes of games into the back of Nicky's station wagon and delivered them to the stores. One department store told us to bring our boxes to the UPS facility on the West Side of Manhattan. When we arrived, we were directed to drive into a huge bay that turned out to be an elevator. The entire car rose up to the fifteenth floor, where the men at the loading dock said, "Here comes Greenwich Village." We didn't make any money, but we had a lot of fun. We developed a second game that we wanted to call "Battle of the Sexes," but someone had already copyrighted the name, so we called it "He She Him Her." It wasn't as much fun as CLASS, and my interest began to wane as I started to think about a potential academic career.

I was pregnant again, and we moved to an apartment with three bedrooms at the Majestic at 115 Central Park West, facing Central Park. It is a beautiful Art Deco building. The doorman showed us a hole in the marble wall of the lobby where a gunman had tried to rub out one of our neighbors, the mafia boss Frank Costello. I later learned that the Majestic had had many famous residents, including other mafia leaders (Meyer Lansky and Lucky Luciano) and celebrities such as Milton Berle, Walter Winchell, Fred Astaire, and the orchestra leader Ted Lewis. When I was raising money to renovate the local playground, I knocked on the doors of neighbors in the building. At one apartment a male voice growled, "Whaddaya want?" I explained, and he said, "Slip the flyer under the door." I did, but never got a contribution. I don't know which mob boss it was.

Our second son, Steven, was born on May 10, 1964. Whereas I labored for 10 hours to give birth to Joey, Steven arrived as soon as I got to the hospital. He was a joyful baby who smiled for everyone. We bought a weekend house on Turkey Hill Road in Westport, Connecticut, a rambling old Victorian with beautiful grounds, where we built a tennis court and spent summers and weekends.

I tried to become engaged in wifely duties. I wasn't especially interested in cooking, but I tried. Dick was a better cook than I was; he excelled at grilling. I wanted to learn more about decorating the apartment, and I studied books about styles and design. I became interested in the work of Lewis Comfort Tiffany, especially his lamps. Every weekend, I would read the listings of furniture auctions in *The New York Times* and occasionally attend an auction just to see the furniture. One Sunday, I read about a sale of authentic Tiffany lamps in Washington Heights in upper Manhattan. I took the subway and got off at Broadway and 168th Street, emerging to a neighborhood I had never visited. As I was walking to my destination, police cars began to converge from every direction. One of the policemen said, "Get out of here as fast as you can!" I asked, "What's happening, officer?" He barked, "Get out of here now!" I ran back to the subway and left as chaos was breaking out around me. I learned when I got home that Malcolm X had been assassinated at the Audubon Ballroom at 165th Street, within a block of where I was blithely heading in search of Tiffany lamps. I had no idea that I was within yards of a historic and tragic event.

As a mother with two small children, I became active in a neighborhood committee seeking to renovate a Depression-era playground in Central Park. We called it the Mothers' Committee for the West 67 Street Playground. The playground was a typical Depression-era installation, paved with asphalt and containing swings, a seesaw, and a slide. We had heard a rumor that the city might turn the playground over to a nearby restaurant, Tavern on the Green, for parking space. We wanted to save the playground, but we also wanted a playground that was more welcoming to little children, with a soft surface and creative things to play on. The committee met with the Parks Department, and they said we could renovate the playground if we raised the money to pay for it. We interviewed architects and selected Richard Dattner, a young architect who was just getting started. I persuaded Leonard Lauder of the Estee Lauder family to underwrite the project, and we called it an "adventure playground." The new playground was covered with a soft but durable material to protect children who fell, and it had tunnels and play spaces and climbing structures that were very engaging for little children. It was the first playground in the city to break the mold of the Depression-era playgrounds. The playground was a success and became a model for other new playgrounds throughout the city and even in other cities. Richard Dattner eventually became a renowned architect. On his website, he has a link to an article about the playground on West Sixty-Seventh Street in Manhattan, titled "Central Park's Iconic Adventure Playground Reopens."

It says:

> The Adventure Playground, designed in 1966 by Richard Dattner, has been completely rebuilt by the Central Park Conservancy and is now open to the public, the second renewal of the playground in its 50-year history. One of the earliest "adventure playgrounds" in the US, this project was the result of a group of young neighborhood mothers preventing Robert Moses' bulldozers from tearing up the asphalt playground formerly on that site for a parking lot for the Tavern on the Green. . . . The success of this iconic space initiated a "playground revolution."

Unbeknownst to the members of the Mothers' Committee for the West Sixty-Seventh Street Playground, we made architectural history.

Things seemed to be going along swimmingly. I was married to a successful businessman whom I loved despite our quarrels, and we had two wonderful little boys. Stevie adored his big brother. He called him "Ojie." He waited for him to come home from school every day and greeted him with a bear hug. The two of them often played together in Stevie's crib. The ceiling of Stevie's room was covered with a fabric of balloons, and it was a joyful space.

But then came the greatest tragedy of my life.

One day, two-year-old Stevie started limping and complained that his "yegs were hurtin.'" We went to the pediatrician, and he could find nothing wrong. He sent us to an orthopedist, who found nothing wrong, then to a neurologist, with the same result. But one doctor suggested that Stevie should have a blood test. We went to Lenox Hill Hospital, where our pediatrician was on staff. Dick and I waited. He brought us into a private waiting room and said, "It is the worst possible thing. Steven has leukemia." I can't describe my feelings. Dick and I held on to one another. A part of me wanted to dissolve, to be nothing and nowhere for this terrible, unbelievable, horrible news.

We went home to our apartment, and by dinnertime the family had gathered. Everyone wanted to show their love and concern. I just wanted to be alone. I didn't want to talk to anyone. I felt that I had fallen into a very deep hole, and I didn't want to come out of it. Our family doctor gave me a shot of something that knocked me out. I was at the very beginning of a nightmare that no parent should ever have.

Stevie got his diagnosis in May 1966, two weeks after his two-year-old birthday. He died six months later on December 14, 1966. During that time, he was hospitalized six times, usually for two weeks at a time. He was in the care of Dr. Carl Smith, a pediatric hematologist who ran the Children's Blood Center at New York Hospital. Dr. Smith said that the odds for survival were next to zero. He said there was always hope for a cure, but it hadn't happened yet. We took Stevie to the hospital whenever the bruises began showing up on his legs, and he would get blood transfusions and experimental drugs. He took prednisone, methotrexate, and many more drugs. He took them in different combinations in an intravenous drug cocktail. The methotrexate gave him ulcers in his mouth, and his hair fell out. As soon as I saw his hair start to fall out, I called a barber to the apartment to shave his head. It was one small way to be in control at a time when we had no control at all.

I scoured the papers every day, hoping that one day I would find an item about that elusive cure. It never happened. Many years later, in 2016, I was watching a television special on PBS, "Cancer: The Emperor of All Maladies." The first episode was about childhood leukemia. I began to relive painful memories as I watched the frightened parents holding on to their doomed babies. But I learned that scientists at the Dana Farber Institute in Boston had found an effective treatment for childhood leukemia consisting of a cocktail of anticancer drugs. The first child to survive began the treatment in 1966, the year that Stevie got his diagnosis and died. I was sad. He didn't get the right drug cocktail. But I was happy for the many children who had lived through this terrible affliction and survived to become adults.

During the time that Stevie was ill, I constantly felt that there was a huge chunk of lead pressed on my heart. I didn't think I would ever laugh again. I cried in the morning. I cried at night. I cried in the shower. I knew what it felt like to say my heart was broken. It *was* broken. But I had to think about Joey. I had to make time to be with him, I had to put on a happy face for him. He was a sensitive child, and he knew something was terribly wrong. He knew that his brother was very sick and that everyone was worried about him.

Sometimes I would take Stevie to the adventure playground. I had to be careful because he was fragile. I couldn't take the risk of him falling. He used to have a lot of friends; now, the children he had played with avoided him. Their mothers were afraid to let their children get too close. They knew he had a fatal disease, and they didn't want to take any chances. People would smile and say hello but keep their distance. I understood. He was oblivious to being shunned. He was just happy not to be in the hospital. Then something happened that put things in perspective, just a bit. One of the other mothers with whom I worked on the playground project reached out to me, and we commiserated about my grief. She had two little children the same ages as mine. I thought she was lucky. Then one weekend, during Stevie's illness, she and her husband drove out of the city to see her parents, and there was an accident. She and the two children were killed instantly. The husband walked away without an injury. How can you understand life's twists and turns? How can you explain fate? You can't.

During Stevie's illness and after his death, I read poetry for solace. I scoured every anthology we had for poems about the loss of a child. There were many, but only one was just right: Ben Jonson's "Oak and Lily." If you read it, you will see why his language affected me.

> It is not growing like a tree
> In bulk doth make man better be;
> Or standing long an oak, three hundred year,
> To fall a log at last, dry, bald, and sere:

> A lily of a day
> Is fairer far in May,
> Although it fall and die that night;
> It was the plant and flower of light.
> In small proportions we just beauties see;
> And in short measures life may perfect be.

I often reread that poem. It didn't ease the pain. But it helped me cope with my sorrow.

Stevie's death didn't make me bitter, but it certainly made me less sympathetic to the hippies who gathered outside our windows in Central Park every weekend. I remember pushing the stroller with my doomed little boy and seeing young adults in flowery clothes, being as ridiculous as they could be, and I found them repulsive. I saw flower beds trampled by the barefoot ones, and I felt no sense of identification with these young rebels. Perhaps that accounts, at least in part, for my philosophical antipathy to the left fringes. I was too old to identify with the carefree hippies on my doorstep and too absorbed in my grief to appreciate their bacchanalias.

After Steven's death, I had one goal: to get pregnant. I wanted two more children. Life was so tenuous, I thought, that parents needed the insurance of having more than one or two children. Ten months after Steven's death, I gave birth to Michael. I was indeed "a mother of men." Michael brought great joy to our home. Like Steven, he was a beautiful and serene child. This little boy was blond and blue-eyed. He had a gentle, sweet temperament. Michael was wanted and loved. He was a beloved child.

8

IN SEARCH OF A CAREER

While Michael was still a baby, I knew the time had come to find my work, to use my mind. I had a small desk in our bedroom that held my portable typewriter. I wanted to write, but I had not figured out what to write about. I remembered Mike Kolatch's advice about finding a subject that I could master and write about with authority. I started casting about.

To help me transition from my grief, my friend May Shayne introduced me to Preston Wilcox, an African American social worker and community organizer whom May had met when they were both students at Columbia's Graduate School of Social Work. I really liked Preston. He was brilliant, militant, warm, and devoted to the Black Power movement. I wanted to know more about the work he did. I am not sure why he accepted the assignment of educating me. He brought me to community meetings in Harlem where I was the only white person in the room. I listened to angry parents express their rage toward the bureaucracy of the New York City public schools. I met the leaders of the community control movement, who were focused on a new middle school in central Harlem called I. S. 201. No one had ever asked them what they wanted or who should lead the school. They realized that the school would open as a segregated school, despite years of promises of integration. They knew that the bureaucracy had chosen a principal without consulting the community. They adopted as their slogan "Integration or Community Control."

About this time, my college classmate, Linda Salzman Gottlieb, the same one who had introduced me to my husband, told me that a friend of hers at the Carnegie Corporation of New York was looking for a part-time research assistant. That sounded intriguing, an opportunity to think and write. I went to the offices of the Carnegie Corporation and met with two senior program officers, Margaret Mahoney and Barbara Finberg. They told me that Carnegie had received proposals from New York City community groups that were unfamiliar to them; since they were accustomed to dealing only with well-established institutions, they needed help in learning about these applicants. Who were they? What problems were they addressing? Should the Carnegie Foundation fund them? It would be like writing a term paper in college, but real work! It sounded great to me. They hired me to do background research at $5 an hour. I didn't need the money, but I needed the assignment. I could work at my own speed. I would have time to take Joey to school and to walk in the park with baby Michael. I jumped at the opportunity.

I wrote some research papers for them that were well-received. Then they gave me a big assignment. The Carnegie Corporation had received a request from the Ford Foundation to join in supporting three experimental decentralization districts in New York City. One was in Brooklyn in Ocean Hill–Brownsville; the second was on the Lower East Side of Manhattan; and the third was in Harlem, in the area around I. S. 201. Would I do the background research to help them make a decision? They wanted me to find out about the dynamics of the decentralized districts: Who was involved? What did they want? Who was opposed? Were their goals attainable? Of course, I accepted the assignment.

When I began working part-time for the Carnegie Corporation, I learned a big secret. When you tell people you are calling from a major foundation, they take your call. I had no trouble getting meetings with the leadership in the experimental districts because I came from the Carnegie Corporation. I listened. I eventually wrote a paper describing the politics surrounding the experimental districts and the battle that was brewing between their militant leadership and the United Federation of

Teachers (UFT), the city's teachers' union. Carnegie was averse to risk and decided not to become involved in the controversial program that Ford supported.

I saw that the decentralization experiment was explosive, and I wanted to write an article about it. Having spent time with parent and community groups in central Harlem, I understood and sympathized with their antagonism toward "the system." I became a daily visitor to the New York Historical Society, a few blocks from my home on Central Park West, where I read about the history of the New York City school system. I wondered why there was a single school system overseeing 1 million students. It made no sense; it was too big to function effectively. The parents I met in Harlem and the other leaders of the decentralization movement wanted to secede from the system. The Ford Foundation backed the community groups that demanded decentralization. So did important political figures in the city, including Mayor John Lindsay. I wanted to learn more about why the school system was organized as it was. I pored through old histories and learned that the city schools had been decentralized in the nineteenth century. Reformers in the late nineteenth century had fought for centralization, hoping to promote efficiency and thereby keep politics out of the system. They wanted the school system to be run by professionals. They complained about the poor results produced by the decentralized schools and about political interference by ward politicians and saloonkeepers who wanted jobs in the schools for their friends and relatives.

At this point, the only articles I had published had appeared in *The New Leader*. I was determined to write an article about the history of the New York City schools and how it affected today's issues. At a dinner party, I met Mike Levitas (son of Sol Levitas, whose death had launched my career at *The New Leader*). Mike was an editor at *The New York Times Magazine*. I told him that I wanted to set the current political demands for decentralization into a historical context and write about how the public schools of New York City had been decentralized and centralized over the years. He told me to write a proposal. I did. He turned me down, saying that if I ever wrote an article titled "I Danced with My Dentist," he would give it serious consideration.

I was not a feminist at the time, but I understood that his response was a sexist put-down. I knew that he would not write with the same sarcasm to a man whose proposal he was rejecting. He implied that I had no authority to write the article I proposed, and he implicitly ridiculed the idea that I could write an article for *The New York Times Magazine.*

Meanwhile, the situation in the experimental school districts was growing more tense. Rhody McCoy, the fiery administrator of the Ocean Hill–Brownsville district in Brooklyn, was at loggerheads with the teachers in the district schools over basic issues of teachers' rights. In 1967, the UFT went on strike for two weeks to force a settlement. In 1968, the situation became even more volatile. McCoy fired nineteen teachers and even the chapter leader of the teachers' union and replaced them with staff members of his own choosing, many of whom had never taught and did not belong to the union. Under the union contract, he did not have the power to fire teachers without formal evaluations and due process. He ignored the contract. When the UFT again went on strike, the entire city's public schools were closed for two months. The union set up picket lines around the schools of Ocean Hill–Brownsville, and the new teachers crossed the lines. There were daily demonstrations and boycotts at I. S. 201 in Harlem and at schools in Ocean Hill–Brownsville. A group of activists disrupted a meeting of the city's august Board of Education, the members of the board walked out, and the dissidents sat in their chairs and called themselves "the People's Board of Education." Black communities in Harlem and Brooklyn grew more strident in their demands for community control. For two months, the city was riveted and dismayed by the drama of 1 million children locked out of school by a confrontation between Black militants and the UFT.

Having interviewed the leaders of the community control movement on behalf of the Carnegie Corporation, I decided to write about what was happening. After Mike Levitas's flippant rejection of my proposal to write a magazine article, I wanted to write the history of the New York City public schools. I began to spend hours every day in the library of the New York Historical Society. I shared my plans with my friends at the Carnegie Corporation, and they had a suggestion: Carnegie was supporting the scholarship of Lawrence Cremin, the nation's leading historian of education, who was a professor at Teachers College, Columbia University. They recommended that I meet with him, using their names as my entrée, and get his advice.

Soon afterwards, I met with Cremin in his office at Teachers College on West 120th Street. He was vivacious and charming, sitting behind a large desk piled high with books in front of a wall lined from floor to ceiling with books. I told him that I wanted to write a history of the New York City public schools; the last one had been published in 1905. He asked me if I had a master's degree, and I said no. He asked me if I had ever written a book, and I said no. He asked me if I had written any articles, and I named the few I had published in *The New Leader*. He said he had a better idea for me. "Why don't you write a few essays? When you are done, let me read them and I will give you feedback." With that, he scanned the bookcase behind him and wrote out a list of books and articles that I should read about the history of urban schools. We spoke for an hour or so, and I thanked him for his time.

I saw a long road ahead of me, and I enthusiastically started the journey. Cremin named me a fellow of the Institute of Politics and Policy at Teachers College, which carried no pay but enabled me to get a library card at Teachers College, where I checked out the books he recommended. I continued to dig through original source documents at the New York Historical Society. I loved what I was doing, and I felt a sense of purpose. I was excited to read documents that no one had looked at in close to a century.

I made a thrilling discovery while I was working in the library of the New York Historical Society. I learned that William M. Tweed (Boss Tweed), one of the legendary figures of New York City history, had begun his career of corruption as a member of a local school board. After he became a state legislator and boss of Tammany Hall, the Democratic Party's organization in New York City, he persuaded the state legislature to dissolve the New York City Board of Education and to turn the public schools into a municipal agency. With the schools under his control, he directed contracts for furniture, books, and supplies to his cronies. And he stopped the purchase of textbooks from the Harper

Company as retaliation for the attacks on him by Thomas Nast in *Harper's Magazine*. Boss Tweed saw the schools as a lucrative source of graft; the independent Board of Education was an obstacle to his control, and he got rid of it.

I set aside my research in the fall of 1968 to participate in the presidential race between Hubert Humphrey and Richard Nixon. My husband had been involved in the Eugene McCarthy campaign, but when Hubert Humphrey won the Democratic nomination, we both worked for the election of Humphrey and his running mate Edmund Muskie. Humphrey was disliked by the antiwar Democrats in New York because he was Lyndon Johnson's vice president and LBJ was responsible for escalating the Vietnam War, which they hated. Dick volunteered to debate on behalf of Humphrey in liberal Democratic clubs where Humphrey was considered a quisling for failing to speak out against the war. I did my part by launching a tiny facet of the New York City campaign called the "New Coalition for Humphrey-Muskie." There was no organization, just a name. I chose the name because the atmosphere was thick with organizations like "New Coalition for Peace and Justice," "New Alliance for a New Day," and "New Revolution for a New Era." I was latching on to the progressive vocabulary from within the inner sanctum of the Humphrey-Muskie campaign to provide a haven for liberals who didn't want to be part of the traditional campaign structure.

My singular contribution to the Humphrey-Muskie campaign was to plan an event—sponsored by the New Coalition for Humphrey-Muskie—on October 31, 1968, days before the election, when a lineup of well-known liberal figures would speak out on behalf of the ticket. The only free venue we could find was a large, dingy hall on West Thirty-Fourth Street called the Manhattan Center, owned by labor unions. As it happened, the Manhattan Center was directly across the street from the cavernous Madison Square Garden, where Nixon was holding a rally on the same night. Our small group was able to line up a star-studded list to speak that night, including John Kenneth Galbraith, Arthur Schlesinger Jr., Herman Badillo (a leader in the Puerto Rican community), Shirley Chisholm (the first Black woman to run for president), Ted Sorensen (John F. Kennedy's speechwriter), and a dozen others, each of whom was supposed to explain in 5 minutes why they were voting for the Democratic ticket. We were told that the vice-presidential candidate, Edmund Muskie, might drop by. The mistress of ceremonies was the actress Shelley Winters. The event was broadcast on a local radio station. We had one security guard.

The evening got off to a good start. The auditorium was full, with several hundred people. The opening speakers talked about how important it was to beat Nixon. But when John Kenneth Galbraith stepped up to the microphone, a young man and young woman jumped up from the first row, threw off their trench coats, and ran onto the stage naked carrying the head of a pig on a platter, which they presented to Galbraith. Shelley Winters grabbed the water pitcher on the podium and threw the water at them. The security guard began chasing them around the stage, reenacting the Keystone Kops but with only one cop. At that moment, a group of about twenty yippies (members of the radical Youth International Party) entered the back of the auditorium, carrying a large Vietcong flag and chanting to a drumbeat, "Ho, Ho, Ho Chi Minh, Viet Cong are gonna win." Someone threw their trench coats over the streakers. The demonstrators marched out, the radio transmission was cut off, and the gathering quickly folded. What had seemed to be a promising event was suddenly deflated, and the auditorium emptied. The Nixon rally across the street, with an audience of nearly twenty thousand, proceeded without interruption. I then knew that Nixon would win and that the Left would help him with demonstrations such as the one I had just watched.

Once again, I was soured by the shenanigans of the militant Left, as I had been when the hippies outside my windows trampled the flowers in Central Park, as I had been while working at *The New Leader* and learning how often the radicals had been their own worst enemy, not only in Russia when the Mensheviks were crushed, but also in the 1930s, when many American leftists were hoodwinked by Stalin.

Nixon won, and I returned to writing a book about the history of the New York City public schools.

9

MOTHERHOOD AND CAREER

Lawrence Cremin had warned me not to write a book. He probably thought he would never see me again. But six months after he had advised me to write a series of essays about the history of the New York City public schools, I made an appointment to see him. I handed him the first 125 pages of the book I was writing. He read it, and his comment was "Go, go, go." And I did.

On the home front, our family was busy. We moved again, in part to leave behind the bedroom with the fabric balloons on the ceiling that had been Stevie's, but also to be closer to where Joey started school at age three. Joey was enrolled at the Dalton School on East Eighty-Ninth Street, and we bought an apartment at 1021 Park Avenue, four blocks away, so that one day he could walk to school. In light of my later life as a passionate advocate of public schools, critics sometimes asked why my own children went to private schools. The answer is simple: I was a new member of the Ravitch family, and I did what they did. Also, I was not then a standard-bearer for public schools; I was a mom doing what my husband expected. My husband had enrolled in the Ethical Culture School in 1936 and completed his education at the Fieldston School; his sister started Dalton in 1941 and graduated from Dalton in 1956. It was a given in the family that our children would do the same. I could have insisted on sending my children to public school, but in the early years of my marriage, I never questioned the practices of the family. I did my best to be accepted as a member of the Ravitch clan, not a rebel. Joey and Michael went to Dalton, which was and is an excellent school. In retrospect, I think they would have flourished at a public school, but I had no reason to defy family tradition. And besides, unlike today's proponents of school choice, we paid for our private choice; we did not ask the government to give us a subsidy.

When Joey entered preschool as a three-year-old at Dalton, his classroom had a sandbox, building blocks, a corner for water play, and every kind of inducement to enjoy school. Joey started reading on his own at age four. Every night before he went to sleep, we read stories, poems, and picture books. Reading was love. He grew up to become a voracious reader. In junior high school and high school, when he found an author he liked, he wanted to read everything that person had ever written. He read every book written by Agatha Christie, Edgar Rice Burroughs, Robert Heinlein, and other writers of mysteries and science fiction. Joey was shy but well-liked by his classmates. In high school, he was elected president of student government and captain of the football team. After high school, he went to Amherst College, where he majored in Russian and history; he then spent a year in London working for *The Times*, and then went on to Yale Law School.

Michael, like Joey, excelled in school. Unlike Joey, he was outgoing and self-directed. When he was six years old, he wrote a "novel" about a family of foxes. One of my friends, Rita Kramer, who authored a regular child-rearing column for *The New York Times Magazine*, wrote a "review" of Michael's book and commended him for its "orthographic novelty." He made friends easily. Both boys studied Greek and Latin, taught by the same teacher. Michael loved theater and was regularly cast in school productions; he was also editor of the Dalton school newspaper. Michael went to Yale, where he majored in English literature. Like his mother, he is a writer, but a writer of fiction. We collaborated on a book called *The English Reader* for Oxford University Press.

To the outside observer, we were a very fortunate family indeed. Dick's business was thriving, and he was involved in city, state, and national politics. He was busy all the time, which is the way he liked it. We had an active social life; we went out to dinner several nights a week, often to meet his political friends. When we entertained, we sometimes had luminaries at our table. Our guests included Barbara Walters, Rupert and Anna Murdoch, Pat and Elizabeth Moynihan, Felix and Liz Rohatyn, and labor leaders like Al Shanker and Victor Gotbaum and their spouses. I made a huge mistake when Barbara Walters came to dinner with her friend, the financier Ace Greenberg. I innocently asked her if she had ever interviewed Nixon: she shot me a venomous look and said, "Certainly! I have interviewed every president!" Benjamin Netanyahu came for drinks one night not long after his brother's death in the raid on Entebbe. It's been a long time, but I never forgot what he said when I asked him what the future held for Israel. He answered, "The best policy is 'No war, no peace.'" It was strangely prophetic of his policy when he assumed leadership of the embattled country.

We frequently went to Broadway plays or opera or concerts. Dick had a deep need for this life-in-constant-motion, and I did my best to keep up while trying to envelop Joey and Michael with time, love, and caring. They were not allowed to watch television for more than an hour each day, and until they were reading on their own, I read to them and with them every night.

But in 1969 I made a fatal error: I got pregnant and did not ask for Dick's permission. The most common form of birth control at the time was a diaphragm, and it was my responsibility to make sure that I had inserted one to protect against pregnancy. Ever since Stevie's death, I had wanted a third child. That didn't seem to be an outlandish wish; my best friends—May, Dotty, and Nicki—each had three children. His cousin and business partner J. R. Horowitz had four children. I almost always wore a diaphragm, but at that time, I did not, hoping to become pregnant.

I thought Dick would be thrilled to learn that he would be a father again. He was not. He was furious. How dare I get pregnant without consulting him! He did not want a third child. He came from a family with two children, him and his sister Susan, and that was the ideal family size. We argued. He stopped speaking to me. For three weeks he did not speak to me. When we did at last talk, we agreed to see a family therapist. We made an appointment with a distinguished older gentleman who was accompanied by two young therapists who were studying with the older man.

We met a few times. I explained how much I wanted a baby. Dick said that it was wrong for me to have a baby without getting his consent first. He insisted it was not the right time. Ultimately, the three therapists agreed that Dick was right and I was wrong. I should not have the baby. Not now. They assured me that there was plenty of time to have another baby—I was only thirty-one—but considering Dick's strong feelings, this was not the right time. It was 1969, and it was not legal to have an abortion in New York State. The next year, the state law was changed, three years before *Roe v. Wade* legalized abortion across the nation.

Four against one. I should have ignored them all, but I didn't. There was always "the next time," they said. I stopped protesting. We went to the family obstetrician, and he performed a D&C in his office, which ended the pregnancy. Dick was pleased; I had obeyed his wishes. I tried to be happy, but I was only pretending, even to myself. I relied on the promise of "next time." Unfortunately, it was the therapists who promised "next time," not my husband.

A few years later, it happened again. I got pregnant and Dick got angry. This time, I knew it was useless to protest. He did not want a third child. There would be no "next time." There was no point seeing a family therapist; I knew how that would turn out. Abortion now was legal, so I lost another child that I desperately wanted. Dick was relieved that I had conceded without a fight.

What I did not understand at the time, and neither did he, was that those two abortions finished our marriage. We remained married for another ten years, but something inside me would never be the same. The losses were grievous; though not nearly as horrible as Stevie's death, I couldn't shake the feeling that I had been bullied into a decision that I hated. Twice. I was ashamed of myself for not having the courage to resist the pressure. Sometimes, when Dick and I were driving without the children, I would start crying without any apparent reason. I told him why I was crying, but it made him angry. He didn't understand. I cried many times again, but he stopped asking why. (When I reminded him of the abortions nearly half a century later, he had no recollection of what had happened.)

You might think that my experiences would have made me into an anti-abortion zealot, but they did not. I felt then and I believe now that it should be a woman's right to decide whether to have a baby. If women oppose abortion, they should not have one. If they want an abortion, it should be their choice, not the choice of the state, the legislature, or the courts. If they want a baby, no one should stop them, as I was stopped.

There would be no third child. But there might be a book, if I kept at it. And I did. I did research when the children were in school. I wrote late at night when the children were in bed. Whenever I completed a chapter, I would bring it to Larry Cremin, who now understood that he was my mentor, and he wrote encouraging words and sometimes suggested additional sources. He never edited what I wrote; that was not his role. He told me he "did not want to put my thumbs on your writing." What I wrote would be mine and mine alone.

Cremin, who was the dean of historians of American education, invited me to be his research assistant. I asked what that entailed. He said that he would give me a topic, I would do research, write it up, give it to him; he would edit it and include it in his new book. He was in the midst of writing a monumental history of American education that reflected his view that education is about all the institutions in a community—the family, the plantation, the church or synagogue, newspapers, radio, clubs and associations, and anything else that educated people. The school was a part, but not necessarily the most important part, of the educating influences in people's lives.

I think I would have done anything for Larry Cremin. I had a secret crush on him; he briefly had a crush on me and once kissed me passionately in my small office. But I was not going to do research and writing for him that would appear as his work, not mine. Just as he would not put his thumbs on my work, I would not be a silent contributor to his.

As I was writing my book about the history of the New York City schools, I wrote a few articles and book reviews drawn from my research. An article that I wrote for *Commentary* magazine in February 1972 had repercussions beyond what I imagined. It was titled "Community

Control Revisited," in which I reviewed the extravagant claims made about the schools of Ocean Hill–Brownsville by such notable figures as I. F. Stone, Nat Hentoff, Alfred Kazin, and Dwight Macdonald. They declared the experiment in community control a stunning success, but they relied on self-reporting by the district's leadership, which refused to administer any tests. When the experiment ended, city tests showed that the children in the district had fallen even farther behind during the chaotic years of community control. How could they not? There were frequent demonstrations around their schools, their veteran teachers were replaced by inexperienced ones, and their classes were often disrupted by adult issues.

After the article appeared, I received a call from the celebrated author Irving Howe, who invited me to lunch to discuss what he called "my little article." We met at a French restaurant on Madison Avenue and immediately engaged in animated conversation. The waiter brought bread and butter; Howe ordered a bowl of soup. I remember the soup because after a few minutes, the waiter came over and said, "Excuse me, Mr. Howe, but you are eating the salad dressing." He laughed and told me that I could have that story about him. It appears here for the first time!

The next response to the article had an important impact on my career.

Cremin spent every summer with his family in Palo Alto, where he was associated with the Center for Advanced Study in the Behavioral Sciences at Stanford University. In the fall of 1972, he returned from his summer sojourn with a message from the famed author Bruno Bettelheim. He said he and Bettelheim were conversing in the swimming pool, and Bettelheim asked Cremin if he knew me. Bettelheim had read my article in *Commentary*. He asked Cremin if I was studying for a doctorate, and Cremin told him that he had advised me against it because I did not need it. He had told me that our society was too obsessed with badges and degrees. Bettelheim said, "Please convey to the young lady that I disagree with you. Tell her that without a doctorate, she will hit a glass ceiling and will not advance beyond it."

When Cremin returned to New York, he gave me the message, and I immediately accepted Bettelheim's advice. Although I did not have a master's degree, I learned that I could register for a PhD awarded by Columbia University's School of Arts and Sciences (not an EdD from Teachers College) if I fulfilled all the requirements. First, I had to pass a foreign language examination. Then I had to pass a course in statistics. And last, I had to submit a dissertation that was satisfactory to a committee of professors. Cremin reiterated that he thought the degree was unnecessary, but I decided that I would ignore his advice and get a doctorate.

About the same time, I took Joey to a birthday party for four-year-olds. While the children played, the parents talked. One of the parents was a prominent historian at Columbia University who was known as a scholar of the new social history that rejected the tradition of centering history on the lives of Great White Men. Given his background, I assumed that he would be sympathetic to my cause. I told him that I planned to earn a doctorate in history and asked for his advice about whether I should apply for admission as a graduate student to the Columbia University Department of History. He told me candidly that I had three strikes against me: One, I was old (thirty-two). Two, I was a woman, and the history department seldom accepted female students. Three, I was interested in education, and the history department was not. Another sexist put-down. That settled it. I would get a PhD at Teachers College, not an EdD, because Cremin had a joint appointment in both Columbia's history department and Teachers College.

I bought a review book in French to revive what I had learned in college and passed the French examination. I signed up for a statistics course at Teachers College and passed the test. I took courses, including Cremin's big lecture course on the history of education. He was an effective lecturer and filled his talks with engaging anecdotes and humor. One memory of that course was Cremin's description of John Dewey, who lectured in that same room on the importance of not lecturing to students but engaging them in purposeful activities. I don't know if Cremin (or Dewey) saw the irony of lecturing about the importance of not lecturing!

By 1973, as I was looking around for a dissertation topic, I was finishing my history of the New York City public schools. I began to search for a publisher that would consider a book by an unknown author. I signed a contract for an advance of $3,000 with a small publisher called Outerbridge & Dienstfrey that was just getting started. Now that I had a publisher, I thought I was set. But one night, Irving Kristol—the so-called father of neoconservatism—and his wife Gertrude (Bea) Himmelfarb came to dinner. Irving warned me not to get a doctorate; he said it would ruin my writing skills. Then he suggested that I send my book to Erwin Glikes, the publisher at Basic Books. I did. Glikes liked the book and bought my contract from Outerbridge & Dienstfrey. Erwin assigned my book to an editor named Paul Neuthaler. Paul was amiable and handsome, and I liked him. But he predicted (not in my presence) that I was a one-book author. When I learned that, I determined to prove him wrong.

The Great School Wars: New York City, 1805–1974 was published in 1975. It received a respectful review in *The New York Times Book Review* and in other publications. Al Shanker, then the powerful president of the United Federation of Teachers, called to introduce himself. He asked if I wanted a good review or a bad review in his weekly paid column in *The New York Times*. Of course, I wanted a good review; that was how I met Al, who became a good friend.

After my book was published, I had many opportunities to write articles about education for the daily press and magazines. I became friendly not only with Irving Kristol but also with other stars of what was known as the neoconservative movement: Nathan Glazer, Daniel Bell, Daniel Patrick Moynihan, Norman Podhoretz and his wife Midge Decter, Thomas Sowell, James Coleman. In 1975, President Gerald Ford invited James Coleman, Nathan Glazer, and me to lunch at the White House to discuss busing. It was just the four of us. President Ford was an amiable man who listened intently as we noted the rising white flight from urban districts and expressed our concern that busing was promoting resegregation.

About the same time, my husband was invited to attend a private dinner of the board of *The Public Interest* at the Plaza Hotel to celebrate its tenth anniversary. *The Public Interest* was the journal of neoconservatism, founded by Daniel Bell and Irving Kristol. I was a contributor to the magazine; Dick was not. He was invited; I was not. The other invitees were all men, including Irving Kristol, Nathan Glazer, and Roger Starr (a member of the *New York Times* editorial board). Roger's wife, Manya (Fifi), was a close friend; we spoke on the phone and commiserated about our sexist husbands. We decided it was time for vengeance. We invited the wives of the other men to join us for dinner at the Plaza Oak Room while our husbands were convening in a private dining room. On the day of the dinner, Fifi and I purchased the head of a pig from an Italian butcher on Ninth Avenue (even in New York City, it was not easy to find a butcher who had the head of a pig). We invited Irving Kristol's wife Bea to our female soiree. Bea Kristol was a prominent historian of Victorian England who shared her husband's conservative values. When we told her of our plan to have a hotel waiter present our husbands with the head of a pig for excluding us from their dinner, she was very upset. Not only was it impudent, she said, not only was it hyperfeminist, but it was not even kosher! We went through with our plan, and a good laugh was had by all, even though it was not in keeping with the conservative values of *The Public Interest* and was not kosher.

Meanwhile, Dick had become friends with Bayard Rustin because of Dick's longtime support for the civil rights movement and labor unions. Bayard was director of the A. Philip Randolph Institute and a proponent of the importance of strong bonds between these two forces. One night Dick got a call about 2:00 a.m. from Bayard. He had been walking on West Forty-Second Street late one night, possibly cruising for another gay man, when a police officer noticed that he was carrying a sword cane and arrested him. The handle of the cane, when pulled out, was attached to a sword. Bayard must have picked it up without thinking twice; from his travels, he had an extensive collection of African art, exotic jewelry, and beautiful carved objects. When Dick got the call from Bayard, he dressed immediately and went to the police station to bail Bayard out. Later, when Bayard wanted to raise money for the Young People's Socialist League (Yipsils, as they were known), we cleared out the furniture in our Park Avenue apartment and Bayard gave an a cappella concert, which was recorded. We did not realize until that evening that, as a young man, Bayard had sung with the famed folk singer Josh White.

Never in the history of 1021 Park Avenue were there as many socialists or Black people in the building as the night of Bayard's concert. Bayard was a fascinating man; although he was born in West Chester, Pennsylvania, he spoke with a pronounced British accent. He was opposed to Black separatism, which he considered a defeatist strategy; he believed in coalition politics—especially alliances with labor unions—as the best way to achieve the goals of the civil rights movement. I consider him one of my teachers. My favorite Bayard story: One year he returned from an AFL-CIO executive committee meeting in Miami, and he was ebullient because he had gone to a nightclub to see Marlene Dietrich perform. "She was gorgeous," he said, "wearing a shimmering, sleek silver gown. I paid extra to get a table by the stage, and I threw a bouquet of flowers to her." I asked him why he was so devoted to Dietrich, and he answered, "I love this woman. She told Hitler to go fuck himself."

The big question I had to solve was what to do about my dissertation. I couldn't find a topic that seemed right. One night, Patricia Graham and her husband Loren came to dinner at our home; she too had been a student of Larry Cremin and later was dean of the Harvard Graduate School of Education. She told me that other writers, like Daniel Bell, had submitted a published work as their dissertation. Why shouldn't I?

The next morning, I asked Larry Cremin about this idea. What if I submitted *The Great School Wars* as my dissertation? It was developed under his tutelage. It had the appropriate scholarly trappings. I had browsed the dissertations in the Teachers College library and felt sure that *The Great School Wars* was equal to or better than those. He said, "It can be done. But this is the risk you take. I will assemble a committee of professors who will interview you and assess the book. You will get a vote of up or down, no chance for revision. Are you willing to take that chance?" I was.

I met with a committee composed of Cremin, Donna Shalala (who taught politics and education and was later President Bill Clinton's secretary of Health and Human Services for eight years), Kenneth Jackson from the Columbia University history department, and Douglas Sloan, a historian of education at Teachers College. They voted unanimously to accept the book as my PhD dissertation, and I was Dr. Ravitch, the first in my family to earn an advanced degree.

Now that I had a doctorate, Cremin discussed my future. He said there were no tenure-track positions open at Teachers College but there was one at a college on Staten Island. I told him that I was more interested in writing than in teaching, and I preferred to be an adjunct at Teachers College than a tenure-track professor anywhere else. And thus began my academic career as adjunct assistant professor of history and education at Teachers College, teaching one course a year, usually the history of urban education. The annual salary was $7,500. I had a career. I was a historian. I would be an academic.

10

SCHOLARSHIP AND A SHOCKING DEVELOPMENT

After I was appointed an adjunct assistant professor of history and education, I had my own office at Teachers College on West 120th Street in Manhattan, where I read and wrote. It was my first office. A room of my own. I had not decided what to write next when Larry Cremin made a request that pointed me toward my next book. The small field of history of education was then riven by a debate between young historians who called themselves radical revisionists and older historians like Cremin. The young radicals believed that the public schools served the nefarious purposes of elites who used them to mold the children of working-class people. They argued that the public schools were created as a means of "social control," to tame the masses and fit them into their preordained roles in the social order. The biggest beneficiaries of public schools, according to this perspective, were the manufacturers and property owners who wanted the schools to train and discipline future workers. The belief that the schools provided social mobility was a myth, nothing more.

I thought this line of reasoning was cynical, even bizarre. I reflected on the issues through my own experience. Where would I be if I had not had the public schools to raise me up and offer me the opportunity for a better life? Where would my mother be? Almost everyone I knew had a better life because of their public-school education. Aside from the family I had married into, I didn't know anyone who had gone to private schools.

The revisionists scorned historians like Cremin because he was a "consensus" historian. Like his contemporary Bernard Bailyn at Harvard University and others of his generation, he downplayed conflict and wrote about unifying themes in history. Without saying it in so many words, Cremin wanted me to defend him. I was glad to do it, and I enthusiastically jumped into the arena. At that point, Cremin was president of the National Academy of Education, an honor society for scholars of education. The academy invited me to write a paper about the radical revisionists. He stayed in the background because it would have been unseemly for him to sponsor my response to his critics.

I read all the books by the revisionists and wrote a paper of one hundred pages or so skewering their claims and reasserting the case for public schools as a means of social mobility and social progress. I sent a copy to Erwin Glikes at Basic Books, and he asked me to expand it into a book. The book was titled *The Revisionists Revised: A Critique of the Radical Attack on the Schools*. It was published in 1978. I intended it to be an evidence-based defense of public schools as progressive, democratic institutions. Ironically, its publication marked me within the scholarly field as a defender of the status quo, a conservative (which was a dreaded thing to be). As a very new professor, however, I enjoyed the prestige of having my latest work sponsored by the august National Academy of Education. Based on the two books I had published, I was invited to become a member of the academy, which was a thank-you note from the Old Guard.

I was by no means a consensus historian myself. I did not hesitate to take on sacred cows and powerful people. I enjoyed the marketplace of ideas, where knowledgeable people debated and exchanged divergent opinions. While I was cowed by my husband and his mother, I was fearless as a historian and writer. Almost all my books deal in one way or another with conflict and struggle, whether it was *The Great School Wars, The Revisionists Revised, The Troubled Crusade, Left Back, The Death and Life of the Great American School System, Reign of Error*, or *Slaying Goliath*. All of them explored the history of ideological and political battles over control of the schools. Other historians of education wrote about fields like instruction and teacher education, where consensus was possible. I was interested in the politics of education seen through a historical perspective, where the turning points were contested. Cremin once told me that he preferred to write about the eras between the "school wars," when consensus was the rule, not the exception. In my lifetime, starting in the Houston public schools, I had seen adults struggle for power over the schools as a way of shaping the minds of children and the future. Whether it was the Minute Women in Houston in the 1950s, snooping for evidence of Communists in the schools, or Moms for Liberty in the 2020s, demanding "parental rights" (but only for white conservative parents like themselves), schools were repeatedly drawn into controversies over race, religion, evolution, censorship, gender, justice, freedom to teach, freedom to learn, and freedom of thought. As I studied the history of education, I saw similar struggles play out in the nineteenth century, the twentieth century, and the early decades of the twenty-first century—struggles for control, struggles for funding, struggles for ideological dominance. I was not looking for trouble. It was there. To ignore it was to distort the truth about the forces that molded American education.

I loved being a historian. I enjoyed doing research. What might be tedious for other people was exciting for me. Nothing was more satisfying than to find exactly the fact or quote or illustrative incident that I was looking for. Nothing was more exciting than to step into the shoes of people who had debated the future of education a century earlier and to see the world as they had seen it.

My articles and essays expressed my meritocratic views, which placed me firmly on the conservative side of contentious issues. I defended standardized testing, which I then believed was an accurate measure of "merit." I believed in color-blind policy because I thought it was the right response to racism. I criticized busing because it contributed to white flight. In 1975, I was invited by *The New York Times Week in Review* to write a full-page article about why busing was "The Solution That Has Failed to Solve." I cited the resegregation of urban schools as whites left the cities for the suburbs and the views of Professor Derrick

Bell of Harvard Law School, who was later recognized as the founder of "critical race theory." I criticized bilingual education because it slowed the assimilation of non-English-speaking people into American society. I criticized affirmative action because I believed that people should be selected based on objective criteria like test scores. In my critique of affirmative action, I was influenced by the views of the conservative Black economist Thomas Sowell, who maintained that, because of affirmative action, Black students were bypassing state universities where they would excel and enrolling in elite universities where they were unlikely to succeed. I wrote an article in *The Wall Street Journal* in the early 1980s opposing the Equal Rights Amendment because I thought it unnecessary. I criticized feminist organizations that complained about gender bias since data showed women overtaking and surpassing men in college enrollments. As someone who believed that society should be color-blind and all people should be treated equally, I was opposed to making public policy color-conscious or gender-conscious. In the mid-1990s, I wrote a regular column in *Forbes* magazine in which I criticized affirmative action, bilingual education, and political correctness and wrote favorably about single-sex schools, Catholic schools, standards, charter schools, and the virtues of competition. On the bright side, I consistently defended teaching the arts, literature, history, and liberal education. I defended teachers and teachers' unions, which defended teachers' rights. I did write one shocking column for *Forbes* in which I contended that no one should be a billionaire, that $100 million should suffice for those who wanted riches. At one point, someone described me as "an egalitarian conservative."

I was often called a neoconservative, although I preferred to think of myself as a maverick. The popular saying at the time—the 1970s and 1980s—was that a neoconservative was a liberal who had been mugged by reality. The scholars I admired, like Bell, Glazer, and Moynihan, were heterodox thinkers who worked in a liberal culture but dared to question its assumptions, and they too were called neoconservatives.

Derrick Bell was not part of the Kristol-Coleman-Glazer neoconservative nexus. He was an original thinker who was revising his own views on remedies for racism. He invited me to participate in a symposium at

Harvard Law School where I presented a paper on the tension between color-blind and color-conscious policies. As a lawyer for the NAACP Legal Defense Fund, Bell had litigated many cases that sought integration and busing. But he had begun to have serious doubts about whether his legal victories were in the best interests of his clients, the parents of Black children, whose main goal was a good education. My paper questioned the widespread view among whites that Black culture was deficient and that the only good schools had a white majority. I questioned whether it might be possible to eliminate all traces of racism while celebrating the achievements of Black culture, rather than viewing it "as a stigma by whites and a handicap to blacks." The essay was published in 1980 in a collection that Derrick Bell edited, titled *Shades of Brown: New Perspectives on School Desegregation*. Derrick was the first African American to win tenure at Harvard Law School, an honor that he relinquished to protest the lack of diversity on the faculty. We became good friends in the mid-1980s, and Derrick visited me at my Upper West Side apartment, where we amicably disagreed about the consequences of the *Brown* decision; he thought it had failed, I thought it had transformed American society.

In 1983 I was invited to contribute an article to a festschrift in honor of James S. Coleman. I decided to write about the three Coleman reports on education. His first report, commissioned by Congress as a study of equality of educational opportunity, concluded in 1966 that integration would improve Black achievement; the report was widely hailed because it was in the mainstream of liberal ideology of the time. In the second report, released in 1975, he concluded that busing was not working because it was promoting white flight and increasing segregation; he was widely condemned in the media for this pessimistic assessment. The president of the American Sociological Association wanted the organization to censure Coleman, one of its most prominent members, but it didn't. The third report in 1981 found that private schools had better outcomes than public schools because of their curricular demands and their discipline; Coleman recommended tuition tax credits or vouchers to enable more Black students to attend Catholic and private schools. I attended a discussion of this report in Washington, D.C., where more than five hundred angry researchers and scholars of education hooted at him. When I told Coleman a year later that I wanted to write about the reactions to his three reports, he shipped me a box of his personal files. In my commentary on the reports, I said that Coleman had a "taste for smashing icons and enduring obloquy." He was willing to correct errors, but no one could make him back down. He had tenure, and his reputation as a scholar was impeccable.

In my role as a scholar, I made some unexpected acquaintances. One of them was Bill Bennett. He came to see me at my office at Teachers College in 1977, looking for a job. He asked if I would put in a good word for him at Teachers College. Being at the very bottom of the hierarchy, a mere adjunct assistant professor, I could not help him, but he had better luck elsewhere. In 1979 he was named director of the National Humanities Center in North Carolina, where he used his background in philosophy to advocate for the humanities in education. In 1981 President Ronald Reagan named him the chair of the National Endowment for the Humanities. He subsequently served as secretary of education in Reagan's second term. He was an outspoken proponent of vouchers and moral values, which made him just right as Reagan's secretary of education.

Bill Bennett was undoubtedly responsible for my invitation to the Reagan White House in 1984. A small group of scholars met with President Reagan, Vice President George H. W. Bush, and a few other officials to talk about education. We were seated around the large table in the room where the Cabinet meets. I was seated next to Vice President Bush. President Reagan opened the meeting by greeting us and telling a few jokes that he had probably told many times. The one I never forgot is his story about his conversation with a group of angry student rebels when he was governor of California. He said they railed about their grievances and insisted that his generation was ignorant compared to their own because they had grown up with computers and space travel, all of which were unknown to Reagan's cohort. The older generation, they insisted, was simply out of touch.

Reagan said he replied to them, in his genial manner, "What you young folks forget is that my generation invented all those marvels of technology."

The president was affable and attentive to the conversation that followed. He listened intently to what others said. I don't recall him interjecting his own views or whether he had any. As the meeting progressed, I whispered to Vice President Bush, "Would you please tell the president that my mother in Texas is worried about the future of Israel?" He said he would. A few weeks later, I received a handsome letter from the White House, signed by President Reagan. After thanking me for attending the meeting, the letter included this line: "Please tell your mother I got her message." Now, I understand that President Reagan did not write the letter; I understand that the letter was signed by a machine. But only Vice President Bush knew about my request, and he made sure it was acknowledged. I thought he was a classy guy.

Around 1980, I struck up a friendship with Checker Finn. He and I were friends immediately. We first met through our mutual friendship with Daniel Patrick Moynihan. Checker worked for Moynihan when he was ambassador to India and then when he was in the Senate. I met Moynihan in 1976 when he was first running for the U.S. Senate in New York and my husband was raising money for him. When we became friends, Checker was teaching education policy at Vanderbilt University and advising Tennessee governor Lamar Alexander. In 1981 we created an informal group called the Educational Excellence Network that circulated a xeroxed monthly newsletter of clippings to other academics around the country who shared our concern about low academic standards in the schools. We didn't raise any money or sell anything, but we built a network of hundreds of like-minded scholars and educators. School choice was not one of our issues. Over the years, Checker and I formed a close bond, almost like siblings. Our families became close, and we frequently shared dinners and holidays.

Meanwhile, I continued my work as a historian. In 1983, I published *The Troubled Crusade: American Education, 1945–1980*. The title was inspired by a message that Thomas Jefferson wrote in 1786 to his friend George Wythe in Virginia, when Jefferson was the American minister to the French government. He was hoping the Virginia legislature would pass a bill to create public schools "for the diffusion of knowledge among the people." He urged Wythe, "Preach, my dear Sir, a crusade against ignorance; establish and improve the law for educating the common people. Let our countrymen know that the people alone can protect us against these evils, and that the tax which will be paid for this purpose is not more than the thousandth part of what will be paid to kings, priests and nobles who will rise up among us if we leave the people in ignorance." The book echoed my deep belief in public schools and the teaching profession.

Meanwhile, my private life continued to flourish. In 1980, Dick and I bought a piece of land on Blue Heron Lake in Pound Ridge, New York, that had previously been the home of Jerry Bock and his family. Bock and his friend Sheldon Harnick were the composer and lyricist for *Fiorello* and *Fiddler on the Roof*. The Bock property was for sale because the house had burned to the ground along with his precious awards. We built a new house with a tennis court on this bucolic spot and spent summers and weekends there, playing tennis, swimming, and boating on the lake. We loved spending time at this idyllic spot.

In the winter, fishermen cut holes in the ice and dropped their fishing lines into the lake. I got an idea one day to go cross-country skiing on the lake while it was frozen solid. That unforgettable day, I went out on the ice alone and traversed the lake from end to end. After an hour or so, I reached a desolate spot where there was no house in sight, and I felt the ice melting under me. I suddenly realized that I was skiing over a spring and the ice was not solid. My skis dropped about 6 inches into the slush, and there was no point screaming for help because no one would hear me. I did what I had to do: I pushed forward with as much strength as I could muster, and I pulled myself out of the slush and back onto solid ice. I had a close call with death; if I had slipped into the lake, there would have been no way to extricate myself. It was one of the most frightening moments of my life.

Aside from my brush with death on the lake, I was leading a good life. Because I was married to a wealthy man, I was invited to join the board of the New York Public Library; at my first meeting, the board learned that the institution was $50 million in debt. Soon after, the board selected Vartan Gregorian as its new president. He was president of the University of Pennsylvania and a scholar of Iranian history. He was a charismatic personality, but more important to the future of the library, he was a prodigious fundraiser. He developed a close friendship with Brooke Astor, who made the New York Public Library the primary beneficiary of her charitable giving. Under his leadership, the library attracted other major donors and philanthropists to the board and wiped out its debt. I was also a member of the board of the American Museum of Folk Art, which had very little money. I was an aficionado of American folk art, and I collected paintings, spatterware, fraktur, and other Americana. I seldom missed an auction of folk art at Sotheby's or the annual Antiques Fair at the Park Avenue Armory in January. During the late 1980s, I was a member of the corporate board of Encyclopaedia Britannica, where I became friendly with Walter Mondale, Mortimer Adler, and the author Theodore (Teddy) White. A few years later, Adler caused me great embarrassment by inviting me to give a lecture at the University of North Carolina; the date of the lecture, I realized belatedly, happened to fall on Yom Kippur, the holiest day in the Jewish calendar. Although I am not an observant Jew, I never do anything outside home or synagogue on Yom Kippur. When I told Mortimer that I had made a terrible mistake, he insisted that I follow through on my commitment. Knowing that he too was Jewish, I did. Only after the day ended did he tell me that he had long ago converted and was an Episcopalian.

Serving on prestigious boards, attending elegant dinner parties, mingling with the elites in academia and society, I had a very privileged life. I fulfilled the obligations of my privileged existence, but my writing was increasingly important to me. After the appearance of *The Troubled Crusade*, a lecture agent—William Leigh of the Leigh Bureau in New Jersey—came to see me at my home and offered to arrange paid speaking engagements. I had never made money, neither as a professor nor as an author, and I signed up with the Leigh Bureau. He arranged speaking engagements about once a month that paid $3,000.

One of my most memorable events occurred when I spoke at Ouachita Baptist University in Arkadelphia, Arkansas. A week before my arrival, I received a phone call from the secretary to the governor of Arkansas, one Bill Clinton. She told me that Governor Clinton would like to invite me to stay in the governor's mansion and meet his wife,

Hillary. I happily agreed; I knew nothing about either of them. I lectured about the importance of a liberal education. Governor Clinton sat in the back of the room and generously asked softball questions during the question-and-answer period. Afterwards, I drove back to Little Rock with him and his state troopers. Hillary was sitting up and waiting to meet me, and we three talked until the wee hours. I had no idea that he aimed for higher office. Hillary and I discovered that we were both graduates of Wellesley: I was in the class of 1960, and she was in the class of 1969. The Clintons were delightful.

But I also remember a less than pleasant event when I spoke at the Young Men's Hebrew Association in Manhattan, an unpaid appearance. I spoke about my work, and at the end of the lecture I was surrounded by about twenty people who wanted to ask questions. This happens at every lecture, and it is customary for the speaker to wait around and answer questions. But my husband broke through the crowd and pulled me out, saying that we had agreed to have dinner with friends of his mother, and we couldn't keep them waiting. I think it was then that I realized that he was jealous of me. I was not acting the appropriate part of wife and mother.

I harbored my own doubts after we spent an evening at the home of former mayor Robert F. Wagner and his wife Phyllis Cerf Wagner. It was a large group of people, and my most vivid memory of the evening was when Chris Cerf, son of Mrs. Wagner from her first marriage to the publisher Bennett Cerf, sat down at the piano after dinner. He was a successful composer and lyricist, and he began playing songs of the 1950s. I was delighted, especially when he played "Earth Angel," which I had not heard since I was in high school. After 10 minutes of his playing and singing, Dick said to me, "We are leaving. Now." I was having a good time, but he hated the music. He loved opera, classical music, and Gilbert & Sullivan. He tastes were rigid, and they did not include the music of my teen years.

Under normal circumstances, I should have been able to pursue my academic interests without worrying about money, but Dick had a disturbing habit of making me feel financially insecure. On many occasions, late at night before going to sleep, he would calculate his assets and his debts and express concern about what might happen if he lost everything. And he would say to me, "What do you think you could earn on your own? Could you support us?" This was frightening because I had never made more than $7,000 or $8,000 a year as an adjunct professor at Teachers College. Even with my new income as a lecturer, I still could not support us. I had no money of my own. I am not sure why he wanted to scare me, but he did. Did he want me to feel inadequate, dependent, unsuccessful?

The Troubled Crusade was the first book that I wrote on a computer. My first computer was a TRS-80 from Radio Shack. The machine was bulky. It broke down so often that I realized I had to buy a second, identical computer because one of them would often be in the Radio Shack repair department. I would save everything I wrote on floppy disks and move from computer to computer. Bringing a computer in for repairs was never easy because only one Radio Shack store in Manhattan repaired computers, and it was located in midtown Manhattan, where parking was impossible. My TRS-80 computers were colloquially (and appropriately) known as Trash-80s.

Despite the problems of maintenance, I was thrilled to write on a computer because I never had to erase the good part of a sentence or paragraph, only delete the bad part. In the pre-computer days, I would have to retype an entire article if there were errors. In the early 1980s, when I was writing *The Troubled Crusade*, I went to a board meeting of the New York Public Library. I sang the praises of writing on a computer to a fellow board member, the historian Barbara Tuchman, and she said she would like to see it. I invited her to my home on Park Avenue and to the tiny maid's room where I worked. After she had watched a demonstration of how a computer works, she told me she used computer paper. I was puzzled. How could she use computer paper when she didn't own a computer? She opened her large bag and pulled out a roll of computer paper, not single sheets but attached ones. On it, she was handwriting her next manuscript. I doubt that she ever changed, but she did use computer paper for her purposes in her own way.

My service on the board of the New York Public Library brought an unfortunate encounter with another famous author, Isaac Asimov. I sat next to him at a formal dinner at the library and was trying to make small talk. Searching for a topic that we might have in common, I fell back on talking about the writing program I was using at the time, which was called WordPerfect. I waxed ecstatic about its virtues; Mr. Asimov was not amused. He said sharply that it was people like me who start wars by thinking that what they do is best. I was stunned into silence. Me, start a war? I never found out whether he used a computer, and if he did, what writing program he used. In any event, when I bought my next computer, a Dell, I had to switch to Microsoft Word. And I never again told anyone my opinion of my writing program (but WordPerfect was far better than Word).

My children quickly learned to do their schoolwork on a computer, using one of mine. One night when I was asleep, I sensed a silent presence next to me and opened my eyes. It was my son, Michael, then about fifteen. He looked shaken. He had been working for hours on a paper for school. He didn't save. Everything he had written had mysteriously disappeared. All his work, gone in a flash because of one wrong click of the mouse. All I could do was commiserate and tell him to get a good night's sleep and start over the next day. The experience was as haunting for me as it was for him. When I was writing *The Troubled Crusade*, I lost the first six pages of a chapter and quickly concluded that it was the best six pages I had ever written or would ever write, and it was now gone forever. I spent days futilely searching for a program to recover the words that were floating in my computer's memory, nameless. I did eventually find someone who had a program called Z that recovered the missing six pages; they were not as good as I thought.

Meanwhile, my friend Checker Finn had a brilliant idea in 1982 about a project we could undertake. He proposed that we ask his friend Bill Bennett, who was chairman of the National Endowment for the Humanities in Reagan's administration, for a grant to hold a series of conferences on the future of the humanities. Bill liked the idea, and we received funding to pay for the conferences and the expenses of its attendees.

This grant had momentous consequences for my life that I could not foresee.

Checker and I invited prominent scholars of history and literature to address issues in their fields. We invited schools across the nation to send teams of teachers to attend the conferences. The conferences were held in 1984, and from those came two edited volumes: one was called *Challenges to the Humanities* and the other *Against Mediocrity*.

One of the speakers was an English professor at the University of Virginia named E. D. Hirsch Jr. I proposed that we invite him to speak after I had read a provocative article that he had written in *The American Scholar* called "Cultural Literacy." Hirsch believed that education required more than a knowledge of skills, processes, and vocabulary. It required "cultural literacy," that is, knowledge of the background and context in which words have meaning. I said to him at the conference, "You know, you really should write a book about this." He did, and it became a national bestseller. After the wild success of his book, Hirsch developed the Core Knowledge Foundation and published books about what knowledge children should learn in each grade. I joined the board of the foundation and enthusiastically promoted his ideas about the importance of knowledge as the basis for learning. Hirsch's ideas about content knowledge resonated with me because I believed then and now that the "furniture of the mind" matters even more than learning processes; too many education professors went overboard for skills and forgot about content. It is content—narrratives and stories—not skills, that ignites love of learning.

But something even more significant happened at our conference in Minneapolis in April 1984. As an organizer of the conference, I was constantly moving from side to side in the back of the auditorium, and at one point during my wanderings a young woman introduced herself. She said she was a social studies teacher from Brooklyn. She told me a story that made me laugh. She said that she had protected our conference secretary, who was being menaced by two men who wanted to use the conference bathroom; they seemed to be stoned, she thought. The secretary told them they would have to go elsewhere, and they were advancing toward her in what seemed to be a threatening manner when the teacher stopped them while holding two scalding cups of coffee in her hands. They left. As she told the story, I laughed out loud. How politically incorrect she was! Later, at a reception, the same young woman saw me standing alone and brought me a glass of wine. I am not a gregarious person, but she was. I learned that she was chairperson of the social studies department at the Edward R. Murrow High School in Brooklyn. She said it was an innovative school. I promised to visit her school. Her name was Mary Butz.

When I returned to New York City, I couldn't stop thinking about how easily Mary had made me laugh. At the time, my husband was berating me for some failure in my household skills, always a sore subject. He was furious that I was unable to find a dry cleaner who could roll his suit collars exactly the way he liked them. I sent his suits to the best, most expensive cleaning services; the collars were never done right. Or it might have been that he had once again found a pair of socks that were mismatched. Or maybe he was angry because I had not quickly picked up the socks that he casually dropped on the floor. He often reminded me that these jobs—picking up after men and keeping their clothes in order—were supposed to come naturally to women, but I needed constant reminders. What was wrong with me? It seemed that the more my career blossomed, the more he criticized me for my inattention to menial household chores. We had full-time household help, but whatever was not right was always my fault.

I had promised Mary that I would visit her school, but I had no idea how to find the Midwood section of Brooklyn, because my life was centered in Manhattan. I had been to Brooklyn only a few times. I called up my friend Charlotte Frank, who was a senior executive at the New York City Board of Education, and told her that I wanted to visit Edward R. Murrow High School. She thought that was a grand idea and arranged a tour of some of Brooklyn's best schools, including not only Murrow but Midwood, John Dewey (a middle school), and a couple of exemplary elementary schools. But I was interested only in Murrow. I met the principal and founder of the school, Saul Bruckner, who was a master teacher. He knew that I was a writer, and he invited me to return to learn more about the school and its progressive philosophy. I gladly accepted. It was a school with unusual programming. The courses lasted only ten weeks, and students hung out in the hallways between classes. The student body was racially integrated, and students from different achievement levels were enrolled, with one quarter chosen from the top test-score strata, one quarter from the lowest, and half the students in the middle. The arts and communications departments were outstanding, and the school boasted a dramatics program that staged highly professional productions. There was much to admire about the school, and I wrote an article about it called "A Good School" that was published in *The American Scholar*.

But in truth, it was not the school that interested me. I was interested in Mary. On one of my trips to see the school, Mr. Bruckner asked her to drive me home, and again she regaled me with hilarious tales about her life as a teacher. We stopped to have drinks at a bar on the Upper East Side. Our legs accidentally brushed, and I felt a jolt of electricity. How could I explain it? Here I was, a serious, conservative scholar, forty-six years old, married to a wealthy man, living on Park Avenue, mother of two sons (one in law school, the other a senior in high school), and I was infatuated with a Roman Catholic high school teacher ten years younger than I.

We had very little in common other than our professional commitments to education. She had grown up in a working-class family in Brooklyn. Her father had been a token clerk for the New York City Transit Authority (when I met her, my husband was chairman of the board of the Metropolitan Transit Authority). Her mother was a housewife who had worked as a cook for a wealthy family. She had gone to Catholic school from first grade through college. I was Jewish and a product of public schools. She was a graduate of St. Joseph's College in Brooklyn. I was a graduate of Wellesley College. She was of German descent; both her parents had come to the United States in the 1920s during Weimar and had suffered anti-German prejudice during and after World War II.

Despite all these differences, I was strongly drawn to her. The more unsatisfactory my home life was, the more I missed her company. I began missing her constantly. With Dick's knowledge, we met a few times for dinner, and we met even more times without his knowledge.

I was at a crisis point in my life. I realized that I was deeply attracted to this woman, but I had a fundamental loyalty to my marriage, to my family, and to everything that constituted my life of the past twenty-five years. It was ingrained in me that marriage was forever. I truly didn't know what I would do, what I should do.

That summer of 1984, Dick and I visited our friends Morris and Carlyn Abram on Cape Cod in Massachusetts. Morris was a renowned civil rights attorney from Georgia. We had settled down to watch the U.S. Open; it was Chris Evert versus Martina Navratilova. Dick was cheering loudly for Evert and shouting, "Beat the dyke!" I squirmed; I had never heard him make a homophobic comment. Was it subliminal? The phone rang; it was someone from CBS, inviting me to appear the next day on *Face the Nation*. But how would I get to Washington, D.C., the next day? The caller said, "Don't worry, we will send a plane for you." I had brought nothing to wear except shorts, T-shirts, and a bathing suit. I scrambled with my host Carlyn to find a presentable skirt and blouse. Dick was not at all pleased that I would be departing in the middle of the weekend. CBS sent a two-engine jet to pick me up very early on Sunday, and I appeared that morning with Bill Clinton, governor of Arkansas; Mary Hatwood Futrell, the president of the National Education Association; and my friend Checker Finn. That was exciting for me, but not good for our shaky marriage.

In the fall of 1984, I began to see a therapist regularly, the same woman who had been part of the group that counseled me to have an abortion a decade earlier. She knew both Dick and me and had seen our interaction. I told her that I was having a clandestine affair with Mary. Should I stay or should I go? I thought she would help me sort out my life and understand what I wanted. She did. She asked me a crucial question: "Haven't you ever heard of the women's liberation movement?" The reality was that it had passed me by or that, in my rank conservatism, I had simply closed it out. She helped me take control of my life and stop absorbing psychic blows.

That Christmas 1984, Dick and I went to London to spend the holiday with Joey, who was working at *The Times* of London for the year between college and law school. Somehow everything went sour. Dick had purchased tickets to see a Shakespeare play at Stratford-on-Avon and exploded in a rage when he discovered that I had not arranged transportation to Stratford. He also became angry when he realized that I had not made a reservation for New Year's Eve dinner at a great restaurant. Joey suggested that we shop for dinner in Harrod's food hall; we did and brought a wonderful, spontaneous meal to his apartment, but Dick could not forgive me for failing to make dinner plans. I felt terrible, but I didn't know about these expectations. He had a secretary. I didn't. I was so tired of feeling like a failure. That weekend, the start of 1985, I decided I could no longer live in this cauldron of disappointment and criticism anymore.

We returned to New York City. I went through the motions for six months. Michael graduated from high school and left for a trip to Europe. Joey had a summer job working for a law firm. On July 11, 1985, I called Mary and asked her to meet me at my building. I packed a bag with a few articles of clothing. I took my computer, my bicycle, and my red Volkswagen convertible. I left Park Avenue and moved to Mary's fourth-floor walk-up apartment in Bay Ridge, a working-class neighborhood in Brooklyn. I had no money other than a bank account that Dick replenished monthly for household bills.

I had taken the most dramatic step of my life. No, not a step, a leap. I dared to leave my home and my well-patterned life, whose arc was completely predictable. I walked into a future that was unknown. I was exhilarated by the thought of my liberation from marriage, yet I was also deeply concerned for Dick. I loved him, but I couldn't bear to live with him any longer. The more I wanted to spread my wings, the more he felt compelled to clip them. Mary made me happy; I marveled at her strength of character, her essential goodness. I knew what I was doing. I abandoned a life of comfort and plenty for the unknown. I was nervous about saying the word *gay* or *lesbian*. I was curious about the new world I had entered. Mary introduced me to gay bars and to her friends, who ranged from teachers to police officers. I was not prepared to announce my new identity to the world. But I was prepared to enjoy my newfound freedom, to shake loose the bonds of convention, and to walk boldly into the future before me, taking life one day at a time.

FIGURE 1 A family photograph at home in 1943, with Diane sitting in the center.

FIGURE 2 Working at the *Washington Post*, 1959.

FIGURE 3 A family portrait: Diane, Dick, Michael, and Joey in 1969.

FIGURE 4 Joey and Steven, 1966.

FIGURE 5 Diane and Mary, 2022.

FIGURE 6 Michael, Diane, and Joe, 2008.

11

A NEW LIFE

In August 1985, Mary and I rented an apartment in Provincetown, Massachusetts, for three weeks. Provincetown is known as a hive of carefree gay life. Everything I saw was a revelation. To say that I was experiencing a major change of life would be an understatement. I felt guilty about leaving my marriage yet happy to be free of the sense of failure and nonstop criticism. I felt guilty about hurting Dick, whom I had loved and protected for twenty-five years. But I had reached a point of no return. And there I was, in Provincetown, suddenly immersed in a new world, surrounded by exuberant gays and lesbians and trying to feel like one of them. It was me but not me. I was very closeted and didn't want anyone to know my last name. Mary had friends there, and we had fun with them, swimming, sailing, biking. They didn't care who I was; I was Mary's friend, and that was all that mattered. Doing things just for fun—that was a new idea at my stage in life (I was forty-seven).

When we returned from vacation, I rented a one-bedroom furnished sublet on the seventeenth floor at Ninety-Seventh Street and West End Avenue with a partial view of the Hudson River and beautiful sunsets. Since I had no money, Dick gave me a monthly stipend to pay for rent and food. Dick continued to think we would reconcile, but I knew that would not happen. I was in love with Mary. I had done my best for twenty-five years and I couldn't do it anymore. I wanted a fresh start.

One by one, I made lunch dates with my closest friends and told them about my decision. They were not surprised. They understood why I had left Dick—they saw the way he ordered me around and berated me—but they did not understand why I was with a woman. One friend asked incredulously, "But what do two women do?" I did not feel obliged to explain.

Dick was very depressed. He couldn't understand why I had left. He had no idea that I was unhappy. He told me that I must be going through menopause, and he was sure I would recover and come to my senses. He did not know how anguished I was by my decision but how eager I was to start a new life.

I spoke with my sons. Joe was not happy; he was home when I left and bore the full burden of taking care of his disconsolate father. He was angry at me for a long time. I understood. Michael and I met for lunch after he returned from Europe. He told me, in somewhat muffled tones—so muffled that he had to say it twice—that he was gay. I reacted calmly. Then he said, "What about you?" He told me he had noticed additions to my bookshelf, such as the poetry of Adrienne Rich. He had also noticed an airline receipt with Mary's name on it that I had mistakenly retained after a trip to South Carolina where she joined me when I gave a Phi Beta Kappa lecture at the state university. Michael and I had a mutual coming-out at a Greek diner on the Upper West Side of Manhattan.

Mary and I were determined to enjoy our lives together. We rode our bicycles from one end of the city to the other. We went to plays. We met Mary's friends, who came from all walks of life. I discovered new friends who were unabashedly gay, like Kate Stimpson, a brilliant academic feminist. I learned that some of my friends had gay daughters or sons whom they had not previously mentioned. Mary won an award from the Kellogg Foundation—the first teacher to be recognized as a Kellogg National Fellow—and I joined her at my own expense on trips to London, China, Thailand, and Japan. We were invited to participate in a trek in the Himalayas in 1986, which included married couples as well as Carol Bellamy, who was later the head of the Peace Corps and UNICEF; the Brookings economist Alice Rivlin; and Donna Shalala, who gave me a shampoo on a mountaintop and told me that I could tell this story in my memoirs if I ever wrote them.

While not traveling or playing, I threw myself into my work with renewed abandon because I was now free to write whenever I wanted and free to travel for work without having to ask permission. Two projects absorbed my attention. The state superintendent of schools in California, Bill Honig, invited me to participate in rewriting the state standards for history and social science. I readily agreed. From start to finish, the California project took close to three years and required monthly trips to California.

At the same time, Checker Finn and I were writing a book together. We had obtained another grant from the National Endowment for the Humanities (NEH) while our friend Bill Bennett was still in charge; the grant paid for the first-ever national test of history and literature by the federal National Assessment of Educational Progress (NAEP). The test sought to determine whether seventeen-year-olds were familiar with basic facts about history and well-known works of American literature. The test was based on E. D. Hirsch Jr.'s ideas about cultural literacy. Knowledge matters. As we expected, the results were dismal, and we wrote a book called *What Do Our 17-Year-Olds Know?*, published in 1987.

By the time the book was in draft form, Checker was working for Bill Bennett at the U.S. Department of Education as assistant secretary of the Office of Educational Research and Improvement and counselor to the secretary. I gave the book my full attention. Mary read the draft copy and advised me to cut Checker's harsh comments about teachers, which I did. After all, the book was about curriculum, and teachers were doing what was expected of them.

Unlike Bill Bennett, who was repulsed by my relationship with Mary, Checker remained a close friend. Mary and I admired Checker's wife, Renu Vermani, who is a wonderful person and a brilliant research cardiologist, and we were friends with their adult children. When I left my marriage, one of the rumors was that I had left to be with Checker!

When Reagan appointed Bill Bennett as secretary of education, he was replaced at the NEH by Lynne Cheney, wife of Congressman Dick

Cheney from Wyoming. Lynne had a doctorate in British literature and was well-qualified for her position. Checker and I were about to publish our book about the national assessment of history and literature that we had commissioned, and she invited us to brief her about our findings. A few days before the book's publication date, the NEH published a pamphlet by Lynne Cheney called "American Memory" that used our data and main conclusions.

The publicist at Harper & Row had arranged for us to talk about our book on one of the network morning shows, but at the last moment we were canceled and replaced by Lynne Cheney. When we complained, she said that our work was paid for by the NEH and that she had every right to publish the findings because they were public property. Maybe she was right, but we were upset. Word of our spat went public, and *The New York Times* published a front-page article about it. Sam Donaldson of ABC News called me and asked whether she had plagiarized our work, and I said I preferred to use a different word, but I don't recall what it was.

Lynne was angry, and she had her general counsel, Brent Hatch (son of Republican senator Orrin Hatch of Utah), launch an investigation of the grant, which was administered by Teachers College, my employer. I was paid $16,000 to oversee the project and write the book, and Checker was paid nothing because he worked for the government. There wasn't much for Brent Hatch to investigate, since almost the entire grant of $400,000 was used to pay for the assessment. But it is very anxiety-provoking to know that a federal government agency is investigating you, because the government has limitless resources. I asked Floyd Abrams, one of the nation's most prominent First Amendment lawyers (and a former neighbor in Pound Ridge), to represent me pro bono, and he did.

The upshot was that nothing happened to me, other than living in fear for months, but Checker had to pay a fine of $4,400 for working on the book on government time, and due to stress, he was rushed to the hospital with a possible heart attack (fortunately, he was OK).

The book achieved a certain notoriety, with conservatives insisting that it proved that American kids today were dumbed down by bad teachers, while others said that the test was stupid because facts mattered less than critical thinking. In retrospect, I think the scores were misleading; high school seniors don't take NAEP tests seriously because they "don't count." High school seniors are not motivated to do well on tests like NAEP because they never get a score and they know the tests don't matter. Younger students haven't figured that out yet.

My role in the rewrite of the California history and social science standards was much more fun than was the nasty tiff with Cheney. Bill Honig, the state superintendent of education, invited me to join a large committee of teachers and scholars, all except me based in California schools and universities. Charlotte Crabtree, professor of elementary education at the University of California, Los Angeles (UCLA), and I were the primary writers. The committee produced a history-based curriculum that contained three years of American history, three years of world history, and a curriculum in the early grades infused with biographies and stories from history. The new curriculum emphasized democracy and human rights, as well as violations of human rights in the United States and the rest of the world. It was decidedly multicultural, demonstrating that people of many cultures had played an important role in American history and that many nations and cultures had histories worthy of study. We were influenced by the ideas of E. D. Hirsch, Jr., and his emphasis on the importance of knowledge.

The California State Education Department held hearings across the state to discuss the new curriculum. Although we thought we had worked diligently to highlight the role of different cultures in American history, many groups complained that their history had been marginalized. Instead of plaudits, our efforts to instantiate multiculturalism set off a litany of grievances. Polish Americans were upset that the curriculum recognized the slaughter of 6 million Jews during the Holocaust but did not give equal time to the millions of Poles who were murdered or sent to slave labor camps. The significant number of Armenian-Americans in the state took their complaints directly to Governor George Deukmejian, a fellow Armenian-American, who required the committee to write a supplement to the human rights curriculum devoted exclusively to the Armenian genocide. African American scholars felt that the role of Black Americans did not get the attention it deserved. No one was satisfied, but the curriculum was adopted by the state board in 1987.

While I was flying back and forth to California, I was also negotiating a divorce from my husband. I interviewed prominent lawyers at major law firms but decided not to hire them because I did not want to embarrass Dick. He had worked professionally with all of them, and I wanted to spare him the humiliation of showing them his income and assets. I also hoped to keep my personal life secret, to avoid embarrassing either of us. I could envision headlines in the tabloid press about both of us. I foolishly sought out two lesbian lawyers who had their own tiny law firm to represent me. Dick did not respect them as he would have respected a peer from a major law firm. He told our sons that I had engaged "bomber" lawyers who would take him for every penny. Nothing could have been further from the truth. He never disclosed his assets. I had none. He kept almost everything, including our apartment on Park Avenue in New York City and our lakefront home in Pound Ridge, New York. My lawyers insisted that I sign a statement saying that they opposed the settlement. I did. I had my freedom but only a small percentage of his net worth. I had protected him but not myself.

Once the divorce was finalized, Mary and I began looking for a place to live together. Mary, a proud Brooklyn native, persuaded me to cross the Brooklyn Bridge, and after many months we found a townhouse to our liking on Garden Place in Brooklyn Heights. I fell for it the moment I walked in and saw the glass wall in the rear of the house that opened onto the garden. The house dated back to 1895. We loved the quiet block and the neighborhood. After some renovations, we moved into the house with her cat Fritzi and my dog Jezebel to start our new life together.

In the spring of 1989, a few months after we settled on Garden Place, I got a call from Al Shanker. He asked if we would be willing to have a reception at our house for the leaders of Teachers Solidarity, the underground Polish teachers' union. We gladly agreed. On the chosen night, about seventy-five people crowded into our home, a mixture of Polish educators and leaders of the teachers' union in New York City. One of our Polish guests invited us to visit Poland that fall. Mary was teaching and couldn't go, but I was eager to go. By the time I got to Poland in early November, the Communist regime had collapsed, and the guests who had been in our home were now government officials. I spoke about democracy and education in Warsaw at the Ministry of Education. A teacher told me that the same words I used—*democracy, debate,* and *criticism*—had also been used by the Communists, and they meant nothing. One of my hosts told me that the building that housed the Ministry of Education had previously been the headquarters of the Nazi Party during the Second World War, and after that, the headquarters of the Communist Party. It had jail cells in the basement. I remember getting goose bumps as I thought about what had happened in that building over the previous half century. I left Warsaw on November 9, 1989. As I sat in the airport, I watched on television as people tore down the Berlin Wall, piece by piece. It was an incredible, emotional time, a breathtaking experience. I thought the world was entering a new and better era.

Al Shanker became a close friend after we met in 1975 following the publication of my book about the history of the New York City public schools. So was his successor Sandy Feldman and her successor Randi Weingarten. Despite my immersion in conservative politics, I was never anti-union. Most conservatives hate unions because unions defend their members, raise wages, and force employers to treat their workers better. That's the job of unions. I always supported unions as a sturdy ladder into a secure middle-class life, the only way that many poor people had a shot at a job with health care, a pension, good wages, and a voice in their workplace. Bayard Rustin had taught me that unions have been especially important for immigrants and people of color.

In the fall of 1990, Al Shanker invited a group of people, including Mary, me, and a few others, to travel to the newly liberated post-Soviet nations and teach about democracy. We visited Bucharest, Budapest, Warsaw, Bratislava, and Prague. Checker Finn joined us, along with the civil rights attorney John Frank from Arizona. I had become friendly with John when we served together on the board of the *Encyclopaedia Britannica*. I did not know that John Frank had clerked for Justice Hugo Black, helped Thurgood Marshall formulate the legal strategy for the *Brown v. Board of Education* decision of 1954, and successfully argued the *Miranda v. Arizona* decision. Janet Napolitano came along with John Frank; we knew her as an Arizona attorney and friend of John's. She subsequently was elected attorney general of Arizona, then governor of Arizona, President Obama's secretary of homeland security, then the first woman president of the University of California.

What we said to our audiences in Eastern Europe was far less important than what we learned about daily life in the former Soviet satellites. In Budapest, young people told us they studied Russian for years but never learned to speak it because they didn't want to. Teachers said that they were ordered to teach that the anti-Soviet uprising in Hungary in 1956 was a counter-revolution. The textbooks said so.

Budapest and Prague were beautiful; nothing, not even decades of Soviet rule, could destroy their elegance. Bucharest, however, was brown, gray, and cheerless. We visited Revolution Square, where there were beautiful old buildings in disrepair, dating from the days of the Austro-Hungarian Empire, as well as drab cinder-block Communist-era buildings. The buildings in the center of Bucharest had many bullet holes. Mary and I visited a large department store in Bucharest to shop for mementoes. The shelves were empty, except for chipped salad bowls and vases. The escalator didn't work. The lights were off. We saw a handmade linen tablecloth and asked a clerk to show it to us; she slid open a broken glass display case to retrieve it, and we bought it for $7.

The nightmare of the Ceausescu regime had ended only six months earlier, in December 1989, with the execution by firing squad of Nicolae Ceausescu and his wife Elena. Life under the dictatorship was hard for everyone other than the party elite. During the winters, there was seldom any heat, electricity, or light. Food was scarce. The dictator and his circle always had electricity, heat, light, and food. Everyone had a tragic story of what had happened to them. Our interpreter told us that under Ceausescu, abortion was illegal. Doctors who performed abortions were sent to prison. Many women died, either because of a bad abortion or self-abortion. In talking to Romanians, we came to understand the meaning of the term *Balkan intrigue*. Everyone had a secret version of all public events. Whatever "they" told you was not true. Everyone thought they knew "what really happened." All elections were fraudulent.

Whatever appeared on television or in the newspapers was false; it was "fake news" before we ever heard the term. No one could be trusted. The truth was always hidden. This was the legacy of dictatorship.

On Sunday, Mary went to mass at a church in Bucharest, and Checker and I went to see Ceausescu's unfinished and abandoned palace. While the populace lived in abject poverty, the dictator tore down apartment buildings and created a grand, wide avenue leading up to his palace. The avenue was lined with imposing facades; most had no buildings behind them, like a Hollywood stage set or a Potemkin village. When we reached the palace, which was fenced in, Checker gave the guard two cigarette lighters in exchange for a guided tour. The large entry rooms had ceilings that were 30 to 40 feet high, with enormous chandeliers, marble floors and walls, and beautiful oriental carpets. There were two marble staircases, one on each side of the room, leading to the "council room," where the president was supposed to meet with his ministers; that room was wood-paneled and contained a huge mahogany table, with dozens of chairs and an opulent chair for the leader. I thought of the song "If I Were a Rich Man" from *Fiddler on the Roof*: "there would be one long staircase just going up and one even longer coming down."

After I returned to New York City, I received an unexpected invitation from Thomas Sobol, the New York State commissioner of education. New York, like California, had decided to rewrite the state's history and social studies curriculum to include the significant roles of people of color. Some of the state's most progressive historians, such as Eric Foner of Columbia University, had participated in writing the new curriculum. But as soon as it was released, it came under fire for not being sufficiently multicultural. Sobol then created a task force composed of representatives of historically underrepresented groups to assess it and make recommendations. Its chief consultant was Professor Leonard Jeffries, a militant professor of African American studies at the City College of New York. The task force report written by Professor Jeffries opened with a fiery statement denouncing centuries of Eurocentric oppression and lambasted the state's new curriculum as part of that long history of white tyranny, cultural oppression, and Eurocentrism. When that controversy erupted, Commissioner Sobol invited a panel of four people, including me, to respond to the task force's scathing critique. I maintained that the new curriculum was multicultural, not Eurocentric. The two years of global studies that it proposed, for example, contained eight units, only one of which was devoted to Western Europe. I argued that we, all of us, had to learn about the histories of different groups while teaching students what we have in common as humans and as Americans. My presentation ended with a quote from W. H. Auden: "We must love one another or die."

I was not the only member of the panel who disagreed with Commissioner Sobol's task force. Edmund W. Gordon, an African American psychologist at Teachers College, told the task force that all children must learn to live together as equals, not as antagonists. I thought that was my message too, but it sounded better coming from him.

My presentation outraged the members of the task force. One of them, Adelaide Sanford, a member of the New York Board of Regents, said scornfully to me, "Your people brought my people to this country on slave ships." She was echoing a Nation of Islam claim that Jews owned the slave ships. I responded that I was quite certain that my grandparents and great-grandparents, who lived in impoverished ghettos in Europe, did not own any slave ships. The facts did not matter. After that meeting, Professor Jeffries saw me as an enemy and denounced me in one of his fiery speeches as "a sophisticated racist Jew from Texas."

Jeffries gained national attention for his extremist views, especially for his claim that Black people were inherently superior to whites because Blacks had melanin in their skin and whites did not. He said that Black people were the "Sun People" and whites were the "Ice People." These assertions brought him great notoriety and coverage in *The New York Times, The Washington Post, The Wall Street Journal*, and national news magazines. I was walking in my Brooklyn neighborhood one day and saw a Black newspaper on a newsstand with a blurry picture of me and a headline that said something like "Who Is This Woman and Why Is She Still Alive?"

It was time for a change.

12

INSIDE THE GEORGE H. W. BUSH ADMINISTRATION

In 1991, I was getting used to living in Brooklyn and adjusting to my new life. I wasn't quite sure which of my friends were still my friends and who had decided to remain Dick's friends. I assumed that most of the people we knew would forget about me because he was important and I was not. Also, I was not "out." I was not yet comfortable in my new role as Mary's "best friend," "partner," or whatever, nor did I know her friends and family well. My closest friends said they were happy for me, but the fact remained that they lived in a couples' world, and I was no longer part of that world. I was in limbo, and I was also uneasy about being a target of Afrocentrists. I had grown up in a decidedly Eurocentric world, and I knew that that worldview was no longer viable. I wanted a better world, but I did not accept that the answer to Eurocentrism was Afrocentrism or other kinds of racial or ethnic separatism.

I continued to write articles about history and multiculturalism, arguing against separatism and in favor of mutual respect among different groups. I assembled and edited a book called *The American Reader*, which was a collection of important songs, poems, speeches, and documents reflecting the views of all kinds of Americans. This was certainly not serious scholarship, but I enjoyed reading widely in old songbooks, poetry, even schoolbooks, to capture the beloved pieces that once united us as a nation. I was a sucker for old chestnuts like

"Casabianca" ("The boy stood on the burning deck, / Whence all but he had fled"). Gathering the contents was relatively easy compared to getting the rights to poems and speeches that had been published in the past seventy-five years and were still covered by copyright. Surprisingly, the most difficult (and expensive) rights to obtain were the speeches of Dr. Martin Luther King Jr. I had assumed that these were in the public domain. They were not.

Just as I was putting the finishing touches on *The American Reader*, I received a phone call from Governor Lamar Alexander of Tennessee. I was taken aback because I had never had any contact with him (his call was Checker Finn's idea). I knew that he had recently been appointed secretary of education by President George H. W. Bush. Governor Alexander invited me to come to D.C. for lunch at the Willard Hotel with him and his new deputy secretary of education, David Kearns—the former CEO of Xerox. They were interested in my views about standards and curricula, he said. My curiosity was piqued, and I quickly agreed.

When I met them for lunch, I was very enthusiastic about standards. I believed (wrongly) that if all students took the same courses and learned the same things, they would all be conversant with the ideas and terminology of the major subjects, and their academic performance would improve and converge. We had a delightful lunch, and later Lamar told me that I talked while they listened. Lamar was charming, thoughtful, and very intelligent. David Kearns was a kind, decent, and energetic man who was willing to give up one of the top executive jobs in America to serve as number two at the Department of Education. I liked them both very much and felt that we were on the same wavelength. I was not the least prepared when Lamar said to me near the end of our lunch that they would like me to join the leadership team at the Department of Education as assistant secretary for the Office of Education Research and Improvement (Checker had held the same job during the Reagan administration). I told him I was a Democrat; he didn't care. I told them that I was not accustomed to going to work every day, that I typically worked at home, wearing jeans and sneakers. Lamar laughed and said, "You can learn to dress for the office. Everybody does it. It's not that hard." I said I would go home to Brooklyn to think about it.

I went home and discussed it with Mary. Coincidentally, she had been offered a job in the Washington office of the American Federation of Teachers, and she was willing to make the move with me. I talked to Checker, my best friend, and he said that I should insist on the additional title of "Counselor to the Secretary" because that would enable me to join the secretary's daily executive staff meetings as well as provide special access to Lamar.

After learning that no decent apartment building would rent to tenants with a dog and a cat, Mary and I went house hunting in the District of Columbia. We bought a small house at 4351 Fessenden Avenue in northwest D.C. for $114,000 and spent a few thousand dollars more renovating the basement and adding a hot tub in the backyard. Each of my sons agreed to live in our house in Brooklyn Heights while we were gone, a good deal for them since they didn't pay rent, and a good deal for us because we didn't want strangers living in our home.

We overlooked one important consideration as we planned our move: I had to be confirmed by the U.S. Senate. My writings would not be a problem; I had written so many hundreds of articles that I knew that no one would bother to read them all. The problem was that we were gay, and the federal government did not knowingly hire gays. I was a security risk. If someone found out our secret, people like me could be blackmailed. I would have no access to national security secrets, but that didn't matter. The FBI sent a team of agents to my Brooklyn block to check me out. Subsequently, after I finished my government service, I requested a copy of my FBI report, and it was astonishingly dull. The neighbors said that we were quiet; we put our garbage cans out on the street on the designated days and brought them back promptly. No one said anything about our relationship. I asked one of Dick's friends, Leonard Garment, a former adviser to Richard Nixon, to draft a letter that I could use in case I was questioned about Mary. I was never asked directly about our relationship, and I never lied. I was confirmed. My work colleagues knew I lived with a woman, but no one ever commented on it. Lamar knew, and he said nothing. It was a nonissue, although I did live in fear that I would be outed.

After I was confirmed, there was an official swearing-in ceremony. I invited my family to witness the event. My mother, brothers, and sisters flew to Washington to celebrate the occasion. I was sworn in by Vice President Dan Quayle at the White House. In my overwhelmingly Democratic family, there were many jokes about my swearing-in. I didn't care. I was launched on a new adventure.

During our nearly two years together in Washington, we led a quiet life. We had no gay friends, but we never escaped our identity. We took a long weekend in Delmarva (the Chesapeake region where the states of Delaware, Maryland, and Virginia converge) and went to a restaurant recommended in one of the guidebooks. The waitress seated us. We waited. And waited. And eventually realized that we were never going to get service. Two women alone. No service for us. At the bed and breakfast where we stayed, the guests joined in a group after dinner and began telling ethnic jokes, and we again knew we were unwelcome. When prejudice starts with any group, we are next in line. We left after one night.

My new office was a large, beautiful corner room with a view of the Capitol. I led an agency of hundreds of people. My chief of staff was an experienced career civil servant named Eunice Henderson, an African American woman. Eunice knew the scoop on everyone and taught me how to act like an executive. I was able to hire a deputy assistant secretary, and I reached out to Francie Alexander, who was one of Superintendent Bill Honig's top staff members in California. She had headed up the revision of the history and social studies curriculum, and I admired her efficiency and brains. To my surprise, she agreed to leave Sacramento and move to D.C. Between Francie and Eunice, I was able to appear to know what I was doing because they did the heavy lifting. The first thing I did was to reassign the speechwriters who worked for my office to other agencies where the assistant secretary needed them. I could not imagine giving a speech that someone else had written.

I started work in mid-1991 and remained at OERI (the Office of Educational Research and Improvement) until the last day of President Bush's term in office. During that time, my work was organized around two responsibilities: (1) supporting the "national education goals," six ambitious (and mostly unrealistic) targets for American education by 2000, set by President Bush and the nation's governors at a meeting in Charlottesville in 1989; and (2) promoting national standards in every subject area. OERI had many ongoing responsibilities, such as supporting educational research and overseeing the nation's regional educational laboratories, which conducted research and provided technical assistance to schools. With few exceptions, the staff at the Department of Education were career civil servants. They did their jobs no matter which party was in power, and most were highly competent. I soon realized that the daily work of OERI would move forward with or without an assistant secretary in the corner office. As one staff member put it, political appointees like me were viewed by the career employees as "the Christmas help." During my stint at the U.S. Department of Education, I learned that very few people who work there are educators; the career employees process grants, oversee projects, and review proposals. Very few were ever teachers. I learned from experience that ED, as it is known, lacks the capacity to shape or direct education policy. The primary functions of the Department of Education are to distribute federal funds to states for programs authorized by Congress and to protect the civil rights of students.

Every morning, I attended the executive staff meeting in Secretary Alexander's office and learned about what other parts of the department were doing. I admired Lamar Alexander and David Kearns, both of whom were moderate Republicans. The team assembled by Lamar shared the belief that American education was in decline and needed a strong dose of innovation and accountability (we were wrong on both points, as I learned later). David Kearns had the idea of setting up a national competition to develop innovative schools. He raised $50 million in private funding to pay for the competition, run by what he called the "New American Schools Development Corporation." Teams of educators submitted proposals, and multimillion-dollar grants were handed out to eleven winning groups to put their ideas into practice. The competition generated great publicity, but in the end it produced nothing of consequence. Three decades later, the models it funded had disappeared without a trace. But the search for the magic bullet to transform the schools or the process of learning did not.

The mission of our team was to deliver on President Bush's 1988 campaign promise to be the "education president." In 1989, he had assembled the nation's governors to agree on a set of goals, not mandates, for the year 2000. As secretary of education, Lamar Alexander created an initiative called "America 2000," a campaign to reach the goals, including the following: America would become number one in math and science scores by the year 2000; America would have a 90 percent high school graduation rate by the year 2000; and all children would arrive in the earliest grade "ready to learn." Essentially, America 2000 was a public relations program to transform American education without paying for anything new. Lamar believed that it was possible to mobilize every community in the nation to support the goals. No mandates or laws or new funding were needed, he believed, and he pointed to the national campaign to ban smoking in public places as a model. Just believe!

Lamar ordered laminated pocket cards listing the six national goals, and he kept one in his shirt pocket. The Bush administration did not propose any new spending to meet the goals, although it did ask Congress for $500 million for a school choice program called "the G.I. Bill of Rights for Kids." Since Democrats controlled Congress, there was no chance that anything would pass, certainly not a penny for school choice. Democrats knew (then) that school choice was a calculated effort to defund public schools. The single worst day that I experienced during my time in D.C. was when I met Jack Jennings, the lead counsel to the House Education and Labor Committee, which had been under Democratic control for many years. I was making a perfunctory courtesy call to introduce myself, and he said, "I don't know why you wasted your time coming to Washington. We won't let the administration pass anything." I felt stupid at that moment and wondered if he was right.

I traveled from one end of the country to the other, talking up the goals. So did Lamar, David, and other members of the team. We assumed that if people knew about the goals, there would be grassroots action to achieve them. I believed, but to this day I don't understand how believing in a goal (like raising student achievement) translates into making it happen. Three decades later, none of the goals has been met except for the one about reaching a 90 percent high school graduation rate. It was not our consciousness-raising that lifted the high school graduation rate, but the economic necessity of having at least that diploma to get hired for most jobs. The doomsayers (of which I was then one) would say that we had not reached the 90 percent mark because we counted only the students who received their diploma in exactly four years; but, as I later realized, if you add in the students who graduated in August, or a year or two later, we surpassed the 90 percent goal.

As for the rest of the goals, there was no chance that our society would reach them without substantial new investments in maternal health, early childhood education, class size reduction, wraparound services, capital improvements, and other costly measures to reduce poverty and improve the quality of schooling and children's lives. The Bush administration did not see a need for new funding. However, cheerleading would take us only so far. To almost no one's surprise, nothing was accomplished.

My most enjoyable experience during my tenure as assistant secretary occurred when First Lady Barbara Bush's staff invited me to join her in a trip to Houston on her private jet, *Air Force 2*. She was flying to Houston but had to leave early for Nashville because the president wanted her to join him at the Grand Ole Opry. Would I stand in for her and deliver a speech? I was thrilled to say yes. Very early in the morning, a White House limousine picked me up at my home and drove me to Andrews Air Force Base, where I boarded her plane. A few minutes later, Mrs. Bush arrived with her press secretary, and we took off, just the three of us. I asked her a million questions to keep the conversation going. In effect, I interviewed her. I grilled her about her predecessor Nancy Reagan, bearing in mind that they allegedly had a rivalry. She was very candid, and her tone was, "Poor Nancy, she had so many problems to deal with," which I interpreted as a sly way of putting her down. At one point, she asked me where I was registered to vote. I told her I had changed my registration to the District of Columbia. She said with mock horror, "Oh, that's a very bad idea. Your vote as a Republican won't count here." She didn't know I was registered as a Democrat.

When we arrived at the airport in Houston, there was a limousine waiting at the foot of the jet stairs to take us to a junior high school.

Outside the school, there was a large marquee that read "Welcome, Mrs. Bush!" We were greeted by the principal and a student mariachi band. Students lined the path from her limousine to the school's front door, and they had their hands out in greeting. She slapped each hand (as Roy Rogers had slapped mine many years earlier). I trailed along as she visited classrooms. In one, she sat down with the students to answer their questions. One said, "Mrs. Bush, what do you have in your purse?" She promptly opened it and dumped out the contents on the table. Nothing unusual. It was exciting to travel to Houston with the First Lady and see the reaction of the students. That evening I spoke to an organization called Communities in Schools which encouraged students to stay in school; I had learned after many months of public speaking to speak eloquently about the importance of education, of staying in school and graduating, and about how the goals of Communities in Schools were perfectly aligned with President Bush's national goals. That was my job: sell the goals! Tell everyone it was up to them to solve their problems! They could do it!

My most fabulous experience as a subcabinet official in the Bush administration occurred when I traveled to San Francisco to speak on behalf of the Department of Education. Out of the blue, I was invited to have lunch with George Lucas at Skywalker Ranch. A limousine picked me up at my hotel and took me north into verdant countryside. We turned into a long driveway that led to his house. He walked me around his enormous, multistory library, which contained thousands of books, interspersed with large display cases containing memorabilia from his films. I recall gazing at the hat and whip of Indiana Jones and wondering how I was lucky enough to be there. I had a very pleasant lunch with Lucas. He talked about his interest in American history and in developing an educational but entertaining television series about history. Of course, I encouraged him. I never understood why I was invited to meet this remarkable man, but I was thrilled to meet him and see Skywalker Ranch.

Then there was the day I went with Lamar Alexander and David Kearns to meet with President Bush. The president wanted an update on how his education team was doing. I talked about the effort to set national standards; he asked me if I had the approval of the National Education Association (NEA), the nation's biggest teachers' union. The question surprised me, coming from a Republican president. I had had no contact at all with the NEA, and I told him so. Why did he care what the NEA thought? As Lamar and David talked, I edged my chair slightly closer to the president. I knew that the White House photographer was taking pictures, and I ended up seated almost next to him, behind his large desk. By the time the photograph was snapped, we were almost side by side. Lamar and David noticed, and they joked about it later that day, but I don't think the president did. If he did, he chose not to notice. He was a gentleman, and I was glad I had the chance to meet him again.

On another occasion, I traveled to Austin to give a speech, and I met Governor Ann Richards in her office. She was wonderful, especially considering whom I was representing; she offered me a tray of freshly baked chocolate chip cookies, and I was awed to be in her presence. A few years later, when I was back in private life and serving on a task force at the Aspen Institute led by Democratic senator Bill Bradley and Republican Bill Bennett, I met Governor Richards again. I waxed on about the theoretical benefits of school choice, and I never forgot her response. She said, "If there is ever school choice in Texas, the hard-right evangelical Christians will get public money to indoctrinate children. You won't like it." How right she was. I wish I had had the wisdom to heed her.

My major assignment as a member of the Department of Education leadership team was to advance the development of national standards for every school subject. Before Bush's election in 1988, the National Council of Teachers of Mathematics (NCTM) had already released its national standards for teaching mathematics, and they seemed to be a good model. NCTM demonstrated that the best way to develop credible national standards was to ask people in the field to write them, especially experienced teachers. My agency, OERI, had a small pot of discretionary money, probably $10 to $20 million, which in terms of the federal budget is hardly a flyspeck. I invited the professional associations in each field to submit proposals to write national standards, and they did. In the short time I was there, the national associations produced aspirational national standards in the arts, science, geography,

English, history, and foreign languages. President Bush's good friend Arnold Schwarzenegger persuaded him to add national standards in physical education, so we did that, too.

Of all the standards, the one that proved to be most contentious was history. OERI reached an agreement with the National Endowment for the Humanities (NEH) to fund the history standards. Lynne Cheney, not my best friend, weighed in to steer the grant to the National Center for the Study of History at UCLA, which NEH had funded. The center was led by Gary Nash, one of the nation's most prominent social historians. Nash disdained traditional history as told through the lives of Great White Men; he cheerfully accepted the assignment of revising the teaching of American and world history to America's children. In this endeavor, he recruited Charlotte Crabtree, who had been my colleague in writing the California standards for history and social science; he also invited Ross Dunn of San Diego State University to oversee the world history standards.

In each of the funded subjects, the professional associations produced a booklet of one hundred pages or so detailing what students should know and be able to do at different grade levels. I hoped that voluntary national standards would unify their respective fields and establish a common ground for a curriculum without telling teachers how to teach. In retrospect, I can't say what effect, if any, the standards had. Since they were voluntary, it is hard to know whether anyone paid attention to them, although apparently textbook publishers did. The history standards, on the other hand, most definitely got widespread attention, the kind that undermined any belief in the value of national standards. The history standards were released in the fall of 1994, long after the George H. W. Bush administration had departed Washington. A few days before their formal release, Lynne Cheney published a scathing denunciation of them in *The Wall Street Journal*. Her blast provoked a vitriolic national conversation about whose history should be taught. Cheney said the standards epitomized left-wing political correctness because they emphasized the nation's failings but paid little attention to its great men. The American history standards mentioned Joseph McCarthy and McCarthyism nineteen times and the Ku Klux Klan seventeen times, she wrote, but mentioned Ulysses S. Grant only once and failed to mention Robert E. Lee at all. Many other notable white men—like Alexander Graham Bell, Thomas Edison, and the Wright brothers—were ignored. The UCLA Center she had funded, she lamented, had turned American history into a story of oppression and failure.

Newspapers and radio talk shows jumped enthusiastically into the controversy. Conservative talk show host Rush Limbaugh declared that the standards should be "flushed down the toilet." In January 1995, the U.S. Senate condemned the standards by a vote of 99–1 (the lone dissenter thought the condemnation was not strong enough). Republicans despised the standards, and Democrats chose not to get involved in an issue of little importance to them. The writers of the standards made a few adjustments but stood by their product. In the end, the idea of national standards was abandoned by almost everyone, at least until the Common Core standards in reading and mathematics came along fifteen years later.

When Governor Bill Clinton defeated President Bush in 1992, our team began to clear out. I was the last one to leave on the last day. I recall sitting in the secretary's empty office, in his big chair, playing the role of "secretary-for-the-day." No one was left but me and the civil servants. I knew where I was going next. The president of the Brookings Institution, Bruce MacLaury, had called on me soon after the election and invited me to accept the newly established Brown Chair in Education Studies at Brookings. I told him I would enjoy spending a year or so at Brookings and helping to create the Brown Center for Education Research, which had been endowed by a wealthy Texas family. But I intended eventually to return to Brooklyn.

Meanwhile, Mary was invited to open a new school in New York City as part of a network of small schools run by the renowned progressive educator Deborah Meier. Having seen the New York City school bureaucracy from many different angles, Mary dreamed of starting her own small school within the public system, and she readily accepted. Although I was staying in D.C. for another year at Brookings, we decided to sell our house, and Mary wanted to sell it herself. Two friends of Mary's came to visit, and one of them, a nun named Sister

Alice, advised her how to sell the house. She said that if you plant a small statue of Joseph upside down in front of your house and put the "for sale" sign on top of the statue, your house will sell quickly. That sounded like a plan, even to nonreligious me, so the next day we went to the shop in the basement of the big cathedral in Washington and bought a small statue of Joseph. (The clerk asked, "Are you selling a house? We are running a special of three St. Joseph statues for the price of two.") We dug a hole in the front lawn and planted the statue as instructed, put a "for sale" sign over the spot, and sat down for dinner. No more than 30 minutes later, a real estate agent called and said she was in a car outside our house with an interested client. Mary said we were having dinner, please come back the next day. I was taken aback by her brushing off a live prospect, but she said the client would be more motivated if we were not eager. Sure enough, the agent called the next day, and we sold the house for what we paid for it, including the cost of renovations. But the buyer didn't want our hot tub, and we had to get rid of it. We put an ad in the local newspaper and promptly got a call from an interested buyer. He stopped by and said he was an FBI agent who had just returned from Waco, where he was part of the fifty-one-day siege of the Branch Davidian cult. He needed a hot tub to calm down. He and a friend carted our hot tub away.

Mary returned to our home on Garden Place in Brooklyn, and she opened her high school on West Twenty-Second Street in Manhattan, a small progressive high school whose students were Dominican, Hispanic, and African American. I rented an apartment near Dupont Circle in D.C., within walking distance of the Brookings Institution. Although I made clear that I did not intend to stay indefinitely in D.C., the Brookings Board of Trustees nonetheless named me the first recipient of the Herman and George R. Brown Chair in Education Studies. While at Brookings, I wrote *National Standards in American Education*, and I convened an annual meeting about major issues in American education, bringing together scholars with different points of view; the results were published as *Brookings Papers on Education Policy*. It was an extraordinary privilege to be a scholar in residence at Brookings because I attended frequent meetings where leading figures in every field, including foreign affairs, spoke about their work. After eighteen months in residency, I left Brookings in 1994 to return to New York City.

I remained a nonresident senior fellow (unpaid) at Brookings until 2012, when I was unceremoniously ousted by my successor, Grover (Russ) Whitehurst. Apparently, the Texans who endowed the Brown Chair in Education Studies wanted it to be held by a solid conservative. Coming out of the George H. W. Bush administration in 1993, I fit the bill. However, in 2009 I was replaced by Whitehurst, who had served as director of the new Institute for Education Sciences (my renamed former agency) in the George W. Bush administration, and his conservative credentials were stronger than mine. After assuming the Brown Chair in Education Studies, he promoted school choice and testing and created a ranking system to recognize the school districts with the most choice. In 2010, I called to ask Russ if I could introduce my new book at Brookings, *The Death and Life of the Great American School System: How Testing and Choice Are Undermining Education*. However, he refused to set up an event unless I paid for all expenses, which would have been customary for an outsider but not for someone who had a long association with Brookings. I turned down his ungracious offer. Rick Hess of the American Enterprise Institute, a conservative think tank, welcomed me without expecting any payment at all, instead paying my expenses, and I spoke to a packed auditorium of Washington insiders. The book went on to reach the *New York Times* bestseller list. In 2012 I wrote an article in *The New York Review of Books* criticizing Republican presidential candidate Mitt Romney's education plan, which emphasized school choice, and the day that my article appeared online, I received an e-mail from Whitehurst—who was advising Romney on education—informing me that I had been terminated as a nonresident senior fellow at Brookings because I was "inactive." In 2015 Brookings removed Whitehurst as the holder of the Brown Chair, an unusual event at that staid think tank. I am not sure why it happened, but I was not sad to hear the news. I did not want Brookings, with its estimable reputation, to be captured by the school choice lobby.

13

BACK TO NEW YORK CITY

When I finished my residency at the Brookings Institution in mid-1994, I expected to return to Teachers College, Columbia University, which had been my academic home from 1970 to 1991. My books and files were there, waiting for me. My mentor Lawrence Cremin had died suddenly in 1990, before I left for Washington, and was replaced by Michael Timpane, who had deep experience in the federal government and in think tanks. I had taught courses with Timpane in the past and considered him a friend. I called him in early 1994 to let him know I was coming home that fall and looked forward to reestablishing my place at Teachers College. Mike hemmed and hawed, then said, somewhat sheepishly, "I'm sorry to say that your colleagues don't want you back." I knew at once that he was referring to the fact that I had served in a Republican administration, which put me far out of bounds at Teachers College, where the academic climate was dominated by political correctness. Without thinking, I said, "I know my colleagues like diversity, but they don't seem to like intellectual diversity." And he replied, "That's the kind of thinking that gets you into trouble."

I had to find a new academic home. I called a friend, Naomi Levine, a prominent civil rights lawyer and a senior vice president at New York University (NYU). With a nudge from Naomi, the dean of the School of Education agreed to hire me. The dean seemed to be as uncomfortable about having me on the faculty as Mike Timpane was; she did not assign me to a department and did not offer a salary. When I asked her if I might teach a course on current education issues or the federal role in education, the dean asked me to submit my reading list, presumably fearful that I was a conservative ideologue. I submitted a list. Since I don't believe in indoctrinating anyone, I passed muster.

I enjoyed being on the faculty at NYU; even though I was never assigned any classes to teach, I occasionally volunteered to teach one per year. I had to find a foundation to pay my salary (my work was underwritten by the foundation of Sandra Priest Rose, a dear friend who was passionate about the teaching of reading and the revival of phonics). The position gave me an office, a library card, and a title. Although I seldom taught, I was very busy. I completed a major writing project, a history of education in the twentieth century. I wanted to call it *Anti-Intellectualism in American Education*, paying tribute to Richard Hofstadter's great book, *Anti-Intellectualism in American Life*. My editor at Simon & Schuster, the legendary Alice Mayhew, wouldn't hear of it. She said it would be remaindered immediately with a title like that. Everyone told me how lucky I was to have Alice as my editor, but she and I got along like oil and water. She wanted the title of the book to scream "failure," but I refused. The book was not a demonstration of persistent failure but a critique of the "movements" that persistently swept through the field, emanating from schools of education. We argued over the title for six weeks and finally compromised on *Left Back: A Century of Failed School Reforms*. I hated that title but not as much as the others she proposed. It was published in 2000. When the book was issued in paperback, I modified the title to *Left Back: A Century of Battles over School Reform*.

I discovered a kindred soul on the NYU faculty, Joseph Viteritti, a political scientist at the Wagner School of Public Policy who shared my interest in education policy and favored school choice, as I did when I arrived in 1994. Joe and I coauthored articles in support of charter schools and edited books together. He was as unwelcome at the Wagner School as I was at the school of education, and he soon accepted a job at Hunter College, where he was named to a prestigious professorship in public policy. New York University's loss was Hunter College's gain. While I was writing this book, Joe sent me a draft of a book he was writing about the four people who had influenced him the most, and I was one of them. He reminded me how active I had been in the 1990s as a supporter of charter schools and even vouchers; he was deeply influenced, he said, by my 1994 article "Somebody's Children," which envisioned vouchers as a tool to promote equity, to give opportunity to the neediest kids. We shared that hope, but it eventually turned out to be a disappointment, leaving me (but not him) to believe that we had been hoaxed.

During this busy period, I rejoined the board of the Thomas B. Fordham Foundation (TBF), whose chair was my close friend Checker Finn; TBF advocated for testing, accountability, and school choice. It had a large foothold in Ohio, where the late Mr. Fordham had made his fortune, and had shown no discernible interest in education policy. I was invited to be a senior fellow at the Manhattan Institute, a conservative outpost in liberal New York City that lobbied for charter schools and that was funded by some of the wealthiest families in the metropolis. At its behest, I traveled to Albany in 1998 to testify on behalf of legislation authorizing charter schools. Governor George Pataki, a Republican, declared that he would not sign a pay raise for legislators unless they signed the charter school bill, and of course they did. My advisers at the Manhattan Institute encouraged me to stress that the goal of charter schools was to help poor Black and brown kids. I did. At the time, I truly thought that was their purpose; I later realized that this argument was a clever ruse to win the votes of Democratic legislators.

After my return from Washington, D.C., I got a call one day from Mayor Rudy Giuliani. I had never met him, so there was no small talk. He went right to the point: "Do you want to be New York City's superintendent of schools?" Maybe I should have said I needed a day to think about it, but instead I answered without hesitation, "No. I am not qualified." That was a conversation stopper right there. I had never been a teacher or principal, never administered anything (the federal agency I "ran" could run itself). I was not qualified.

Because of my activity at the Brookings Institution, I kept up my contacts in D.C. President Bill Clinton remembered me long after my visit to Arkansas in 1984. On February 11, 1997, I received an invitation to come to the White House for a screening of Ken Burns's documentary *Thomas Jefferson*. Mary was invited too. It was a grand occasion. I had been to the White House on several occasions—a state dinner hosted by President Lyndon B. Johnson, lunch with President Ford, a meeting with President Reagan and Vice President Bush, and my conversation with President George H. W. Bush, along with Secretary Alexander and Deputy Secretary Kearns—but Mary had never been there, and she was thrilled. We were the first to arrive and the last to leave. As we walked up the grand staircase, the Marine Band was playing "Edelweiss" from *The Sound of Music*, and Mary started crying. She thought of her parents, who had emigrated from Austria and Germany during the Weimar years, who had borne the shame of being called Nazis when they were loyal Americans, and she wished they could see her now. Politicians, journalists, and various luminaries arrived, and we savored every moment of being guests in the White House, chatting with the Clintons, and mingling with distinguished guests.

In late 1997, President Clinton appointed me to the National Assessment Governing Board (and issued a presidential press release announcing my appointment), the agency in charge of the federal testing program. On March 16, 1998, his staff invited me to join thirty other educators to discuss the importance of science and mathematics education. We met at the White House and then boarded buses to go to a nearby Virginia high school. There in a large meeting room was the White House press corps, with dozens of cameras and microphones. At first I was puzzled, but I soon realized the reason for their presence: the previous night, a woman named Kathleen Willey had appeared on *60 Minutes* to accuse President Clinton of sexually assaulting her during his first term in office, some five years earlier. The press corps shouted questions at the president, who vigorously denied her accusations. His face turned red and blotchy. After a few questions, a press aide stood up and said, "That's it. No more questions on this topic. We are here to discuss science and math education." Then the entire press corps turned off their cameras, closed their notebooks, and departed. A few education reporters remained, but no cameras or lights. The meeting was sad and desultory, and the president was noticeably distracted.

A different kind of invitation came in 1998 from John Raisian, the economist who was director of the Hoover Institution at Stanford University. I flew to California, and we discussed ways to raise public support for school choice. He asked me to become a resident senior fellow at Hoover, but I did not want to move to California. I had a better idea. I suggested that he gather ten or twelve conservative scholars to meet regularly at the Hoover Institution. Our discussions would sharpen our thinking and our productivity. He liked the proposal and set up the Koret Task Force, generously funded by a local foundation. Its members were Eric Hanushek, Terry Moe, John Chubb, Caroline Hoxby, Paul Peterson, Herbert Walberg, Paul Hill, Checker Finn, Williamson Evers, E. D. Hirsch Jr., and me. As a group, we supported rigorous standards and assessments, test-based incentives, teacher accountability, competition among schools, and school choice. We did not entirely agree with one another: E. D. Hirsch Jr. and I engaged in a formal debate with Caroline Hoxby and Paul Peterson about which reform strategy was better: a stronger curriculum or more choice? Our team supported curriculum; their team supported choice. The audience, composed of wealthy patrons of the Hoover Institution, voted Hoxby and Peterson the winners.

The Hoover Institution is a beautiful, well-funded center in the midst of the Stanford University campus (Eric Hanushek, a member of the Koret Task Force, was noted for saying that money doesn't make a difference in schooling, but it surely made a difference at the Hoover Institution, which has an endowment of hundreds of millions of dollars). Our group met four times a year, each time with a fabulous meal, exquisite wine, and the opportunity to mingle with the illustrious scholars and wealthy benefactors of the Hoover Institution. Because I had suffered a near-fatal pulmonary embolism in 1998, I had permission to fly first class, so my quarterly trips to Stanford were delightful. We stayed in a luxurious hotel near campus and were paid $5,000 to attend meetings. We earned additional stipends for publications: I received the Hoover

Institution's Uncommon Book Award in 2004 for my book *The Language Police* and a prize of $10,000.

Around the same time that the Koret Task Force was getting started, I was invited to fly to Austin to meet with Governor George W. Bush, who planned to run for president. About a dozen educators were there, including Lynne Cheney and Eric Hanushek. Governor Bush talked about how he would make education reform a major part of his campaign as a "compassionate conservative." He intended to use the formula that he thought had been successful in Texas (standards, tests, and accountability). He talked enthusiastically about "the Texas Miracle" (which later turned out to be the Texas Mirage). Someone asked him what he would say if the subject of teacher pay came up, and he said, with a grin, "Teachers are so wonderful that we can never pay them enough." That was his way of saying he would dodge the question. I told his aide Margaret Spellings how much I liked barbecue, and she took me to a barbecue restaurant that night. She later was George W. Bush's second secretary of education, after Rod Paige, who was the superintendent of schools in Houston.

Despite my congenial meeting with George W. Bush, I supported Lamar Alexander when he ran for president in 2000. Having worked for him, I greatly admired his intelligence and integrity. For the first time, I switched my voter registration from Democrat to Republican so I could vote for Lamar in the Republican primary in New York. Unfortunately, Lamar was out of the race by the time the New York primaries occurred. I had to re-register.

After the election, I attended the unveiling of Bush's No Child Left Behind (NCLB) program in the East Room of the White House on January 23, 2001, along with about two hundred other educators. It was a twenty-eight-page document that featured the policies that conservatives had been seeking for years: annual testing, accountability, and charter schools (when Bush's proposal was turned into legislation, passed by Congress, and signed into law on January 8, 2002, the NCLB legislation was more than one thousand pages long). NCLB was the most dramatic expansion of federal control of education in history, a surprising move for a Republican president. Conservatives thought that testing and accountability were just common sense. If kids know they will be tested, they will focus on what is taught and work harder; it didn't occur to me then that testing in reading and math would devalue everything in the curriculum that was not tested. If teachers know they will be held accountable for student test scores, said the wisdom of the day, they will push the students and get better results. If the students don't improve their test scores, the teachers will be shamed, and if the students do improve their test scores, the teachers might win a bonus. Those claims were directly challenged by Al Shanker at one of the Brookings conferences I ran every year. Shanker said, "Let me get this right, kids will try harder so that their teachers can win a bonus?" His question was irrefutable, and it stuck in the back of my head for many years. He was right. The idea that students would work harder so their teachers could win more money made no sense, and—as we learned from research and experience—neither did the idea that teachers could raise test scores if they only tried harder, and they would try harder only if they were offered a bonus for higher scores.

But it was not only Republicans and conservatives who fell for the idea that test scores would go up if students were tested more often and if there were consequences—rewards or punishments—attached for teachers and schools. More Democrats voted for Bush's NCLB than Republicans, and the bill was cosponsored by the liberal icon Ted Kennedy, senator from Massachusetts. I too supported NCLB, so I can't fault others who did as well.

Not long after the 2000 election, which was not resolved until five weeks after election day, I was invited to be a member of a high-level commission to make recommendations to improve the fairness and security of future elections. The chairmen of the National Commission on Federal Election Reform were former presidents Jimmy Carter and Gerald R. Ford. The members of the commission were a remarkable group of individuals from both parties with deep experience in government, politics, and the law; it included former senators, members of the House, attorneys general, a university president, and a law school dean. The commission hoped to see an electoral process that was fair and effective. It wanted to avoid the spectacle in 2000 when paper ballots were disputed because of the way they were punched by hand, leaving what was known as "hanging chads" that sometimes made the voter's intent uncertain. The commission recommended that each state maintain a computerized voter roll; that Congress adopt legislation to simplify absentee balloting; that states should pass legislation to restore the voting rights of convicted felons who had finished their time in prison; and that states should consider switching from paper ballots to computer technology. There were many other recommendations, but the gist was this: every eligible voter should be encouraged to vote, and every vote should be accurately counted. The report inspired the passage of federal legislation, the Help America Vote Act of 2002.

At the time, these recommendations were uncontroversial and commonsense. Who could possibly dispute that every qualified voter should vote and every vote should be counted? A quarter century later, these ideas seem antique. Instead of sensible reforms to make it easier to vote, state legislatures have passed laws to suppress the vote, especially the votes of racial minorities. Instead of the sound principle of one person, one vote, and all votes counted, state legislatures have brazenly, shamelessly gerrymandered districts to maximize their partisan advantage. The camaraderie and fair dealing that characterized the work of that bipartisan commission seems now to have happened on a planet long ago and far away.

When the charter school idea took off in the late 1980s, I was there, and again it involved Al Shanker. We were both attending a conference at the Princeton home of the Educational Testing Service, and we took a break from the discussions to talk in an empty dining room. He wanted to get my reaction to an idea. He said, "What if teachers could say to their principal or superintendent, 'We want to start a new school within the school, using different methods. We want to gather the kids who have given up, the kids who are in the back of the classroom with their heads on their desks, the kids who are troublemakers. Give us a five-year contract and let us see if we can turn these students around'?" The teachers would seek the endorsement of the other teachers in the building, he said, as well as the local teachers' union and the local school board, so there would be no enmity. I thought it was an interesting concept, and I encouraged him to promote it. He brought the idea to the American Federation of Teachers' national conference in 1988 and talked about it in his weekly paid column in *The New York Times* and on his travels. He saw the charter idea as a way to get more attention for the most difficult, least motivated students, but also as a way to get them out of regular classrooms so that regular classroom teachers did not have to spend time disciplining recalcitrant students.

When the first state charter law was passed in Minnesota in 1991, it bore little resemblance to Shanker's concept. His proposal had been sabotaged by charter zealots who opposed regulation, accountability, and unions. Anyone—not just teachers—could open a charter, without the endorsement of the local teachers' union or the local school board. The charter sponsors did not even need to be educators. Any student—not just those who were bored or failing in school—could enroll, and charters were free to seek the best students, not the most difficult or lowest-performing. Collaboration was abandoned and replaced by competition. The first charter lobbying group, the Center for Education Reform, was founded in 1993 by a former staffer from the right-wing Heritage Foundation with the specific purpose of increasing the number of charter schools while opposing any public regulation or accountability, criticizing public schools, and rejecting unions. Pandora's box opened wide, and lobbyists for charter schools encouraged states to pass laws encouraging entrepreneurs, for-profit corporations, and corporate charter chains to start charter schools. Often, the state charter laws were written by lobbyists for the new charter industry. By 1994, Shanker realized that his grand idea to promote innovation had been hijacked, and he turned against the charter school idea, writing in his *New York Times* column that charters were no different from vouchers, and both were meant to smash unions and destroy public education. But for years to come, charter promoters claimed him as one of their founding fathers, neglecting to mention that he turned against the charter movement.

In the beginning, the charter school idea was a blank slate. Checker Finn and I embraced it enthusiastically and wrote articles extolling the virtues of competition and accountability. We imagined that charter schools would be free to hire the best teachers and to get rid of the dead wood; that their freedom from time-wasting regulations would enable them to be innovative and get better academic outcomes than public schools; that they would close if they did not meet their academic goals; and that they would produce better results at less cost because they would not be burdened by bureaucracy. I envisioned universities, hospitals, museums, and other responsible institutions opening charter schools and taking their obligations seriously. I did not imagine that the charter sector would attract for-profit entrepreneurs, grifters, and corporate chains that paid lobbyists to seek federal grants and to oppose accountability and transparency. I thought that charter schools would seek out the neediest students, not that they would inflate their test scores by admitting students likeliest to succeed and pushing out those with the highest needs. Nor did I anticipate that the charter sector would become the darling of Wall Street tycoons and billionaires who made campaign contributions to elected officials to win their support for charter schools. The august institutions I expected to open and manage charters were busy attending to their own responsibilities.

My high hopes for charters were eventually destroyed. So was my belief that standardized testing was a valuable tool for teachers, parents, principals, and policymakers. My seven years of experience on the federal testing board should have made me skeptical, and it eventually did. I learned about the ingrained flaws of standardized testing as a result of my service on the National Assessment Governing Board (NAGB) from 1997 to 2004. The board oversaw the national testing program called NAEP (the National Assessment of Educational Progress). The media wrote breathlessly about the results of every NAEP test, and the headlines were predictably dismal: "Most Students Not Proficient" in math, reading, history, science, and so on. Few journalists bothered to read the fine print; on NAEP, "proficient" was equivalent to an A grade. Why would anyone expect that most students would score an A? If by some miracle they did, the headlines would complain about grade inflation.

As a member of NAGB, I read the test results carefully and saw that they were always—always!—arrayed by family income: the students from families with the highest income received the highest scores, and the students from families with the lowest income received the lowest scores. Of course, there were exceptions: the low-income students who received high scores, and the rich ones who got low scores. But the overall result remained the same: the rich kids at the top, the poor kids at the bottom. I reviewed test questions on the reading, history, and civics tests for fourth- and eighth-grade students. I did not attempt to read the math questions, as the eighth-grade questions were much more advanced than any math I had studied in high school. I found myself wishing that the politicians and journalists who were outraged by student scores would take the eighth-grade math test and publish their own scores. I felt certain that most adults would perform worse than the students they criticized.

In reviewing the test questions, I sometimes spotted questions that had more than one right answer (e.g., "How did the central character feel about her bad luck? Sad? Angry? Depressed? Rebellious?") and even some that had no right answer. I began to doubt the objectivity of the tests; the questions and answers were written by fallible human beings. On the reading tests, students were sometimes asked to choose an answer that described the author's purpose or meaning. These were fishy questions because the author's thinking was not always easy to discern. I recall reading an article at *HuffPost* in 2017 by a poet named Sara Holbrook, who learned that two of her poems appeared on Texas tests for grades seven and eight; she was outraged to see that students were asked questions about her "purpose," with answers that were just plain wrong. The "right answers" were not the right answers. She apologized to the students.

My NAGB service inspired me to write a book about censorship published in 2004 called *The Language Police: How Pressure Groups Restrict What Students Learn*. The book was the by-product of a failed effort by the George W. Bush administration to create a voluntary national test at a cost of $50 million. NAGB was assigned to oversee its development, and several major publishers collaborated to create the test. The consortium of publishers sent a copy of their "bias and sensitivity guidelines" to every member of NAGB, demonstrating how careful they were to weed out words, phrases, and illustrations that might be offensive to racial, ethnic, gender, religious, or age groups. Never having known about this careful scrubbing of the language on tests, I began collecting similar guidelines from other major publishers. Eventually I compiled a list of hundreds of common words and phrases that were routinely censored by education publishers, not only on tests but in textbooks as well. These lists led me to write a book about the history of censorship of textbooks and tests, which was both fun to write and horrifying to learn about. Words like *cowboy*, *landlord*, *actress*, *yes-man*, and *heiress* were forbidden, as were illustrations that suggested stereotypes, such as elderly people with canes or women in the kitchen or a Mexican wearing a sombrero or an illustration of a rainbow (too gay). Any mention of death or serious illness or evolution or witches or Halloween was forbidden, as it might upset the student taking the test. The bans and censorship were coming from every direction. The book was neither right-wing nor left-wing; I ridiculed censorship.

The voluntary national test never came to be because no one could figure out for whom the test would be "voluntary." For states? For districts? For schools? For students? $50 million was wasted on an ill-conceived idea.

The Language Police, however, was a media sensation. I was interviewed on FOX News by Sean Hannity and Alan Colmes (who then had a show called *Hannity & Colmes* with Hannity on the right and Colmes on the left); by Tucker Carlson on CNN, who admired the book for its excoriation of political correctness; by Bill O'Reilly on FOX News; by the conservative radio host Laura Ingraham; and by Terry Gross for her NPR program *Fresh Air*. Morley Safer interviewed me for *60 Minutes*, but it never aired.

The best event of all was an interview with Jon Stewart of *The Daily Show*. The publicist at Knopf called to tell me, in great excitement, that I had been booked for the interview, and it was a very big deal. I had never heard of Jon Stewart or his show. I watched that night; Caroline Kennedy was his guest. Oh, my god, I thought. What am I doing on this show? This is way out of my league. The next night, a limousine picked me up and brought me to the studio. I was ushered into the green room to await my turn. Jon Stewart came in, and he immediately sensed that I was nervous. He said, "Don't worry about being funny; that's my job." He could not have been nicer. When the time came for my interview, the producer brought me behind the curtain on the side of the stage. I could see the audience, mostly young people. Jon Stewart started introducing me and said my name, and the crowd started to applaud, but then when he said I was "a historian of education," the applause died out. I hesitated, as he waited for me to appear, and the producer, a young woman, literally shoved me out onto the set. Jon cracked jokes about the book, and the next day *The Language Police* was number one on Amazon. Such was the power of Jon Stewart.

In the aftermath of the publicity, I was invited to attend the 2006 meeting of the World Economic Forum in Davos, Switzerland, as a panelist, all expenses paid. I asked if the forum would pay for my domestic partner; I didn't want to travel alone. The answer came back, to my dismay, "Absolutely not. No domestic partners." We exchanged e-mails, but the staff at Davos was adamant. My son Joseph, who worked in the financial sector, was delighted to hear that I was invited to attend Davos and very disappointed when I told him that I would not go because they would not pay for Mary to accompany me. He made a few phone calls and learned that the Davos staff thought that I wanted to bring a "domestic" with me, and they would not allow anyone to include their household staff. Once they understood what a "domestic partner" was, everything was OK.

Visiting Davos was a remarkable experience. Before we left Brooklyn, we began to get invitations to parties: to the Japanese reception (where we enjoyed sushi flown in daily from Japan) and to half a dozen other stellar events involving world leaders. We accepted all invitations! Once we arrived, we signed up for sessions in which the speakers were kings, prime ministers, world-renowned experts, even one on cybersecurity featuring Robert Mueller, then the director of the FBI. The variety of sessions was akin to a graduate university whose faculty were very important people and we were the students. At one point, we saw a large crowd gather around a couple of people. Was it a king, a president? From a distance, we could not see their faces. Then we did: Brad Pitt and Angelina Jolie. We got on the rope line to say hello to former president Clinton, and he lit up when he saw me (he never forgets a face). We saw Angela Merkel, one of Mary's heroes; Mary yelled out, "Angela, America loves you," and she responded, "And I love America." We dined with Gavin Newsom and the scientist Francis Collins. On the last day, we attended a spectacular brunch on top of a mountain. Expecting bitter cold, we wore heavy fur coats and traveled by funicular to the mountaintop. Waiters passed trays of elegant hors d'oeuvre, and tabletops were carved out of ice and covered with trays of smoked salmon, caviar, and other delicacies. After an hour or so, we shed our coats because the heat from the sun was so intense. Our eyes were popping as we walked past celebrities from all over the world. We were told that corporate executives paid $25,000 each to attend. I was thrilled to be there with my domestic partner, all expenses paid.

Returning to New York City meant resettling in our house on Garden Place and returning to my new life as a commentator, author, and occasional NYU professor. Our street was like a mews, only one block long. Our neighborhood, Brooklyn Heights, was first in the city to receive landmark status. Brownstone living is an experience in itself. We had a narrow brownstone, only 17 feet wide, but it had four stories and a full basement. I had a book-lined office on the fourth floor, which was flooded with sunlight. I never ran out of space for books because the living room had floor-to-ceiling bookcases. As Thomas Jefferson once wrote, "I cannot live without books."

Life on Garden Place was a series of adventures and misadventures. When we first moved back into the house after our time in Washington, I was cleaning out stuff left behind by my second son, who had lived there with his friends while we were away. While cleaning up, I found some unknown grain and dumped it into the garbage disposal, thinking that was the best way to get rid of it. I didn't realize that I had stuffed two cups of raw couscous into the drain; instead of dissolving, it blew up and clogged the drain, even backed up into the dishwasher. We called a plumber, and he said he had never seen anything like it. It was like a scene from an old *I Love Lucy* show. It took a couple of days to clear the couscous out of the pipes in the kitchen.

We were once again in full possession of our house, but I continued to live in Washington, D.C., and work at Brookings while Mary lived in Brooklyn. She was very busy as principal of a new high school in Manhattan that she created from scratch. We spent weekends together, knowing that the separation was temporary. On Martin Luther King Jr. weekend in January 1994, I took the train to New York City. The weather was typically wintry. First there was a heavy snowfall, which turned to solid ice, and then rain. When I got to the house, Mary was still at her school, and I arrived to see the water level in the outdoor entryway rising dangerously close to the ground floor entrance because the rainwater was trapped by the ice. I went into the house and saw that the water level in the backyard was also rising and that before long the first floor would be inundated from both the front and the back of the house. I realized that the only way to reduce the water level was to create an internal drain. I hurried to a pet store and bought 80 feet of clear plastic tubing, the sort that would be used in an aquarium. I took one end to the backyard and covered it with a brick. I unrolled the tubing and placed the other end in the laundry drain in the basement. Then I sucked long and hard until water from the backyard began to flow down into the sink. Whenever the tube slipped away from the brick, I had to start the process over, sucking filthy water from the yard into the tubing. Eventually the water level fell enough to avert the danger. And the next day, we engaged a plumber to build drains in the front and back of the house.

We lived on Garden Place for twenty-five years. It was home. We were married there in 2012 in an ecumenical service by Rabbi Sharon Kleinbaum (Randi Weingarten's wife), surrounded by family and a few close friends. Mary's priest sat quietly, without any of his priestly attire. Garden Place will always be home, even though we sold it in 2013;

we both lived there longer than any other place we lived. Both of us had bad knees, and we couldn't handle the stairs anymore. We found our next home in a century-old cooperative building in the same neighborhood that had a superintendent who dealt with all the physical problems that had caused us so much grief at Garden Place. And an elevator.

In 1999, despite the demands of the house on Garden Place, we bought a big antique house on Long Island Sound in Southold. Like the house on Garden Place, the house on Hyatt Road was built in 1895. It too had seen many updates, and it too had an endless series of physical problems, including a mouse population that resisted every attempt to remove them. For the next twenty years, we split our time between Brooklyn and Southold. Both houses required constant care, and that burden fell to Mary, since I was useless when it came to issues involving boilers, plumbing, roofing, and the mechanics of houses. Early in our relationship, we had seen a Jackie Mason one-man show on Broadway. Mason was the master of ethnic and religious jokes. He said that the way you could tell the difference between a Jew and a goy is when they are house hunting. The Jew wants to know about closet space, the goy wants to see the mechanicals. That was us.

14

DISILLUSIONMENT SETS IN

In 2001 New York City, the nation, and the world was stunned by the terrorist attack of September 11, which left the city shaken and fearful. I was at home that morning, enjoying a cup of coffee at my dining table, when I felt and heard an enormous boom. At first, I thought it was a car crash on the Brooklyn-Queens Expressway, only a few blocks away. But a few minutes later, Mary called from her office at the Board of Education headquarters to tell me to turn on the television. Something terrible had happened at the World Trade Center, she said. I did. I saw the smoke rising from one of the two buildings, and the commentators speculated about a small airplane crashing into the building. A tragic accident, it seemed. I grabbed one of our two dogs and hurried down to the Promenade, a scenic walkway that overlooks New York Harbor and has a direct view of lower Manhattan. Just as I looked up, I saw a large aircraft plunge directly into the one remaining tower. I stood there speechless, along with several other people. I ran home to watch television to learn more about what was happening, and the news was about terrorism, not an accident. I ran back to the Promenade and watched smoke rising from both towers; fortunately, I could not see people leaping from the upper floors to their deaths. When I got home, Mary was there. We went to the nearest hospital to offer blood, but they weren't accepting donations because no ambulances were bringing victims. When we walked closer to the harbor, we saw a steady stream of people who had walked across the Brooklyn Bridge, downcast, covered in soot and ashes. The air was heavy with debris that was fluttering from the wreckage. The cars on the street were blanketed in ashes. In our backyard, we found pieces of paper that were pockmarked with burn holes; they had been on someone's desk that morning. An hour after the second plane hit the second tower, what had been a beautiful, cloudless day turned dark. The wind shifted in our direction, and the entire sky was blotted out by the smoke rising from the remains of the Twin Towers.

Everyone in the city, it seemed, felt a personal connection to the tragedy. A niece of Mary's got out of the second tower before it collapsed. A neighbor on our block died. Like other New Yorkers, I was in a state of shock. Night after night, I imagined the scene on the upper floors where people were trapped and knew they were going to die. The city shut down. The bridges and tunnels were closed. Traffic was halted. The subways and buses stopped running. For days, there were no sounds in the air except sirens and military jet planes. We watched the news obsessively, trying to understand, learning about the good people who died that day. Photographs of missing people were plastered on walls and hung on fences—in downtown Manhattan, in Grand Central Station, in many other public places: "Have you seen this person?"

Depressed as I was about the terrorist attack on September 11, I realized that I had a date to lecture at Wheaton College in Massachusetts just a few weeks later. I contacted the lecture agent, Alan Walker of the Program Corporation of America, to tell him that I had to cancel; I could not travel or speak. I didn't know Walker well, having never booked a lecture through his agency before. He responded harshly that if I didn't perform the lecture, for which I was going to be paid $10,000, he would sue me. So, being lawsuit averse, I went to Wheaton, gave the lecture, and returned home. Weeks went by, and I didn't get a check. When I called Walker's office, his assistant assured me that I would get a check soon. Then Walker sent a letter telling me that he would not pay me because I had been under exclusive contract with his agency since 1993, when I left the federal government. He wrote that I had given many lectures in those eight years but had not paid his commission. He said he would not give me the money paid by Wheaton until I paid him the thousands of dollars I owed him.

I was stunned because I had never signed a contract with him. I called my friend David Blasband, an intellectual property lawyer, who agreed to represent me pro bono. David had married my friend Francie Alexander, whom I met in California when I worked on the state's history curriculum and who then joined me in the Bush administration as my top deputy. The only recourse I had in my Wheaton contract was to go to mediation with Walker, with the mediator's decision being final. The American Arbitration Association supplied a professional mediator. David and I traveled several times to Westchester County to make our case, and we won. Walker refused to pay.

Meanwhile, I had been doing research about Walker's very impressive client list. I obtained an affidavit from the head of the lectures department of the William Morris Agency, stating that a dozen of its exclusive clients—including Carol Channing, Queen Latifah, and Bernadette Peters—were listed in the Program Corporation of America catalogue but that the corporation represented none of them. I contacted everyone I knew on the list, and some I barely knew (like former president Jimmy Carter and former president George H. W. Bush). Every one of them (or in the case of the two presidents, their representatives) replied either that they were not represented by Walker or that they gave a speech for him once and never got paid. As I reached out, I began to hear from people who learned that I was seeking information. The historian Arthur Schlesinger Jr., who was a friend, wrote to tell me that he had given a lecture at Walker's behest and was not paid until he brought in his lawyer. Lani Guinier, a brilliant law professor at Harvard, called to tell me that Walker had never paid her fee.

Coincidentally I learned that Andy Rooney, a humorist on CBS's *60 Minutes*, had not received his speaking fee from Walker; Rooney brought a camera crew to Walker's office, but Walker refused to come to the door. Rooney's stunt got some national attention, and the astronaut Scott Carpenter saw it and called his attorney. Carpenter, another of Walker's victims, then brought his complaint to the FBI.

Once the FBI began contacting Walker's list of clients, the case escalated, as did the number of aggrieved victims. Walker went to trial in federal court in White Plains, New York, in 2005. The number and stature of people who had been defrauded by Walker were impressive. Walker had a special section of his program called *Roots* that was devoted to African American speakers. He had stiffed many of them. A partial list of other celebrity clients who had not been paid included the basketball star Magic Johnson; the boxer Hurricane Carter; Robert Ballard, who discovered the wreck of the *Titanic*; the poet Nikki Giovanni; Senator Carol Moseley Braun; the labor organizer Erin Brockovich; the political consultant James Carville; the actor James Earl Jones; the late comedian Alan King; the late Ossie Davis; and Martin Luther King III. Walker's defense was that he needed the money to save his financially stressed business. The judge was not impressed. She sentenced him to five years in prison on sixty counts of fraud and one of conspiracy. I never received any part of my fee, but I was satisfied.

Even as the ruins of the World Trade Center continued to smolder in November 2021, the city held an election for mayor, and the billionaire Michael Bloomberg handily won. Education was high on the new mayor's list of priorities. As a candidate, he promised to take control of the public schools and fix them. He made it sound easy. He was a technocrat with no political ties or debts, so of course he was the one to fix them. On January 1, 2002, Michael Bloomberg was sworn in as mayor. Most voters seemed grateful that the city would be run by a successful businessman, not an ordinary politician who bowed to campaign contributors. Michael Bloomberg bowed to no one. Once he took charge of the city's public schools, he pledged, he would infuse them with innovation, efficiency, and results. After years of divided authority and fitful leadership, Bloomberg's promise to take charge was exciting to many voters, including me. I wrote articles in the tabloids welcoming his arrival. He seemed to be the "man on a white horse" that everyone was waiting for.

A few weeks after Bloomberg was sworn in, he called me personally at my home and invited me to have breakfast at the mayor's official residence, Gracie Mansion, a beautiful nineteenth-century home in Manhattan on the East River and Ninety-Second Street. I had been there only once before, when Mayor Ed Koch had invited me and Mary to a small dinner party that included Billy Joel and his wife Christie Brinkley.

Mayor Bloomberg sent one of his big SUVs to Brooklyn Heights to bring me to breakfast. We had a delightful chat, and he told me that he had asked the state legislature to give him full charge of the public school system. He intended to turn it into a department of city government. I warned him that actual change in education is always incremental and not the stuff of headlines because many different factors affect students' academic performance, including ones completely outside the control of schools, like students' home circumstances. Toward the end of our breakfast, he surprised me by asking if I would like to go on his "personal payroll." I was confused because I didn't want a job. He said that he wasn't offering me a city job but a place on his "personal payroll," as a behind-the-scenes adviser, working in the background for him. He knew that I wrote frequently in the local press about the schools and appeared on local TV news shows. He wanted to pay me to be his ally. I could not do that. I could not sell my voice and my independence. I blurted out that I was "independently wealthy" and did not need his money. That wasn't literally true. I was well off, but not independently wealthy. I did not want to be his bought puppet. I told him there was one thing he could do that would satisfy my sense of independence, and that was to pay the opening installment of $25,000 to create the Mary Butz Scholarship Fund at St. Joseph's College in Brooklyn, her alma mater. He said the college would receive an "anonymous donation" the very next day, and it did. That way, I reasoned, his money would go to a good cause, and I would feel no obligation to compromise my integrity in my writing or speaking engagements. From that time forward, as I saw certain academics on the local television news station defend whatever Bloomberg did, I wondered if they were on his "personal payroll." Meanwhile, we have continually replenished the scholarship fund at St. Joseph's, and over the past two decades it has enabled a few dozen worthy students to get a college education.

A few weeks later, Bloomberg's secretary called and asked if he could come to dinner. Poor man, I thought. He has no one to have dinner with! We bought a huge steak at Balducci's, a high-end grocer in Greenwich Village, Mary brought out her best wines, and I made a salad. We had hors d'oeuvre on the parlor floor of the brownstone, and it was a bit uncomfortable because Mary had recently moved all the living room furniture except the sofa to our new vacation house on the North Fork of Long Island. The three of us sat side by side on the sofa, turning awkwardly to talk to one another. At dinner, we were both nervous about entertaining the mayor. But he had a delightful sense of humor, and we enjoyed bantering with him. Mary asked him if he knew much about wine, and he responded, "Sure, there is red and white, and the bottles are sealed with either corks or screw tops." Becoming animated about wine, Mary made a sweeping gesture with one hand and knocked a wine glass to the floor, where it shattered. One piece of glass bounced up and landed on the mayor's plate. He immediately worried about our dog lest she step on the shards of glass. Then he set aside his plate and pulled the entire cutting board in front of him to chow down on the steak, saying, "I'm so strong, I eat broken glass!"

It was all very jolly, and every so often over the next few weeks, Bloomberg called to ask my opinions on various education issues. The mayor decided to abolish the lay Board of Education that had managed the city's public schools since 1842 (with a brief exception in the 1870s during the reign of the Tweed Ring) and turn the management of the schools into a department of city government—like the Police Department, the Fire Department, the Sanitation Department—run by someone he appointed (just as Tweed had). At one point, he told me that the legislature insisted on retaining some kind of school board, but he insisted that the mayor appoint a majority of its members who would serve at his pleasure, not for a set term. He told me that he had decided to rename the school board—once the powerful New York City Board of Education—the "Panel on Education Policy" to show how toothless it was. The new board soon became known as the "PEP."

The mayor selected the chancellor and the board majority and controlled the budget.

Mayor Bloomberg announced that he was selling the Board of Education's historic headquarters at 110 Livingston Street in Brooklyn to a real estate developer (who converted it into luxury condominiums) and moving the central headquarters of his new Department of Education to the Tweed Courthouse next door to City Hall, so he could keep a close watch on it. The Tweed Courthouse was named for Boss Tweed; the elegant building was a symbol of municipal corruption because the Tweed Ring embezzled millions of dollars during its construction.

In early June 2002, the state legislature handed control of the New York City public schools to Mayor Bloomberg. Several weeks later, the mayor called to tell me he had chosen Joel Klein, an antitrust lawyer who had served in the Clinton administration, to be the new chancellor of the New York City public schools, and he asked my opinion. I was not familiar with Klein. I asked him if Klein knew anything about education. Bloomberg said "No, but he's smart. He will learn."

I wanted Bloomberg and Klein to succeed. I believed in Michael Bloomberg; he was a phenomenal businessman and remarkably confident of his ability to solve any problem. He was also charming. I liked him. He seemed to have the fresh perspective that the school system needed. Soon after Klein was hired, I sent him an e-mail and asked him to try to find a way to use my partner Mary in his new regime because he would find her to be knowledgeable, experienced, and loyal; she also had deep institutional memory. At the time, Mary had a high-level job in the Board of Education. She had been a teacher, an assistant principal, a principal, and a mentor to other principals. When Klein arrived, she was executive director in charge of a principal-training institute that she created at the behest of the previous chancellor, Harold O. Levy. He had asked her to devise a program to help new principals improve at their jobs. Her idea was to gather fifty of the system's best principals, dub them "the Distinguished Faculty," and pay each of them a stipend of $5,000 a year to mentor ten new principals. At minimal cost, the school system had a functional leadership training program for five hundred principals that relied on the wisdom of its most successful leaders. The U.S.

Department of Education held a national competition for principal training programs, and New York City's Distinguished Faculty mentoring program was recognized as one of the best in the nation and won $3 million. I thought Klein would be pleased, but he was noncommittal. I did not realize that Klein was trying to purge the school system of people like Mary; he wanted disruptive change and believed that veterans were an obstacle, not a resource.

Klein and a host of consultants from foundations and the corporate world spent six months preparing a plan to overhaul the schools. They announced their program—called Children First—on Martin Luther King Jr. Day in January 2003. Although Bloomberg was an independent and Klein was a Democrat, they quickly embraced a test-driven, top-down model that was closely aligned with George W. Bush's No Child Left Behind (NCLB) law. Schools had to raise their test scores or face punishment. Bloomberg and Klein worked closely with the billionaire philanthropists Bill Gates and Eli Broad, both of whom believed in disrupting the old way of doing things, breaking up public schools, closing those that didn't get results, and giving public funding to privately managed charter schools. What mattered most was test scores, data, and accountability. Klein reorganized the school system from top to bottom, and he did it again and again. He closed large high schools, most of which enrolled thousands of students, often in the face of protests by students, teachers, parents, and alumni. He opened scores of new, small schools—as many as four or six located in the same high school building that was closed, each with its own theme and its own principal. The large high schools offered many special programs and many electives; they enrolled students with disabilities and newcomers who didn't speak English. But the new regime, abetted by funding from the Gates Foundation, favored small schools and considered them to be innovative, even though students had fewer choices than they did in large schools and the schools had less ability to help students with disabilities or English-language learners. As the maelstrom of planned chaos intensified, experienced educators were unceremoniously ousted or retired.

Klein was not interested in Mary's Distinguished Faculty program for new principals. He had other, grander plans. He turned to Jack Welch, former CEO of General Electric, for advice about leadership training. Welch was known for his belief in "stack ranking," which involved ranking employees on a "20-70-10" model. The top 20 percent, in this approach, were the most productive employees; the middle 70 percent were adequate; the bottom 10 percent should be fired. Klein also sought advice on leadership from a partner at Goldman Sachs. He trusted businessmen, not educators. He eliminated Mary's Distinguished Faculty program, replaced it with his own "Leadership Academy," and selected as its leader a computer executive from Colorado whose business had just imploded. The businessman brought a large staff with him to New York City. Mary was allowed to remain as a figurehead vice president of the Leadership Academy but was never trusted by the new team because she was tainted by her long experience in the Old Order.

Near the end of the first year of the new administration, the Goldman Sachs partner whom Klein relied on to find a CEO for the new Leadership Academy asked me to meet him for breakfast at a diner in my neighborhood. I don't know why he sought me out. He told me he was bailing out because the reorganization was "amateur hour." He disapproved of the person selected to lead the Leadership Academy, a man with no experience in education whose business had failed. However, on his website today, two decades later, he claims credit for restructuring the school system.

Mary realized that Klein wanted to fire her, but she was kept on staff because Klein's Leadership Academy, which was privately funded with $75 million in philanthropic gifts, wanted the $3 million that her program had won from the federal government and needed her signature to get the money. Since she was very close to retirement age, she swallowed her pride and stayed on. She soon realized that the goal of the new team was to bring ambitious young people directly from the classroom or the business world into the principal's job, completely bypassing the position of assistant principal, where would-be principals traditionally learned their jobs over several years of apprenticeship.

Klein later claimed that I turned against him and Bloomberg because he wouldn't give her a promotion. That was not true. Mary didn't need a promotion; she was an "executive director." She had risen as far as she could go in the school system. She wanted to contribute to a team effort, but she was not allowed to join the team. She knew too much. As long as she worked in the school system, I did not write anything about the new regime, but when she retired in 2003, I was free to speak out against Klein's policies. I wrote critically in the city's tabloids about Klein's decision to mandate citywide reading and mathematics programs, both of which were very controversial. Klein chose a reading program called Balanced Literacy that was developed by Teachers College professor Lucy Calkins, and he mandated a little-known "discovery" math program called Everyday Mathematics.

Balanced Literacy was a refined version of the "Whole Language" method of teaching reading that swept the field in the 1980s. Advocates of Whole Language eschewed phonics and instead focused on "authentic" reading in real children's books. Instead of sounding out words, children were encouraged to guess at the meaning of words from pictures and "context clues." After extended criticism of Whole Language by dissatisfied parents and the media, Calkins led the way in developing "Balanced Literacy," which was intended to be a combination of Whole Language and phonics. In the 1990s and early 2000s, Balanced Literacy became the dominant mode of teaching reading in many districts. In 2022, the death knell for Balanced Literacy was a podcast by the journalist Emily Hanford called *Sold a Story: How Teaching Kids to Read Went So Wrong*. The podcast criticized Balanced Literacy for its neglect of phonics and "the science of reading." The Hanford critique was devastating to Balanced Literacy, as dozens of states responded by passing legislation banning Balanced Literacy and requiring the teaching of phonics and "the science of reading."

For myself, I object to any state or district mandates that tell teachers how to teach. I do not believe in mandating "phonics only," "whole language with no phonics," "Balanced Literacy," or the current "science of reading." No single method of teaching reading is right for all children. Well-prepared teachers should know a variety of methods and use them as needed, based on their judgment about the children in their classroom. As a historian of education, I have seen the pendulum repeatedly swing from phonics-only to no-phonics-at-all, then back again. The "science of reading" had its origins in the report of the National Reading Panel, created in 1997 by Reid Lyon of the National Institute of Child Health and Human Development. Lyon, a neuroscientist, is a specialist in learning disorders and an advocate of phonics. The panel's report was released in 2000 and became the basis for federal literacy policy in George W. Bush's No Child Left Behind law. Lyon became an adviser to President Bush and First Lady Laura Bush on education research. The report endorsed explicit and systematic instruction in phonics and called it "the science of reading." Bush's NCLB law incorporated the panel's findings into a six-year, $6 billion program called "Reading First." The program was tarnished by conflict-of-interest scandals involving U.S. Department of Education officials who awarded grants to states and districts to buy designated instructional products. Reading First fell under a cloud and was not renewed by Congress. Evaluations of the program's effectiveness showed some gains, some losses, but no improvement in students' comprehension of what they read.

When Klein took office as chancellor of the New York City public schools, he knew none of this background. He mandated Balanced Literacy in 2003, at the peak of its influence, and I was an outspoken critic of the decision. I also was critical of Everyday Math, which was mandated citywide, although it was little known and untested. Everyday Math was heavy on conceptual learning and light on learning basic mathematical processes, like addition, subtraction, multiplication, and division. It was the mathematical counterpart to Whole Language, mathematics as a way of thinking but without the basics.

It was curious to see the Children First reformers embracing conservative strategies like high-stakes testing and charter schools while simultaneously mandating what was then known as constructivist pedagogy. It was an ideological mishmash. The heavy emphasis on testing and privatization was associated with Republicans; constructivist pedagogy was consonant with the freewheeling pedagogy favored by educational progressives. I began to see Klein as an ambitious know-it-all who was flailing about for quick fixes and hostile to anyone who knew more than he did, which was almost every teacher and principal in the school system.

I did not abandon my conservative views, but I began to rethink them. My ideological transformation occurred almost four years later. However, what I saw during the Bloomberg-Klein years showed me the downside of my beliefs. I saw up close how easily test score gains were gamed by shrewd administrators whose jobs and reputations depended on those gains. In 2009, as he ran for reelection, Mayor Bloomberg called a news conference to laud the principal of an elementary school where scores had miraculously soared in a single year. The timing was auspicious for his controversial reelection campaign (he had persuaded the City Council to let him run for a third term even though the city charter limited the mayor and councilmembers to only two terms; he sealed the deal by agreeing that they too could run for a third term). The principal who had achieved those miraculous test score gains collected her bonus and promptly retired. A year later, under a new principal, the school's test scores collapsed and returned to where they had been before the election.

What mattered most was not what was happening in the schools but what the media said about what was happening in the schools. The Bloomberg publicity machine was relentless and skillful. The department expanded its public relations team from three people to more than a dozen to sell "the New York City Miracle" to the national media and the public; it was aided by the mayor's own sizable public relations staff and Joel Klein's Fund for Public Schools, whose board members included Mort Zuckerman, the publisher of the New York *Daily News*, and Wendi Murdoch, wife of Rupert Murdoch, the publisher of the *New York Post*. The public relations narrative touted the remarkable renaissance of the New York City public schools, asserting that they had been transformed into a national model in a few short years under the wise leadership of Michael Bloomberg; by every measure, the stories said, the city's schools demonstrated unparalleled success upon success.

Cheered on by Wall Street titans, the mayor and chancellor opened dozens of charter schools; they persuaded the state legislature to require the city to give free space in public schools to charter schools or to pay their rent in private space—even for charter schools whose board of trustees included billionaires—a requirement that took space and funding from the public schools. Bloomberg and Klein frequently praised charter schools, which was odd, because they did not control them. They often disparaged the schools they did control, the public schools. The path to academic success for charter schools was to choose students and families carefully and to push out those who did not meet the goals of the charter school. Success Academy, the city's most celebrated charter chain, won national acclaim for its remarkable test scores, but its equally remarkable student attrition rates and teacher turnover rates garnered little attention.

The experiments came and went with rapidity during the dozen years of Bloomberg's reign over the schools. A citywide merit pay plan was announced and declared a great success until studies showed that it failed to make a difference in test scores, an outcome that characterized merit pay plans in other cities. The department's leadership imposed an elaborate accountability plan on every school, which received a report card and a letter grade. The school grades were puzzling. The elementary school in my neighborhood (Brooklyn Heights) received an A one year; Chancellor Klein came to the school to offer his personal congratulations and pledged to expand the school. The next year, the same school received an F, even though nothing had changed. Same staff, same pedagogy, from A to F in one year. The school system's accountability system demanded improvement every year, and even high-performing schools might fail to improve. Teachers of gifted students were at risk of receiving low grades on the city's evaluation model because the students who scored at the top of last year's test did not raise their scores the following year.

I wrote articles in the local newspapers about the arrival and departure of new programs, new policies, new reorganizations; the only constant was disruption. I was living with Mary, but our relationship was not public. I was afraid about being outed as gay. One day, an article in the gossip column ("Page Six") of Murdoch's *New York Post* referred to our relationship. A friend who worked in the highest echelon at the Department of Education visited my home and warned me that if I continued to write critical articles, I would regret it. I not only continued to write articles but also gave speeches to civic groups and university audiences about why the Bloomberg reforms were floundering. I had not yet given up on testing or even on charter schools. But I was dismayed by the transfer of corporate practices to schools, which meant indifference to the culture of schools that were summarily closed, contempt for educators, and the treatment of students, teachers, and administrators as interchangeable widgets, callously moved from school to school.

When I gave lectures, I noticed that the same man often sat in the front row of the audience, recording my speeches. I eventually learned that he worked on the public relations staff of the Department of Education. I realized what he was up to when a full-page article appeared in the *New York Post* in the fall of 2007 attacking me as a hypocrite for criticizing the Bloomberg plan of high-stakes testing and charter schools, policies that I had long endorsed. The article was signed by the leader of a major business association. I learned through journalist friends that it had been written by the public relations firm that worked for Bloomberg, using the dossier that had been compiled by the Department of Education's staff.

I refused to be intimidated by the public attack on me. I continued to write about the idiocy of imposing a one-size-fits-all reading program and an untested math program on the entire school system and the lack of any vision about education beyond raising test scores. But whoever wrote the article was right about the central point. Bloomberg and Klein were faithfully, if erratically, imposing the right-wing policies that I had once endorsed and demonstrating their ineffectiveness. The Bloomberg-Klein regime was obsessed with raising test scores, but testing was distorting education and stripping the joy of teaching and learning from the classroom. The team at the Tweed Courthouse was giving me hard lessons about how wrong I was and had been for many years. Even so, I kept thinking they were doing the right things in the wrong way. It did not yet occur to me that they were doing the wrong things in the wrong way. I continued to be a dedicated member of the Koret Task Force at the Hoover Institution and the board of the Thomas B. Fordham Foundation (TBF). I continued to support standardized testing and charter schools, despite what I saw happening in New York City. I thought what was happening was a bug, not a feature.

In late 2006, Rick Hess of the American Enterprise Institute (AEI) invited me to take part in a conference about the progress of the No Child Left Behind law after half a decade. I accepted, eager to learn from a dozen scholars what was happening in different cities and states. I was looking for hopeful stories about the strategies I had long championed. The conference was in late November at AEI headquarters in Washington, D.C. My assignment that day was to sum up the lessons from the papers.

This is what I heard and was later able to read in a book comprising the conference papers, called *No Remedy Left Behind: Lessons from a Half-Decade of NCLB*, edited by Frederick M. Hess and Chester E. Finn Jr. NCLB had set a fourteen-year timetable for schools to reach the ambitious goal of 100 percent proficiency for their students in reading and mathematics. Under that pressure, more students were expected to raise their scores every year. If schools were not on track to meet that utopian goal, they had to use certain remedies: first, allow students to transfer to a better school, or second, provide after-school tutoring to help students make progress. If schools tried these remedies and still failed to make progress, they were subject to a cascade of sanctions that might culminate in the firing of the staff and the closing of the school.

The scholars said that very few students—typically only 1 or 2 percent—in low-performing urban schools took the opportunity to transfer to a higher-performing school; some parents did not want their children taking long bus rides to school, or they believed that the student's current school was as good as the other options, or they were frustrated by paperwork. Most students did not want after-school tutoring because they did not want a longer school day. The scholars said that the U.S. Department of Education required districts to use private providers of tutoring, but they were more expensive and no better than tutoring offered by the district. They said that members of Congress liked the idea of private organizations offering tutoring to low-performing students because they thought that the market would spur improvement. Competition among public and private providers, they believed, would be a good thing. What they did not anticipate was that some private providers offered cash incentives to school officials, even to parents, to hire their services, regardless of their quality. In some states, like California, there were so many English-language learners that the goal of 100 percent proficiency was impossible; by 2010, a majority of the schools in the state would be labeled "failing." In some states and cities, there was already so much choice—within districts, across districts, and to charter schools—that the offer of more choice was irrelevant. Many educators, they reported, saw NCLB as a guarantee of failure for almost all public schools. Across the papers, the story was the same: the NCLB sanctions were having little effect. Even Rick Hess and Checker Finn, the organizers of the conference, wrote that NCLB's accountability goals were "more a form of moral advocacy than a sensibly designed set of institutional improvement mechanisms and incentives." They acknowledged that NCLB's "patently unreachable" goal of 100 percent proficiency had the effect of focusing educators on compliance, rather than the impossible goal.

At the end of the day's presentations, I summarized what I had learned: NCLB was failing. The sanctions were ineffective. Urban districts already had plenty of school choice or lacked high-performing schools to accept transfers, and very few students wanted to leave their local public school. After-school tutoring had more participants than choice programs, but most students did not enroll because they did not want to lengthen their school day. Everything I heard convinced me that NCLB was not working. That was the day when I began to look at the issues in a different way. Threats and compulsion did not work. Punitive accountability did not work.

I began to see "education reform" in a different light. In its current state, it did not mean funding schools with ample resources, strengthening the entry requirements for new teachers, helping new teachers get better at their work, improving instructional materials and the curriculum, providing the arts and music in every school, or raising teachers' salaries. Reform in its present guise meant strategies of test-and-punish. It meant high-stakes testing, punishment of teachers, principals, and schools if scores did not improve, rewards if they did, and choice for students to move to a different school. Reformers assumed that students earned low scores because their teachers and principals were not trying hard enough and needed threats and incentives to motivate them. They believed that "failing schools" needed to be closed and their staff fired en masse. This was the version of "reform" that was riding high. The Gates Foundation continued to pour millions of dollars into New York City to open new small high schools, although in 2008 the foundation abandoned its own small-schools initiative and declared that it was ineffectual; the Broad Foundation awarded New York City its $1 million prize for "most-improved urban district" in 2007, although the city's scores on the federal National Assessment of Educational Progress (NAEP) tests for that year showed no improvement at all.

Eli Broad's secretary called to invite me to meet the great man in his elegant penthouse overlooking Central Park on Fifth Avenue, a temporary residence (he lived in Los Angeles). When we met, he explained that what schools needed more than anything else was tight managerial control. That "tight managerial control" felt very much like micromanagement that crushed teachers' sense of autonomy. When I brought up education issues, he said he knew nothing about "reading or curriculum or any of that stuff." He was right about that. He was an expert about management, nothing more.

As I grew increasingly skeptical about my conservative views, I became a dissenter on the TBF board and the Koret Task Force at Hoover. TBF had become a sponsor of charter schools in Ohio in 2004, which I opposed at that time because I thought that a think tank should be independent of entanglements; how could we evaluate charter schools if we were sponsoring them? Sponsorship of charter schools was lucrative, however, and hopes were high for the promise of charter schools. I was outvoted by the other members of the board. The results were not pretty, however. About half the charters we sponsored eventually failed and reopened with new leadership.

In 2009, shortly before leaving the TBF board, I opposed a motion to accept funding from the Bill & Melinda Gates Foundation. Again, I wondered, how could a think tank independently evaluate the projects of the biggest funder of education reform if it was getting millions from the same organization? I was outvoted. The rest of the board liked the idea of accepting Gates's money. When I left the board, the Gates Foundation paid TBF millions of dollars to promote the Common Core state standards, creating exactly the kind of conflict I foresaw. TBF should have been evaluating the standards, not advocating for them. When the Common Core standards became available in 2010, I was an outspoken critic because the standards were assembled in record time, without any field testing by teachers, and states were asked to sign on without reviewing the standards so as to be eligible to compete for the Obama administration's $5 billion race-to-the-top jackpot. Most states agreed to adopt the Common Core standards because they hoped to win the federal dollars. Common Core was a bonanza for publishers of textbooks and tests, but ultimately it had no effect on student test scores.

I became an increasingly outspoken dissenter at meetings of the Koret Task Force at Hoover. When we discussed the future of NCLB, which was supposed to be reauthorized in 2008, I was a solitary outlier. The other members of the task force knew that it was not accomplishing anything, but they did not see the harm it was doing to students, teachers, and the quality of education. I argued that it was a disaster and could not be fixed. I called NCLB "the death star" of American education, ranking schools solely by test scores and imposing sanctions for not meeting an impossible goal of 100 percent proficiency. I argued that test scores measured family income, not the quality of teachers; they did not agree. Ultimately, the task force issued a report on how to fix NCLB. My name was not on it. But I was not left out entirely. In 2008, *Education Next*, a magazine based at Harvard, funded by Hoover Institution allies, and edited by Koret Task Force member Paul Peterson, published a debate about NCLB between John Chubb and me. His article was titled "NCLB: Mend It." My article was titled "NCLB: End It."

Step by step, I was abandoning my long-held views about education. I wasn't sure that I could sever ties with people I had known and cared about for many years, especially Checker Finn. They were my friends. But I no longer believed in the conservative ideas I had long championed. I had lost the faith. I offered my resignation to the TBF board and to the Koret Task Force in 2008 and told my colleagues that I no longer shared their views. Both rejected my resignation and urged me to stay on and be a dissident on the board. They enjoyed the banter and the debates, which I always lost, a minority of one. I lasted another year, then tendered my irrevocable resignation in 2009. It was no fun to work with people, even friends, as the perpetual dissenter. I was no longer certain about what I believed. But I did know that I no longer believed in the power of testing or the promise of choice.

15

REFORMING MY VIEWS

I began working on a book about my change of views, and I set about examining the research on every important question on which I had changed my mind. I determined to write a critique of standardized testing, merit pay, charter schools, and vouchers with the intention of evaluating the case for "education reform," as it was currently defined. I intended to show that I had been wrong in my public stances for three decades. It wasn't easy to admit that I was wrong, but I had no choice. I also intended to expose the big money propelling the cause of what I called corporate education reform.

The book was eventually published in 2010. Its title was *The Death and Life of the Great American School System: How Testing and Choice Are Undermining Education*. The question I was asked most frequently was "Why did you change your mind?" The short answer was that I changed my mind when I realized I was wrong. When the policies I had supported were put into practice in the city where I lived, I learned that they had terrible effects. They didn't improve education; they distorted its purpose. Making testing the central measure of schooling crushed the joy of learning and discouraged both students and teachers. The joy of learning was no longer a goal; it became irrelevant and disappeared. Using public money to fund privately managed charters and vouchers disrupted communities without improving education. It also diverted funds and top students away from public schools, which left them with a disproportionate share of the neediest students. I quoted John Maynard Keynes in *Death and Life*, who said, "When the facts change, I change my mind. What do you do, sir?"

I changed my mind when I realized that the ideas I had championed sounded good in theory but were failures in practice. I thought that standards, tests, and accountability would lead to higher achievement (test scores). They didn't. Even if they had, the scores would not signify better education, just a fortunate upbringing and the mastery of test-taking skills. I originally thought, like other so-called reformers, that competition and merit pay would encourage teachers and principals to work harder and get better results. They didn't. The teachers were already working as hard as they knew how. Many of my colleagues in the "reform" movement blamed bad teachers for low test scores; they believed that teachers who did not raise test scores should be fired every year. I did not agree; I foresaw that punitive measures would demoralize teachers and discourage others from entering the profession. In fact, enrollment in teacher colleges plummeted after the "reform" movement gained traction.

My colleagues on the Koret Task Force knew, just as I did, that our ideas were unsuccessful. In our private conversations, we often discussed why so many charter schools failed to produce academic gains, why they were not generating innovation, why so many attracted incompetent leaders, why so many closed soon after opening. We also knew that No Child Left Behind (NCLB) was a bust. However, everyone but me had ideas about how to make our theories successful in the future. No one but me gave up on the conservative agenda of standards, testing, competition, choice, and accountability.

As I turned skeptical about the remedies I once believed in, I decided to take a closer look at the origins of the new "reform movement," as well as to answer my own questions. I started my investigation in San Diego because I had read that Joel Klein borrowed many of his ideas from Alan Bersin, the lawyer and former "border czar" for the Clinton administration who was chosen by the San Diego Board of Education to overhaul its public schools. Like Klein, Bersin had no prior experience as a professional teacher or a school administrator, but both Bersin and the San Diego board believed that his lack of experience or knowledge about schools was a plus. Bersin and his team would be untethered to old ideas. Before I visited San Diego, I read several new books by scholars who were hopeful about the dramatic changes implemented by Bersin in San Diego. I wanted to see for myself what the excitement was about.

I spent a week in San Diego interviewing teachers and principals, as well as Alan Bersin and his successor Carl Cohn. Although Bersin had been ousted by a new board in 2005, he was proud of the disruptive policies he had imposed; he believed that he had been successful. Carl Cohn was a veteran educator who was respected among other superintendents in California. He spoke to me about the importance of trust among educators. Genuine school reform is built on collaboration, he said, not bullying from the top. He pointed out that there are no quick fixes, no perfect theories. Cohn's advice resonated with me and helped me as I was letting go of my long-standing infatuation with testing, accountability, and charter schools, all of which were imposed by politicians and so-called experts from outside the classroom.

The San Diego school board elected in 1998 was led by critics of the city's public schools, who held a margin of 3–2. Most of them were convinced that the public schools were failing; they wanted bold new leadership. The board hired Bersin as the district's superintendent and encouraged him to impose sweeping changes. This seemed strange because I knew from my experience on the federal testing board that San Diego was the nation's highest-performing urban district. The board wanted Bersin to disrupt the status quo. Disrupt he did, but what he put in place was an authoritarian workplace that had no room for debate or dissent. He provided bold new leadership, but he demoralized the teachers and principals who worked for him.

Bersin had a genuine sense of urgency about the importance of rapid change. He disdained collaboration, which was slow and cumbersome. Bersin used metaphors like "pedal to the metal" and "you don't cross a chasm in two leaps" to demonstrate his commitment to action. A study commissioned by the Bersin administration summed up his philosophy as "do it fast; do it deep; take no prisoners."

He did not trust educators; he preferred people from the military or the business world. Experienced administrators and principals who resisted the new order were demoted or fired. Professional development in Balanced Literacy and constructivist mathematics was mandatory. Reform-minded foundations like Gates and Broad and the think tanks they funded raved about this decisive approach to education reform. But teachers and principals were angry. They protested at board meetings. They engaged in petty acts of rebellion. They created a book of anti-Bersin songs. They created a bingo game using the rhetoric of reform as squares on the board. The pro-Bersin bloc on the board held three seats; the anti-Bersin bloc held two. Eventually the tide turned. In 2005, the voters elected a different board, and San Diego abandoned Bersin's reform plan.

Based on what I learned in San Diego and New York City, I saw the outline of the book: I would show how NCLB was warping education by its slavish devotion to standardized tests; why market-driven dependence on rewards and punishments failed to improve test scores and alienated staff; why higher test scores were not the same as better education; how dependence on test scores narrowed the curriculum and promoted gaming of the system, even cheating; why teacher evaluations based on student test scores were flawed drivers of teacher "performance"; and why testing, competition, merit pay, charter schools, and school choice were not solutions to the problems of education. I knew from my years on the National Assessment of Educational Progress (NAEP) board that test scores are highly correlated with family income and education. That being the case, the best way to improve school performance would require taking significant steps to improve the quality of life for those who do not have a decent standard of living. It is easier and less costly to blame teachers and schools than to work for significant social and economic change; the "reformers" blamed teachers and schools for conditions beyond their control.

The big story behind the new book was not what happened in San Diego or New York City. The big story was my public renunciation of views I had confidently expressed in the public square for three decades. It was my mea culpa, my recantation, that made news. I looked at data and research, but even more important in my personal transformation was what I learned by talking to teachers and principals in places that were undergoing reform. As I learned from Carl Cohn, if the people tasked with doing the work feel disrespected, if there is a culture of distrust, if the frontline workers do not share in shaping the agenda and the goals, reforms will not take root. The ideas that look great on the drawing board will fail when they are imposed in an authoritarian manner and when they are not informed by practical experience. What seems to work in business cannot be transferred to schools; education is not a business. Without trust, mutual respect, and an atmosphere of professionalism, reform will be a chimera.

George W. Bush's NCLB law institutionalized the top-down method of reform. It was written by politicians, not educators. It relied on using carrots and sticks to motivate professional educators in hopes of improving test scores. The law embodied disrespect for professional educators. It imposed ideas drawn from the business world (competition, data-based decision-making, and sanctions for failure to produce measurable results). It ignored the knowledge of experienced teachers and principals. It also disregarded common sense. NCLB's requirement that "all students" would score "proficient" in reading and mathematics by the year 2013–2014 was pie-in-the-sky thinking. Districts that failed to meet that ridiculous goal would be subject to a series of escalating sanctions: teachers and principals would be fired, schools would be handed over to private management, and schools would close. No other nation in the world had adopted a policy that threatened eventually to terminate every school in the nation if wildly unrealistic goals were not met.

Soon after NCLB was signed into law in 2002 by President Bush, I attended an event sponsored by the Hoover Institution at the historic Willard Hotel in Washington, D.C., the same hotel where I first met Lamar Alexander and David Kearns in 1991. A panel of senators, including Lamar Alexander from Tennessee, explained how NCLB would transform American education. When it came time for questions, I stood and asked my former boss a question: "Senator Alexander, do you really believe that every child in every district will be proficient in reading and math in a dozen years?" He answered: "It's not likely, Diane, but it is good to have goals." Even though the senators knew the goals were absurdly unrealistic, teachers and principals would be fired and schools would be closed if they could not achieve the impossible. Would the public tolerate a federal crime bill that pledged to abolish all crime within twelve years or fire every police officer and give their badges to inexperienced amateurs?

In 2002, I, along with members of both parties and the George W. Bush administration, chose to believe the impossible and to justify that belief with the rationalization "It's good to have goals." As time went by, as NCLB ended careers and closed schools in low-income districts, the goal of 100 percent proficiency began to seem not only impossible but cynical and cruel. Its authors believed that students got low scores because their teachers were not trying hard enough or didn't have high expectations. Offering bonuses and threatening to fire educators should motivate them, the reformers assumed. But no number of carrots and sticks could produce 100 percent proficiency when a significant number of students lived in poverty, didn't get medical care, didn't read or speak English, had cognitive disabilities, missed school to babysit so their mother could go to work, or just didn't care about schoolwork. A decade after passage of NCLB, at least 80 percent of American public schools were on track to be labeled as failures and to be eventually closed or privatized. This was not sane policy. The real-world effect of NCLB was to punish teachers and schools in the poorest communities, waste billions of dollars, and encourage public demand for any alternatives to public schools, be they charters, religious schools, online schools, or homeschooling.

After the election of President Barack Obama, his education team—led by Secretary of Education Arne Duncan and allies from the Gates and Broad foundations—embraced the principles of NCLB. They made matters far worse for schools and teachers by creating the Race to the Top competition for states. Race to the Top, like NCLB, was based on testing, accountability, and incentives. Race to the Top was a program, while NCLB remained the law. The Obama administration spent billions of dollars to encourage new charter schools, more merit pay, and additional punishments for teachers, principals, and low-performing schools. Arne Duncan sang the praises of standardized testing and applauded districts that fired the entire staff of schools that had low scores. Teachers knew that the way to get a high rating was to teach in an affluent district and to avoid teaching students who were poor, had disabilities, or had limited ability to read English.

Why did I change my mind? I saw that the toxic policy of federally mandated high-stakes testing was inflicting harm on students and teachers by establishing unattainable goals and demonizing public schools, thus creating a demand for school choice. Once I broke free of my long-standing faith in standardized testing, my eyes were open to other views. I learned about Campbell's Law, which had been written by the sociologist Donald T. Campbell in 1975: "The more any quantitative social indicator is used for social decision-making, the more subject it will be to corruption pressures and the more apt it will be to distort and corrupt the social processes it is intended to monitor." In other words, the emphasis that NCLB placed on testing corrupted testing as a measure of learning. Educators were focused on satisfying the measure rather than on pursuing the real goals of education. Students were rewarded for their test-taking skills, not their pursuit of knowledge. The test took precedence over the cultivation of curiosity, motivation, innovation, creativity, imagination, and love of learning. And, because the federally mandated high-stakes tests were only in two areas, mathematics and English-language arts, other subject areas—civics, history, science, the arts, even recess—got short shrift, and in some schools disappeared. Both as a conservative and as a liberal, I had a rock-solid belief in cultivating the joy of learning, in learning to love classic literature in the Western tradition and in other cultural traditions, in engaging with the drama and excitement of history, in studying whatever sparks a student's passion. The path of standardized testing and accountability, of rewards and punishments, was an absolute barrier to my beliefs.

In one of my last public events as a conservative intellectual, I participated in a meeting of the Philanthropy Roundtable, an organization composed of conservative foundations. I was asked to be a judge of a competition for the best proposal to disrupt education in the coming decade, sort of like "America's Got Talent," but for conservative policy wonks. One especially disturbing presentation was presented by a lobbyist who had created an organization called the Center for Union Facts, whose purpose was to attack unions. He explained that he had plastered major highways in New Jersey with billboards blaming the state teachers' union for declining test scores. His pitch was straightforward: teachers' unions are greedy and don't care about students. When it was time for questions, I asked him to name a state with high test scores that had banned unions. He was stumped. Then he said, somewhat pathetically, "I am a PR guy, not a researcher."

When I was an advocate of testing, accountability, and choice, I read articles and books that reinforced my views. As I turned skeptical, my reading broadened to include the critics of what I had once championed. There's a lesson there for all of us: not to get trapped in our own bubbles.

In 2008, I read Daniel Koretz's book *Measuring Up: What Educational Testing Really Tells Us*. He said that coaching students for state tests produces test score inflation and the illusion of progress. Students who are well-prepared for the state tests may be poorly prepared for different tests of the same subject or for applying what they have learned to real life. Excessive test preparation distorts the very purpose of tests, which should be to assess learning and knowledge, not test-taking skills. Excessive attention to test preparation distorts curricula and pedagogy, yet every school district needed to invest time and resources to test preparation in a desperate effort to satisfy federal law. Teaching to the test was once considered unethical and unprofessional, but in the era of NCLB and Race to the Top, it became a common practice.

The next year, I read Todd Farley's *Making the Grades: My Misadventures in the Standardized Testing Industry*, in which he describes his fifteen years as a grader of answers to questions that were "open response"—a short written answer—and to essay questions written by high school students. The book is alternatively hilarious and appalling. Farley utterly demolishes any faith the reader ever had in the fairness of standardized tests, at least those in which any part of a student's answer is in writing. He was a test scorer, a job he picked up to make money. He didn't make a lot of money because he and other test scorers were paid hourly at or slightly above minimum wage. The answers to test questions were scored according to rules that were "ambiguous, arbitrary, superficial, and bizarre" by temporary workers who would otherwise be unemployed; the test scorers skimmed student answers for a minute or less as they rushed to meet their daily quotas. To be a test scorer, he writes, it was best not to be too intelligent or experienced in the classroom. The snap decisions of these test scorers determined whether students would be promoted or receive a high school diploma. Nothing about the tests, he maintains, was standardized, and the results were not credible to anyone but newspaper reporters who touted the latest scores as "evidence" of something important. What mattered most, he concluded, was the profits of the testing corporation.

My newly acquired disdain for standardized testing grew stronger when New York, along with other states, implemented the Common Core tests called PARCC (the federally funded Partnership for Assessment of Readiness for College and Careers) in 2013. The tests in reading and math were first given to students in the spring, and the results were reported in September. The test-publishing organization forbade teachers and anyone else from posting or discussing any of the questions with students, other teachers, or parents. A teacher's critique of the fourth-grade Common Core test was posted anonymously on the blog of Celia Oyler, a professor at Teachers College, Columbia University, to hide the teacher's identity. The teacher wrote that she was required to sign a form agreeing not to reveal or discuss items that appeared on the test with anyone, including students or school staff, not verbally or on social media or in any other form. The teacher wondered on her post how she might assess her students' progress if she was barred from examining and discussing their test results with them. She pointed out that the test given to her students was "developmentally inappropriate," meaning that some of the readings were written for students in middle school, even high school. What is the point, she wondered, of expecting students in fourth grade to read and respond to texts written well above their grade level? The examples that she cited were removed from her post "under legal threat" at the direction of the testing organization PARCC.

I put the anonymous teacher's post on my blog and was promptly contacted by the office of the president of PARCC and told to remove the copyrighted material from my post or face legal action. I did.

But I was left with these questions. What is the value of the test if students and their teachers are not allowed to discuss the questions and answers? The student's teacher in the spring, when the test is given, is no longer the student's teacher in the fall, when the scores are returned to the schools. So the student receives a score that no one can interpret to help the student; the teachers don't know what the student got right or wrong. Neither does the student. What is the purpose of giving students questions that are two or three grade levels above them? Of what value is the score without any diagnostics, any information about what the student needs to do to improve? I likened it to going to a doctor with a pain in your stomach and being told that you will get a report from the doctor in six months. When the report arrives, the doctor tells you that you rank above or below others with the same symptoms but she can't really prescribe any medication because all she knows is your ranking relative to others in the same situation. That's crazy. It was crazy enough to inspire a parent-led movement to opt out of state testing in New York and other states. In some schools, the opt-out rate was over 50 percent, and state officials in New York complained that they were unable to rank the schools where the opt-out rate was high.

It seemed that collecting data and ranking students and schools had become an end in itself that had nothing to do with improving the ability of students to read well.

Two treatises by Richard Rothstein reshaped my thinking about accountability. Richard became a friend when he was the education editor of *The New York Times* from 1999 to 2002. We used to have long conversations about education issues, and he tried—fruitlessly at the time—to convince me that I was wrong about testing and accountability. At the height of my success as a conservative, I was unmoved. But when I began to reconsider my views, Rothstein's work on accountability and on the effects of poverty on students' performance in school redirected my thinking.

His paper on accountability, called "Holding Accountability to Account," was posted on the Internet in 2008 by the Economic Policy Institute, a think tank with which Richard is affiliated. He reviewed a large body of research about performance incentives in noneducation fields, all of which showed that quantitative goals encourage gaming of the system and goal displacement. He told a story about the Soviet Union that may have been apocryphal: when the central planners measured output from nail factories, one factory produced the biggest nail in the world to win the competition for output by weight; if the competition had been based on quantity, the factory would have produced millions of tiny but useless nails. Measurement doesn't improve services, he wrote; it distorts goals. In medicine, for example, cardiac surgeons got the highest scores for survival rates by rejecting the sickest patients. In many fields, quantitative measurements caused providers to neglect whatever was not measured.

After reading Richard's work on accountability, I turned to his 2004 book *Class and Schools: Using Social, Economic, and Educational Reform to Close the Black-White Achievement Gap*. Like so many other reformers, I had been inclined to think of students as a blank slate on which teachers write. I naively believed that "fixing schools" would fix poverty. Students who earned high test scores would get good jobs, and presto, the problem of poverty would be solved. I ignored the fact that teachers have less effect on students' academic outcomes than do their home environments. This is a fact, not a hypothesis, that has been demonstrated repeatedly in social science literature, most forcefully by the American Statistical Association (ASA) in 2014 when it criticized the Obama administration's plan to evaluate teacher effectiveness by student test scores. ASA pointed out that most studies find that teachers contribute only 1 to 14 percent of the variability in test scores, and that "the majority of opportunities for quality improvement are found in the system-level conditions." ASA warned that ranking teachers by changes in their students' test scores "can have unintended consequences that reduce quality." The "unintended consequences" include teacher demoralization, teacher avoidance of classes that are unlikely to show test score gains, teachers taking early retirement, and the deprofessionalization of teaching.

Then there is the inconvenient reality that standardized tests are always normed on a bell curve, which guarantees that half the test takers will be above the midpoint and half will always be below. The bell curve never closes. The gap between those at the top and those at the bottom persists. Furthermore, the most affluent students always cluster in the top half of the bell curve, and the poorest students always cluster in the bottom half. By design, the standardized tests guarantee that most poor students will have no escape from low test scores, low self-esteem, and in all likelihood, a life of poverty.

Standardized tests, I came to understand, confer privilege on the already privileged. Sure, there are exceptions to the rule that the most affluent rank at the top of the bell curve and the poorest score at the bottom. There are poor kids who get high scores, despite the obstacles they face, and there are rich kids who don't. But they are exceptions. The rule holds in every standardized test, whether it is a state test, a national test, or an international test: the most affluent students get the highest scores, and the poorest get the lowest scores.

And that brought me to an insight I garnered from Michael Young's 1994 introduction to his classic *The Rise of the Meritocracy* (which was originally published in 1958):

> If the rich and powerful were encouraged by the general culture to believe that they fully deserved all they had, how arrogant they could become, and, if they were convinced it was all for the common good, how ruthless in pursuing their own advantage. . . . Even if it could be demonstrated that ordinary people had less native ability than those selected for high position, that would not mean that they deserved to get less. Being a member of the "lucky sperm club" confers no moral right to advantage. What one is born with, or without, is not of one's own doing.

The tests are the foundation of our meritocracy; they determine who gets promoted or fails, who graduates or fails, who gains admission to the best colleges and universities. If meritocracy cements the good fortune of those who already enjoy the advantages conferred by their affluence, I wondered why our society was using this rigged methodology to harden class lines. I wondered, why shouldn't all people in our rich society—regardless of their wealth or class or race or personal attributes—have a decent life, meaning health care, decent housing, good schools, food security, and physical safety? Some people consider that aspiration to be "socialist" or "communist" or "woke," but I don't. I think these are preconditions for a good society.

Standardized tests reproduce and confirm inequality. Why would we want to cut off the bottom rungs of the ladder of social mobility? If more evidence were needed, I discovered *The Spirit Level: Why Greater Equality Makes Societies Stronger*, written by two British sociologists, Richard Wilkinson and Kate Pickett. They demonstrated that greater income equality produces societies that are happier, more physically and mentally healthy, less violent, and more educated. In our society, we expect better educational outcomes to produce equality, but Wilkinson and Pickett assert that better educational outcomes are a result, not a cause, of greater income equality. I did not read *The Spirit Level* until after the publication of *Death and Life*; it reinforced my new view of the causes of educational inequality.

The Common Core standards were intended to reduce educational inequality. The theory behind the standards was that classroom instruction could overcome socioeconomic differences if all children were taught the same things in the same way by teachers who had studied the Common Core curriculum, used textbooks aligned with Common Core, and were tested by examinations based on Common Core. Under all these conditions, all students supposedly would get the same high scores. When the Common Core standards were released in 2010, I knew they would fail because their assumptions were naïve. And fail they did. Achievement gaps on tests persisted. Scores on national tests remained stagnant for the decade after their widespread adoption. I once heard Bill Gates speak to an audience of teachers about the virtues of standardization, comparing school standards to electrical outlets. He said, "Isn't it marvelous to know you can plug your appliance in anywhere and anticipate that it will work?" He was wrong. Students are not toasters, and neither are teachers. Students in the same classroom with the same teachers, using the same textbooks and taking the same tests, have very different outcomes.

Rothstein's book *Class and Schools* explains why. What happens in school is an important part of academic outcomes, but other aspects of students' lives are even more important. Students' academic performance is influenced by their family, by prenatal conditions, by the health care they receive, by their nutrition, by the quality of the housing in which they live, by whether they are exposed to lead or smoke or vermin. Growing up in economic security with educated parents is a tremendous boon to children; growing up in poverty with worries about food, a roof over one's head, medical care, and physical safety is a combination of stress factors that interferes with learning.

When studying merit pay and incentive plans, I was influenced by Andrea Gabor's *The Man Who Discovered Quality*, about the important work of W. Edwards Deming, a business expert who abhorred merit bonuses. In business, merit bonuses set employee against employee, undermining teamwork and shared goals; each employee looks out for himself, not for the organization. Raymond E. Callahan's powerful book *Education and the Cult of Efficiency* taught me how the work of the schools and their administrators in the early twentieth century had been corrupted by the ideas of "efficiency experts" who imposed business ideas on them. Books by social psychologist Edward Deci, behavioral economist Dan Ariely, and author Daniel Pink taught me how motivation is dampened by extrinsic rewards. When people are paid extra to complete a task, they stop working when the extra pay stops. Intrinsic motivation, they show, matters far more than rewards.

The book *Seeing like a State* by the Yale political scientist James C. Scott taught me the dangers of trying to fix other people's lives from a distance of 20,000 feet in the sky. That is what I had been doing for many years. Trust those closest to the work, those on the ground, those trained to do the job more than consultants, experts, and politicians. Scott's book taught me an important lesson about my work: *I literally didn't know what I was talking about.* I was a historian, not a classroom teacher. Like most other reformers, I offered advice in op-ed articles about how to reform the schools, but my ideas were not grounded in experience or reality. Very few of the reformers had ever been teachers; the few who were had spent two years in the schools as Teach for America (TFA) recruits. Experienced educators were missing from the top ranks of the reform movement. The most influential of the reformers had worked in foundation offices or think tanks. They had been employed at desk jobs for their entire professional lives, or they were billionaires who had never attended public schools or even visited them. I realized with embarrassment that I was no different from them. As I considered the overwhelming evidence against the policies I had abandoned, I began to feel very foolish indeed.

My views on racism were influenced by my friendship with Derrick Bell. When I met Derrick in the late 1970s, he was an experienced civil rights lawyer and a professor at Harvard Law School who was rethinking his views about the persistence of racial segregation and racism. I naively believed that our society was making steady progress and that racism would eventually be stigmatized so much that it would never appear in public again. In time, I imagined, Americans would accept our nation's founding ideals as a guide to living. But Derrick believed that systemic racism was baked into our laws and institutions. Later, as I reevaluated my worldview, his doubts became my doubts. When Nicole Hannah-Jones published *The 1619 Project* in 2019, I read it with admiration and defended it. I appreciated critical race theory, a field of study in law schools Derrick Bell helped to found that examined the historical and institutional roots of racism. I realized that our lengthy discussions about the consequences of the *Brown* decision were an exercise in critical race theory, from which I learned and benefited. I shed my belief that racism would wither away; it had not, it has not, and I knew it. The evidence was everywhere, despite the election of Barack Obama. The election of Donald Trump in 2016 and 2024 exposed the persistence of racism and enabled racists to express their bigotry in public. As I turned against testing and choice, I also abandoned my Panglossian view that racism would magically disappear.

Aside from my reading, certain people changed my way of thinking, including my partner Mary, who was the founder and principal of an innovative high school. She shared with me her students' pressing everyday problems, few of which had to do with their academic program: they had been kicked out of their homes or they needed a coat or a shirt or their parents beat them. Standards and testing would not solve their problems. I was also influenced by the passionate activist Leonie Haimson, who has devoted her life to improving public schools in New York City, especially by reducing class size. She showed me the research on the value of smaller class sizes, and it was compelling. And I was changed too by my seven-year-long blog debate with the veteran progressive educator Deborah Meier in *Education Week* from 2005 to 2012; exchanging ideas every week with her took me out of my ideological bubble and compelled me to engage with very different views. Listening and talking to someone who holds different views, I realized, were all too rare; the people I knew, the books and articles I read, the ideas I encountered, reinforced my preexisting beliefs. Debating weekly with Deborah broadened my perspectives.

When the book was finished, I handed it over to my literary agent. Every few days, she would call to tell me it had been turned down by another publisher. At least a dozen major publishers rejected it. An editor at Holt wanted to talk to me. He told me that the book should be either a personal book or a policy book, but it could not be both. I refused his advice. The book had to be both personal and political.

Finally, a publisher liked it as it was. It was Basic Books, which had published my first two books in 1975 and 1978. The publisher who accepted my new book in 2009 was John Sherer, who later became director of the University of North Carolina Press. My editor, Tim Sullivan, suggested the title, borrowed from Jane Jacobs's classic book about the rebirth of American cities. The final title was *The Death and Life of the Great American School System: How Testing and Choice are Undermining Education*.

The book was released in the spring of 2010. The months before its publication were a torment. I remembered an animated Monty Python sketch in which a giant foot comes down and crushes an unsuspecting character. The giant foot, in my fears, belonged to the powerful billionaires, whose errors and arrogance I described in a chapter called "The Billionaire Boys' Club." That chapter was devoted to the power wielded by the Gates Foundation, which supported high-stakes testing, test-based teacher evaluation, and charter schools; by the Broad Foundation, which supported charter schools and offered a training program for school superintendents, where they were taught the value of top-down management, school closings, and disruption; and by the Walton Foundation, which poured millions every year into opening more charter schools. I imagined bad reviews for taking issue with "reform," because the mainstream media loves stories about "miracle" schools and teachers. I imagined the disappointment of my former colleagues, who would see my critique of testing and choice as a betrayal, not an awakening. I lost close friends who could not accept that my change of mind was genuine. I became a pariah in my former world of conservative intellectuals. A few conservative stalwarts asserted that I was bribed by the teachers' unions. A few education journalists wrote hostile articles, complaining that my change of views was "too sudden" and therefore not credible. One blogger wrote that I was like an unfaithful wife and that no one should ever trust me. Another journalist wrote that I was a lousy historian and a liar. Much to my surprise, the book reached the national bestseller list of *The New York Times*.

I learned how teachers would respond when I accepted my first speaking invitation from the San Jose, California, teachers' union. After I spoke, the room of three hundred people rose with a standing ovation. Then I spoke at the annual education conference sponsored by Channel 13, the New York City public television station. I made my way to the front of a large, empty ballroom 30 minutes early and sat in the first row, awaiting my introduction. When I went to the podium and looked out at the audience, I saw that the room was packed with more than one thousand people. Some were sitting in the aisles; others were standing on the sidelines against the walls. I described my change of mind and heart and again received a standing ovation.

I stopped reading personal attacks. I realized that if I spent my time pulling arrows out of my back, I would not be able to move forward. And I wanted to move forward because I felt a great sense of urgency about the gathering movement to privatize public education, divert public funding to charter schools and vouchers, tear down the wall of separation between church and state on behalf of public funding for religious schools, micromanage education from the top, demoralize the teaching profession, replace professional teachers with technology or amateur teachers from Teach for America, and reduce the remaining teacher workforce to gig workers without unions, pensions, or job security of any kind.

The reaction to the book was not the giant billionaire boot that I feared; it was surprisingly positive. *The New York Times* published a feature story about my change of views. The political scientist Alan Wolfe wrote a wonderful review in *The New York Times Book Review*. The *Washington Post* journalist Valerie Strauss interviewed me about the book on C-SPAN's *Book TV* show and wrote a glowing review. I was invited to speak to teachers and administrators across the country. Teachers were so hungry for support and affirmation that some actually cried as they thanked me for writing the book that, they said, told their story. The most important question they asked me was hardest to answer: How do we protect our public schools and our profession from this juggernaut of terrible ideas? All I could say was, inform yourselves; stay true to your professional ethics; join with others, including parents and other supporters of public education; attend school board meetings; run for school board; get active, stay active. We are many, and they are few; our numbers can overcome their vast resources.

The book opened doors.

I received an invitation to meet with Arne Duncan, the secretary of education, to share my views about testing. I told him why I thought that the emphasis on standardized testing in his Race to the Top program would have harmful effects, even if it raised test scores. He took notes but didn't say much. His assistant secretary for communications, Peter Cunningham, said to me later, "You measure what you treasure." I responded that I treasured my children, my partner, and my pets, and I asked, "How should I measure them? With a standardized test?" I don't recall his answer.

In 2010, the same year that *Death and Life* was published, I was invited to the Obama White House to meet with the administration's education leaders: Melody Barnes, director of the White House Domestic Policy

Council; Roberto Rodriguez, the White House education adviser; and Rahm Emanuel, the president's chief of staff. For whatever reason, Arne Duncan was not in attendance (after our meeting, he may have had enough of my advice). They asked me what I thought about the Common Core state standards, which were almost finished. I urged them to try the standards out in three to five states before imposing them on the nation. Work the kinks out, I said. Newly minted standards may look good on paper, but they need to be implemented in the classroom so that teachers can determine whether they are grade-appropriate; some might be too hard or too easy, and teachers are the best judge. The standards will be better if you get feedback on how they work, I said. They said that the standards had to be in place before the 2012 elections and there would not be time for trials. The group asked me what I thought of merit pay. I told them it had been tried repeatedly and never worked. They said that the president would be announcing a $1 billion merit pay program in the next few days. I loved being in the White House, but the meeting was disheartening.

I was also invited to speak to the Rainbow Push Coalition in Chicago. I eagerly accepted and was thrilled to meet the Reverend Jesse Jackson. In my conservative days, I disliked him. When I met him, he was kind, warm, and welcoming. I spoke at his church, and he took me by the hand and introduced me to his parishioners, then escorted me to an outdoor lunch for the members of his congregation. I was with him not just for my talk but all day. That evening he took me to a steak dinner with his closest associates. I saw a different man, different from the one I had seen many times on television. I felt enveloped by his presence and his warmth.

The high point of my travels after the publication of *Death and Life* occurred in Sacramento, California, where a group of teachers' unions from Sacramento and surrounding districts organized a spectacular rally in 2012. The unions hired the city's conference center and filled it with more than three thousand teachers and their friends on a rainy Friday night. I was introduced by California's leading educators, including the state commissioner of education. It was a thrilling, unforgettable night.

I followed up my visit to Sacramento with a side trip to the University of California at Berkeley to meet the famed linguist George Lakoff. I had read his bestseller *Don't Think of an Elephant! Know Your Values and Frame the Debate*, and I wanted his advice. How, I asked him, can I break through to the public about the dangers of privatization? How can I alert them to the gathering attack on their public schools? I described the drumbeat of propaganda engineered to undermine public confidence in public schools and the crisis of confidence it had created. Poll after poll showed that the public had a low opinion of "American education" but a high opinion of their own public schools, especially if they had children in them. Lakoff explained that liberals rely on facts and reason to make their arguments on any topic, while conservatives tell stories. Having facts on your side, he said, is never enough; you must frame the narrative so that it tells a compelling story. We talked for 2 hours. Our conversation was taped by a film crew that intended to make a documentary. They did, in fact, make a documentary called *Backpack Full of Cash*, about the dangers of privatizing public schools, directed by Sarah Mondale, produced by her and Vera Aronow, and narrated by Matt Damon. Unfortunately for me, but no doubt best for the film, my conversation with Lakoff ended up on the cutting-room floor. Mondale had previously produced a documentary series called *School: The Story of American Public Education* that was narrated by Meryl Streep and shown on PBS. However, PBS was not interested in airing *Backpack Full of Cash*, so its producers released it to community groups across the nation.

In Denver, I was supposed to address the Denver Teachers' Association in an auditorium at the University of Colorado. Denver's power elite was committed to the choice and testing policies I opposed. The day before I spoke, *The Denver Post* ran an editorial saying that I should not be allowed to speak at the university because I was "political." The university canceled my appearance, but the sponsors quickly shifted the venue to a local church, and the event proceeded as planned with a large and enthusiastic audience, mainly teachers.

As the author of *Death and Life*, I was invited to meet with the Democratic members of the House Committee on Education and the Workforce in Washington, D.C. The members gathered around a large conference table in the U.S. Capitol. Soon after the meeting started, Congressman Jared Polis of Colorado pulled out his copy of my book and said loudly that it was "the worst book" he had ever read. He then threw it across the table at me and said that he wanted his money back. One of the other members pulled out a $20 bill and bought Polis's copy. I later learned that Polis was one of the wealthiest members of Congress and that he had founded two charter schools in Colorado. Polis later became governor of Colorado, where he continued to promote charter schools.

That night, Connecticut congresswoman Rosa DeLauro hosted a dinner in her home for the members of the House Committee, and I was the featured speaker. The minority chair of the committee, George Miller of California, reacted with sullen anger to everything I said. In response to my criticism of George W. Bush's NCLB, he muttered that NCLB was the best thing that had ever happened for poor children. I disagreed with him, pointing out that NCLB testing was not only stigmatizing them but also robbing them of instructional time, while the closing of their neighborhood schools was disrupting their communities and their education. He sat with his arms crossed over his chest, and DeLauro chided him, saying, "George, don't act like a baby." I later learned that Nancy Pelosi considered him the ultimate decider of the Democratic position on education issues; in addition, he was a favorite recipient of funding by the corporate reform group called "Democrats for Education Reform" (DFER), an organization of hedge fund managers that lobbied vigorously for high-stakes testing, evaluation of teachers by student scores, and privately managed charter schools. DFER repeatedly endorsed George Miller and raised money for his campaigns, as well as the campaigns of other Democrats.

Death and Life was published in the same year as the release of the documentary *Waiting for "Superman."* Robert Silvers, the founding editor of *The New York Review of Books*, asked me to review the film. I went with Mary to a plush screening room that held about two hundred people in the headquarters of Viacom in Manhattan. We took our seats and waited for the film to begin. The lights were dimmed. But then we saw Barbara Walters walking down the carpeted stairs; she tripped and landed on her face. Mary jumped up and pulled her to her feet as everyone else sat still and watched in horror.

The film's thesis was that public schools were failing and damaging their students and that the only hope to save them was charter schools. It followed four students who were struggling in their public schools (and one in a Catholic school) but had the good fortune to gain admission to a charter school, where they flourished. The film heaped praise on the corporate reform movement and poured scorn on public schools, their teachers, teacher tenure, and teachers' unions. The heroes of the film were Michelle Rhee, Joel Klein, Bill Gates, Geoffrey Canada, and other leaders of the reform movement. In my review of the film for *The New York Review of Books*, I pointed out that it distorted the statistics of the National Assessment of Educational Progress to make public schools look bad. The narrator mentioned, but quickly glossed over, a major charter school study showing that only 17 percent of charter schools registered higher test scores than public schools. The film failed to get an Academy Award nomination, and one Hollywood publication (*The Hollywood Reporter*) cited my review as one of the reasons (the other, more important, reason was that the documentary included a staged scene).

It struck me as peculiar that the charter movement had the financial support of billionaires on the far right, like the Walton Family Foundation, the Koch brothers, the DeVos family, and Philip Anschutz, but also centrists like Bill Gates, Reed Hastings (the billionaire founder of Netflix), and Michael Bloomberg. I have long suspected that the very determined people on the far right play the long game and that they snookered the technocratic billionaires into supporting the privatization of public education.

What was especially frustrating was to see conservatives using the language of civil rights to promote their attack on the public sector, on public education, and on unions. They sold privatization by claiming that it would benefit Black kids and poor kids, as if the market were ever beneficial to those who were at the bottom. This was a dishonest strategy. I knew about it from my own experience as a senior fellow at the Manhattan Institute, when I testified on behalf of charter legislation in New York State. Charter schools and vouchers, their promoters promised, would "save poor kids from failing public schools." This claim made their cause seem liberal, but it was not true. "Rich white kids have choice, why shouldn't poor Black kids have choice too?," said billionaires like Betsy DeVos, who was Donald Trump's secretary of education. DeVos, Jeb Bush, the Koch brothers, and other promoters of vouchers knew that the choices available to students who left public schools would not be Andover or Exeter or Sidwell Friends, or whatever the local equivalent was, where tuition was many times higher than any voucher and where there were no empty seats and no interest in accepting struggling students from impoverished communities. Their choices would be religious schools and underresourced private schools. School choice meant that schools would choose the students they wanted and reject or remove those they did not want.

What school choice advocates glossed over was the history of their cause; it originated in the South in the 1950s, after the *Brown* decision of 1954, as white segregationists sought public money to subsidize vouchers and white flight academies so that white students would not have to attend school with Black students. Despite lots of rhetorical footwork, the reality was that "school choice" was launched as a ruse to avoid desegregation. In our own time, voucher schools operated outside of the constraints of anti-discrimination law; they could choose students of their own religion and exclude students for any reason, including their race or disability status or test scores or sexual orientation.

My busy lecture schedule included a lecture in the fall of 2010 at Wayne State University in Detroit. The next day, I was going to fly to Los Angeles, changing planes in Chicago. I realized that it would be a chance to meet the new leader of the Chicago Teachers Union, Karen Lewis. As head of the upstart Caucus of Rank-and-File Educators (CORE), she had won a surprise victory in June 2010 over the established union leadership and became an outspoken opponent of school privatization. Chicago's superintendent Arne Duncan (later, Obama's secretary of education) had launched a plan in 2004 called Renaissance 2010 to close public schools and replace them with charter schools; he eventually closed nearly one hundred public schools and encouraged their replacement by nonunion charter schools. I contacted Michael Klonsky, a new friend whom I had met (thanks to Deborah Meier) on a previous visit to Chicago, and Mike connected me to Karen (irony of ironies: in the 1960s, Mike Klonsky had been a leader of Students for a Democratic Society, a group that I detested at the time for its radicalism). I told

Karen in an e-mail that I could arrange a 90-minute layover in Chicago to give us time to talk. She responded: "Oh, no, you must have a 4-hour layover. We have a lot to talk about." I changed my flight schedule.

When I landed in Chicago, Karen and her husband John brought me to an airport hotel, where we sat in an empty ballroom and talked for 3 hours. I felt I was talking to my sister. We exchanged stories about our lives, our values, and the issues that concerned us. She had a dog-eared copy of *Death and Life*, with underlining, exclamation points, and Post-its all over its pages. I felt that I could open my soul to Karen, as she opened hers. I was sorry when the time came for me to leave.

Two years later, Karen led the Chicago Teachers Union (CTU) in a citywide strike. The privatizers, acting with the aid of a group called Stand for Children, enacted legislation that barred any strike that had a vote of less than 75 percent of its membership. In a widely circulated video from the Aspen Ideas Festival of 2011, Jonah Edelman, the leader of Stand for Children, boasted about how he had outsmarted the unions by hiring all the best lobbyists, spending money from conservative billionaires to secure the votes of Democratic members of the legislature, and winning passage of a bill that set a threshold for teachers' strikes that he believed would never be met. His belief proved wrong in 2012 when Karen took the strike vote to her members and nearly 90 percent voted to strike. When the video of Edelman's Aspen anti-union talk went online, he apologized for his remarks, but Stand for Children continued to promote corporate reform.

Karen became a dear friend; she was warm, bold, brilliant, and brassy. She was a graduate of Dartmouth College, and she was never cowed by the powerful billionaires who hated teachers, unions, and public schools. I recall when we discussed the billionaire Bruce Rauner, a major supporter of charter schools and a future governor of Illinois, elected in 2015. She said he had tried to intimidate her, and she told him, "Listen, buster, I wore the green jacket too" (like Karen, Rauner was a graduate of Dartmouth, the home of the green jacket). When Rauner launched his campaign, Karen referred to him in *Chicago* magazine as "a menace to society."

In 2012, I won an award from a private foundation (the Dolores Kohl Education Prize) in Chicago and attended a private dinner for sixteen people, where I met Rauner. We debated his fealty to charter schools across our table. I asked him, "What about the children with disabilities? What about the children who have learning issues?" He said bluntly that he didn't care what happened to them. His charter schools were for strivers who were likely to succeed. On a different occasion, Karen told me that Mayor Emanuel had told her matter-of-factly that one quarter of the children in Chicago were "uneducable." We were appalled by their indifference to the most vulnerable children.

She was preparing to run against Rahm Emanuel for mayor of Chicago in 2014 when she was stricken with a brain tumor. She stepped down as the CTU president. I continued to visit with her during her illness whenever I was in Chicago, and she never lost her sharp wit. She died in 2021 at the age of sixty-seven. Her death was a great loss for teachers and public schools across the nation. I loved her dearly.

In 2011, I was invited to debate the founder of TFA, Wendy Kopp, at the Aspen Institute, the same one where Jonah Edelman made his infamous boast about outfoxing the teachers' unions in Illinois to prevent them from striking. The conference was dedicated to "reform" of the kind I opposed. At our debate, Kopp spoke corporate-speak, the kind of sloganeering that you would give to a friendly CEO, replete with uplifting phrases: "It can be done. It is being done. We are doing it." Of course, I disagreed. TFA was a huge financial success, with revenues of hundreds of millions of dollars each year, but it had little impact on the nation's classrooms, especially in impoverished communities. Education cannot be improved by replacing experienced teachers with young college graduates who have five weeks of training and plan to leave after two years. Founded in 1989, TFA had drawn about seventy thousand young people into teaching over the course of thirty-five years, of whom about fifteen thousand continued to work in the classroom. In a profession of more than 3 million teachers, TFA was less than a drop in the bucket. Worse, it created the illusion of solving a national problem: a shortage of excellent teachers who are committed to their profession for the long haul and who would teach the neediest students.

Later that same day at Aspen, I gave a lecture contending that the current school reform movement was on the wrong track because it ignored the devastating effects of poverty on children, families, and communities. David Brooks of *The New York Times* was in the audience. We spoke afterwards, and he was very cordial. Imagine how surprised I was when, several days later, he wrote a scathing column rebuking my views. He challenged my critique of testing and insisted that the very best charter schools emphasize testing but also have a wonderful array of engaging classes. He accused me of parroting the line of the teachers' unions that poverty is the real issue, not bad schools (which I believe is a fact, not a union excuse). *The New York Times* allowed me to respond to him, and I did, by pointing out that tests should be used for diagnostics, not to hand out bonuses, fire teachers, and close schools. I repeated that poverty has an indisputable influence on academic achievement, and our society must both improve schools and reduce poverty.

That exchange occurred in 2011. Two years earlier, Brooks had lavishly praised the charter schools of Geoffrey Canada's Harlem Children's Zone as "the Harlem Miracle," proof that poor children can become excellent scholars. (Canada was one of the stars of *Waiting for "Superman."*) Brooks gushed over the "no excuses culture" and admired the schools for weaving standardized tests "into the fabric of school life." Only a year later, *The New York Times* published a long article about the problems of the "Harlem Miracle" schools. Despite their lavish spending, their hefty endowment, and their small class sizes, student performance on state tests was mediocre. The 2009 scores that Brooks hailed, it turns out, were based on state tests that were dumbed down, the same tests that enabled Michael Bloomberg to win a third term as mayor. Geoffrey Canada burnished his reform credentials when he ousted the entire first-year class of students because of their persistently low scores on state tests. I debated Canada on an NBC program called *Education Nation*, funded by Bill Gates. I asked him why he ousted every one of the first-year students he had recruited with a promise that they would go to college. He didn't deny it; he boasted that it was the right thing to do, and the reform-dominated audience applauded vigorously. No one seemed to care that booting out a whole class of students is profoundly demoralizing.

A few weeks after returning from my debate with Wendy Kopp in Aspen, the public park on the other side of the Brooklyn Bridge was filled by protesters against economic inequality and the 1 Percent, who hoarded more and more of society's wealth. I got a call one day from a young man who asked me to speak to the protesters and to donate a copy of *Death and Life* to the Occupy Wall Street library, an open-air library in the park consisting of wooden bookcases shielded from the weather by a canvas tarp. We agreed to meet; he told me to look for him in a red jacket. I went to Zuccotti Park and wandered among the protesters; most of the men were wearing red jackets. I never found him, but I overcame my hostility toward radicals and protesters: *I was one of them*. I did find the library and gave the volunteer librarian a copy of the book. A few days later, Mayor Bloomberg decided it was time to clean up Zuccotti Park, and the police cleared out all the protesters, tore down their tents, and threw the Occupy Wall Street library into a dumpster, where the books were left to rot. I was proud that my book was among those in that rain-soaked dumpster.

One of the most memorable of my speaking engagements was a peculiar nondebate with Michelle Rhee. Rhee was the brightest star of the "reform movement," selected as chancellor of the District of Columbia public schools despite her lack of any administrative experience. After preparation by TFA, she had taught in Baltimore, where she claimed to have dramatically raised her students' test scores (a claim that was subsequently debunked by the retired teacher and blogger G. F. Brandenburg). As chancellor, she pledged to fire principals and teachers, clearing out all the deadwood until the district's scores rose to become the highest of any urban school district in the nation. She appeared on the covers of both *TIME* and *Newsweek* magazines based on her bold stances. When the mayor who appointed her was defeated in 2010, she left her position and led a campaign for charter schools and vouchers.

Lehigh University wanted to sponsor a debate between Rhee and me. The university contacted my speaking agent and her speaking agent, and we agreed to debate. Then Rhee's agent said she wanted two people on each side; I agreed. Then the agent came back to say that Rhee wanted three people on each side. I noted that it was turning into a panel discussion but agreed. Then she dropped out. She would not debate me, whether it was one versus one, two versus two, or three versus three. Lehigh asked me to speak without her, and I agreed. I decided to hold the debate as intended and to represent both sides. I asked questions. I answered as I thought Rhee would have. Then, I answered Rhee. I kept this up for about 45 minutes, and in my personal view, it was hilarious and thoroughly enjoyable. Of course, I won.

At the time I was out on the lecture trail, the "reform movement" was celebrated in the media. I hammered their harmful ideas, and teachers were thrilled to have someone supporting them and validating their hard work. I criticized the reformers' claim that the way to fix schools was to fire teachers, fire principals, and close schools. They believed that new teachers, new principals, and new schools would somehow be superior to those they replaced. They believed that this sort of punitive action would lead to a "miracle." All children would get high test scores, go to college, and escape poverty. Sadly, it never happened in any district. School improvement is never "a miracle." The search for miracles and panaceas is a persistent fantasy that harms American education and sets up educators and students for failure.

My philosophy of education had changed. Whereas I had long advocated for high-stakes testing and considered test scores as a measure of success, I now knew that test scores reflect the advantages enjoyed by well-to-do students: being secure in their homes and well-fed; having regular visits to the doctor, trips to the library, museums, and other places of cultural value; having dinner-table discussions about politics and the world; and being exposed to a large vocabulary and correct syntax. Test scores reflect the demographics of the classroom and the school, not the skill of the teacher.

I had always believed that schools should be places of learning, where the curriculum should be rich with possibilities for deepening the joy of learning. School should be where students encounter great literature, become immersed in history and in debates about history, where they learn the sciences they need to understand important public issues, where they master mathematics, where they are introduced to the arts, and where they gain the knowledge and skills to appreciate democracy and to engage in civic life. And of course, students should participate in athletics to the best of their ability and learn the essentials of good health.

But after my transformation, I saw the role of the school in a broader context. School is about much more than test taking and competition for scores. School should be a place where well-educated, well-prepared teachers guide and inspire students as they learn new skills and knowledge and self-discipline. School should be a place where everyone discovers new worlds and learns what interests them most, how to be a responsible person, and how to work collaboratively with others. For the adults who teach, the work should bring them honor, respect, professional wages, and satisfaction, which it seldom does in a world where human value is measured in dollar signs, not in service to others. The experience of schooling should prepare young people to live and work with others in a democratic society and to contribute to the improvement of that society. Schools should encourage students to be the best they can be, not to be standardized into a preset mold.

Through hard experience and my own mistakes, I learned that schools cannot be measured solely by test scores, nor should anyone believe in tales of "miracle schools." As Carl Cohn, former superintendent of the Long Beach Unified School District and the San Diego Unified School District in California, wrote in an article in *Education Week*, which I quoted in *Death and Life*: "There are no quick fixes or perfect educational theories. School reform is a slow, steady labor-intensive process" that depends on harnessing the talent of individuals "instead of punishing them for noncompliance with bureaucratic mandates and destroying their initiative." He predicted that "ground-level solutions, such as high-quality leadership, staff collaboration, committed teachers, and clean and safe environments, have the best chance of success." A precondition for success is trust, trust among administrators and teachers, teachers and parents, and teachers and students. This trust is endangered when the schools are targets of abuse, when teachers are disrespected by the media, when the complex work of education is reduced to test scores, and when legislators insert themselves into education, usurp the roles of professional educators, and make decisions that affect curriculum and teaching methods and that determine which books are permitted in classrooms and libraries.

16

ACTIVISM

Having worked inside right-wing think tanks, having heard the inside chatter, I came to understand that the end goal of testing and corporate school reform was privatization. The rhetoric of "failing schools" was intended to persuade the public that radical change was needed and that the "crisis" of "failing public schools" justified public funds for privately managed charter schools and vouchers for private and religious schools, for-profit schools, even homeschooling. Reformers were certain that the alternatives would get higher scores than the beleaguered public schools would. After more than thirty years of charters and twenty-five years of vouchers, it is now obvious that the alternatives are not better than the public schools and are often far worse. Some charters (those that choose their students with care and oust those they do not want) get higher scores than public schools, most charters get about the same scores, and some charters are abysmal. A significant number of charters close their doors every year, either because of financial or academic failure or outright fraud by their owners. Voucher schools are worse for kids than the public schools they left. Students who leave public schools for private or religious schools using a voucher typically see declines in their academic performance as compared to the peers they left behind in public schools. In every state with vouchers, most students who take them were already enrolled in private or religious schools.

Vouchers benefit religious schools that indoctrinate their students into their beliefs and, unlike public schools, are free to discriminate against students who have disabilities or are gay or do not share their religion. Some voucher-funded religious schools use the Bible as their primary textbook. As the voucher movement became the ultimate education reform in Republican-dominated states, vouchers were extended to all students, even rich kids in private schools. Vouchers turned into a giveaway of public funds to affluent families, not to poor kids "escaping" public schools. Wherever universal vouchers were introduced, they were an enormous drain on the state budget, which had not previously subsidized the tuition of all private school students, even the children of the wealthy.

I determined to use my knowledge and experience to expose the reformers' goal of destroying public education. Beginning with the publication of *The Death and Life of the Great American School System*, I dedicated myself to the singular mission of revealing the well-funded cabal that seeks to privatize the funding of education. I wrote. I spoke. I continued to do research. I made it my mission to connect the dots, to expose the right-wing billionaires, the religious zealots, and the free marketeers behind privatization, and to strip away the pretense that school choice is "the civil rights issue of our time." I knew, and I wanted the world to know, that privatization originated in white flight to avoid desegregation and invariably exacerbates segregation and disadvantages the poorest and neediest children. It is neither progressive nor liberal to support privatization of public services. Privatization is theft of what belongs to the citizenry.

I came across this excellent commentary in English folklore:

> *The law doth punish man or woman,*
> *That steals the goose from off the common.*
> *But lets the greater felon loose,*
> *That steals the common from the goose.*

Would the public awaken to the theft of what belonged to them?

But nothing I did alone would ever be enough to counter the money and power of the billionaires behind the sham reform movement.

I placed my bets on democracy, on the hope that an aroused public could change the odds. In July 2011, I joined with other education activists at the Save Our Schools (SOS) march on Washington, where several thousands of teachers, parents, students, and concerned citizens joined to protest the toxic policies of George W. Bush's No Child Left Behind (NCLB) and Barack Obama's Race to the Top. At the march, I met Anthony Cody, a middle-school science teacher from Oakland, California, and a well-known blogger. Anthony and I had corresponded before the SOS march but met there for the first time. We stayed in contact, trying to think of ways to sustain the movement against the punitive Bush-Obama policies. We knew that wealthy individuals and financiers funded anti-public-school candidates in state and local races. Anthony thought we should start a PAC, a political action committee, to support pro-public-school candidates. We had no money to give to candidates, but we thought that an endorsement might serve as a "Good Housekeeping" seal of approval. Neither of us is a lawyer, so we asked Randi Weingarten if someone at the American Federation of Teachers (AFT) could give us advice. The AFT lawyer said it was very expensive to start a PAC because every state has different laws governing PACs. We decided to start an organization that was not a PAC, one that would facilitate connections among the many grassroots groups across the country. After many e-mails and conversations, we assembled a board, and in March 2013 we announced the creation of the Network for Public Education (NPE).

NPE is now a thriving organization with 350,000 followers, located in every state, and a paid staff: one full-time executive director—Carol Burris, who had a distinguished career as a teacher and principal in New York and is a statistical whiz as well as a terrific writer—and two part-time employees.

NPE holds an annual conference that brings together activists from across the nation to meet and learn from one another. It publishes deeply researched reports about the failures of privatization. Its reports have been valuable in demonstrating, for example, the waste, fraud, and abuse in the federal Charter Schools Program, which dispenses $440 million every year for new charter schools and charter school expansion, mostly handed out to well-funded charter chains. NPE's reports about the poor results of the Charter Schools Program prompted the U.S. Department of Education to issue regulations in 2021 for the program, for the first time since it was created in 1994 as a $6 million program to spur charter school growth. At that time, there were only a few dozen charter schools in the whole country; now there are more than seven thousand. The need for the federal payout has disappeared, but the charter lobby fiercely defends it and fights for more funding, less oversight, and no accountability. After the election of Donald Trump in 2024, federal funding of charter schools is certain to grow, despite ample evidence that they do not provide better education than public schools and, in some states, are supporting white flight academies.

In 2012, while Anthony and I were planning the launch of the NPE, I started my own blog. I had been blogging weekly at *Education Week* since 2007 with Deborah Meier. I will never forget how I became friends with Deborah, the quintessential progressive educator. In 1984, Deborah wrote a scathing review of my book *The Troubled Crusade* in a left-wing publication called *Dissent*, edited by the estimable Irving Howe. Deborah and I had never met. I let it go, but a few years later, I spoke to Al Shanker about my bad relationship with her. He said, "Why don't you call her?" I did. I reached her at her school, Central Park East Elementary School in East Harlem, and when she answered, I said, "Hi, Deborah, this is Diane Ravitch. I know you are familiar with my work, but I am not familiar with yours. May I come and visit your school?" She readily agreed, and a day later I spent two hours walking around her school and talking about education with her. Despite our disagreements, we became good friends, and it was easy to start blogging together, which we did from 2007 to 2012. In 2012, I started my own blog.

I liked the format of blogging because it encouraged informality and ease of expression. Unlike when submitting a piece to a major newspaper, I didn't have to worry if it would be accepted or if an overzealous editor would chop it up. I posted multiple pieces every day, usually something I read that I wanted to share. Occasionally I wrote original pieces. A decade later, the blog passed 40 million page views.

One day in 2012, I spoke at the Education Law Center at Rutgers University, a civil rights organization in New Jersey. I was accompanied by

David Denby of *The New Yorker*, who was writing a piece about me. He told me that he had interviewed my detractors, and they said that I had only criticisms, no solutions. So I decided to write another book that answered their criticisms and offered specific solutions.

I determined to debunk every phony claim that the corporate reform movement made about the alleged failure of the public schools. I demonstrated with graphs and other data that the public schools were not failing. Using U.S. Department of Education data, I showed that test scores and graduation rates were at that time the highest ever for students of every group; and that scores on international tests, where the United States usually placed in the middle, bore no relationship to economic progress. I offered specific, research-based solutions to the problems of children and the schools. I had chapters on the need for prenatal health care, the value of reduced class sizes, and the importance of school-based health clinics. If anything was failing, it was the quack "reforms" being imposed on the public schools by the federal government and a bevy of arrogant billionaires; these so-called reforms were hurting the schools and demoralizing teachers. I wanted to arm readers with the information they needed to fend off attacks on their community's schools. The book was published in 2013 and titled *Reign of Error: The Hoax of the Privatization Movement and the Danger to America's Public Schools*. I was fortunate that the new book was published by Knopf and edited by the legendary Victoria Wilson. Like the previous book, *Reign of Error* was a national bestseller. Again, there was a flurry of media appearances. I was interviewed by Bill Moyers, Dan Rather, and Charlie Rose. Again, I traveled the country, appearing on local television shows and speaking at universities.

Things were going well, but then I had a horrific accident. In April 2014, I tripped and fell while hurrying down the front steps of our house in Southold. I landed on a paving stone with my full body weight on my left knee. I heard a loud crack. I couldn't stand up. Mary was away visiting her college friends in Georgia. I dragged myself up the stairs and called a neighbor. The neighbor called an ambulance, which took me to the local hospital, which didn't have the equipment to diagnose the extent of the damage. My son Michael took a bus to Southold and drove me back to Brooklyn that night. A surgeon at the Hospital for Special Surgery told me I needed a total knee replacement, which he could not perform until two weeks later. Meanwhile, I was planning to go to Louisville, Kentucky, to receive the Grawemeyer Award from the University of Louisville for *The Death and Life of the Great American School System*. The prize carried an award of $100,000. I had to appear in person or sacrifice the award. I wasn't sure I could make the trip safely because my knee kept collapsing, and I crashed into a few walls. Nonetheless, Mary and I went to Louisville, shared some splendid Kentucky bourbon with the wonderful staff at the university, and on the appointed day I walked up to the podium without a cane or crutches or walker, not sure whether I would topple over. I made it through the ceremony and the dinner with no falls and returned home to prepare for surgery. A life lesson: Always hold on to the handrail!

Unlike my recovery in 1998 from a pulmonary embolism, which was life-threatening but pain-free, the period after knee surgery was a nightmare. I was in agony, could not straighten my leg, and went into a deep depression. Physical therapy did not help. I imagined a lifetime of disability, pushing a walker.

Then my college classmate Linda Gottlieb (always there at crucial moments in my life) recommended a new physical therapist, who said my knee was encased in scar tissue and would never heal unless I saw a specialist. Mary and I flew to Cincinnati to see Dr. Frank Noyes, a specialist in arthrofibrosis (scar tissue). Dr. Noyes brought me to a small room, where I sat on a table and stretched my bent knee to another table. Two husky men pressed down as hard as they could until my leg was forced straight. Tears were rolling down my cheeks. While they held my leg straight, another aide built a cast around my entire leg. When it was dry a few minutes later, the aide split the cast open and lined it with cotton and gauze. Dr. Noyes told me to wear it on my leg for 8 to 10 hours a day for at least six weeks. I followed his instructions, and six weeks later my leg was straight.

My period of recuperation slowed down my travels and speaking, but I continued to write my blog. The toxic years of the Trump administration absorbed my creative energies. I blogged daily, but I—and everyone who cared about the future of the nation's public schools and about the future of democracy—were constantly taken aback by Trump's vicious attacks on the press, on his rivals, on the Constitution, and on the dignity of his office. I was appalled by Secretary of Education Betsy DeVos's vitriolic criticism of public schools, our most democratic institution, and the growing political power of right-wing billionaires, their libertarian allies, religious zealots, and white-supremacist militant groups.

I wasn't sure I had another book to write, but I was inspired by the wave of teachers' strikes that began in West Virginia in 2018 and swept across the country. I began to collect stories about parents, students, teachers, and community leaders who courageously fought back against school privatization. I wrote a book about these heroes who stood up to the powerful and won. It was called *Slaying Goliath: The Passionate Resistance to Privatization and the Fight to Save America's Public Schools*. It was published by Knopf in January 2020. I began my book tour in Brooklyn that January, then traveled to Seattle, San Francisco, Los Angeles, Chicago, Miami, Boston, and D.C. My last stop, fittingly enough, was the capital of West Virginia, where I met with and addressed the teachers who had participated in the historic strike of 2018. They ended their strike after the governor promised that he would not allow charter schools or vouchers. They went back to work, and the governor went back on his promises. West Virginia's Republican legislature passed both charter schools in 2019 and vouchers in 2021, with the intention that vouchers would be available to all students by 2026. And, as in other states, vouchers in West Virginia will mostly subsidize families whose children are already enrolled in private schools.

By the time I got back to Brooklyn, the country was starting to close down due to the COVID pandemic. When the book tour was over, a month after publication, the biggest education issues were whether schools should remain open or closed and whether students should wear masks. Privatization and robber barons and teachers' strikes were no longer near the top of the public agenda. It didn't help that, for the first time in my life, the book got a lousy review in *The New York Times Book Review*. The reviewer did not agree with my concerns about privatization or my belief that public schools are a public good. Those are the breaks.

Meanwhile, the struggle to save our public schools goes on. Republicans have made school choice—charters, vouchers, cyberschooling, even homeschooling—a central issue in their state and national platforms. Thanks to Arne Duncan's Race to the Top, almost every state has authorized charter schools. Two-thirds of states have endorsed vouchers for private and religious schools, and a growing number of conservative states make vouchers available to all students, without regard to family income. Thanks to Donald Trump's three appointees to the Supreme Court, the High Court directed the state of Maine to pay tuition for students at two evangelical religious schools because the state already paid tuition for private high schools in communities where no public high schools were available. These two religious schools discriminate against students who do not share their religious views and against gay students, their families, and staff. The Court majority ruled that the students' inability to choose a religious school violated their religious freedom. Only a few years ago, such a decision from the Supreme Court would have been unimaginable. The Court has always tried to balance the First Amendment's "freedom of religion" clause with its prohibition against an "establishment" of religion. Thomas Jefferson's description of a "wall of separation between church and state" guided state funding most (but not all) of the time; exceptions were made for bus transportation, textbooks, tests, and any services mandated by the state. That wall is crumbling, and the public is likely to be stuck with paying for religious schools, subsidizing wealthy families in elite private schools, and underwriting segregation and discrimination. The research on the negative effects of vouchers is clear: in every state that has adopted vouchers, the majority of students who use them were already enrolled in private and religious schools; the students who leave public schools to use a voucher do not enroll in a better school and do not experience academic gains. In fact, most fall behind their peers in public schools. Josh Cowen, a professor of education policy at Michigan State University, spelled out the research on vouchers in his book *The Privateers: How Billionaires Created a Culture War and Sold School Vouchers*. States with universal voucher programs have experienced budget-busting costs by sending money to families who previously paid for their children's tuition. Yet

Republicans continue to demand universal vouchers, no doubt to solidify their support among affluent voters.

Those who believe in the importance of free public education, devoid of religious indoctrination, free of discrimination, will have to fight for it, not only state by state but also at the national level. The re-election of Donald Trump exponentially increased the hazards of privatization for public schools. Ten days after his 2025 inauguration, he signed executive orders that directly threatened the funding and curriculum of public schools. One executive order, called "Expanding Educational Freedom and Opportunity for Families," promised to turn federal funds over to the states to be used for school choice; even formula-driven funds for low-income students and students with disabilities would be converted to "block grants" that states could use for school choice. The second executive order, titled "Ending Radical Indoctrination in K-12 Schooling," threatened to cut off federal funding to any school that taught diversity, equity, or inclusion, or, as the order put it, "radical gender ideology" or "discriminatory equity ideology." The schools were also ordered to teach "patriotic education," meaning to celebrate the nation's greatness. Whoever wrote that order apparently was unaware that since 1970 federal law has forbidden any federal officials from exercising any "direction, supervision, or control over the curriculum, program of instruction . . . or over the selection of library resources, textbooks, or other printed or published instructional materials."

Trump's efforts to ban diversity, equity, and inclusion (DEI) are doomed to fail. He may force schools, universities, and large organizations that receive federal funding to stop using those words, but the words represent genuine changes in society. DEI, as its critics call these ideas, was not hatched by the U.S. Department of Education. No one forced these ideas on public schools and workplaces. They arose from sincere efforts to create opportunities for women and people of color to succeed. They are baked into our American ideals of fairness for all. There is certainly more indoctrination happening in religious schools than in public schools; indoctrination is one of the central purposes of religious schools.

It is undeniably a fact that our nation is diverse. Banning the word doesn't change the reality. We are a nation whose inhabitants include people of every race, religion, national origin, and ethnicity. We are a nation of men and women, and yes, people who are LGBT. Yes, our population does include transgender men and women, and not even Trump can erase them.

Equity is a necessity if we are serious about reducing the vast economic and social gaps in our society. Equity does not mean hiring or admitting unqualified people because of their race or gender; it means making a conscious effort to expand opportunity for qualified applicants who are not white males. In my lifetime, it was President Lyndon B. Johnson who offered the classic definition of equity in a speech he delivered at Howard University on June 4, 1965 (written by his aide Daniel Patrick Moynihan).

He said:

> You do not take a person who, for years has been hobbled by chains and liberate him, bring him up to the starting line of a race and then say, "you are free to compete with all the others," and still justly believe that you have been completely fair.
>
> Thus it is not enough just to open the gates of opportunity. All our citizens must have the ability to walk through those gates.
>
> This is the next and the more profound stage of the battle for civil rights. We seek not just freedom but opportunity. We seek not just legal equity but human ability, not just equality as a right and a theory but equality as a fact and equality as a result.

As for inclusion, it means nothing more nor less than *all*. When we say the Pledge of Allegiance, as I did every school day in Houston, we spoke of "liberty and justice for all," not for some. *All* means all. *All* means inclusion.

When the U.S. team marches together into the Olympic stadium, it is the most diverse team in the world. I feel proud when I see them. If I had buttons on my shirt, they would surely burst.

The hateful, calculated attack on our nation's public schools is motivated by a fervent desire to reverse the strides our nation has made in protecting the civil rights of everyone. It is driven by racism and a desire to return to the 1950s, to a time before the legislative achievements of the civil rights movement.

This retrograde activism is driven not only by bigotry but also by Christian nationalism, by religious zealots who want to impose their religious ideology on everyone else. They want to obscure the Founding Fathers' unqualified commitment to a secular nation, in which no religion is favored over another, in which all Americans are free to practice their religion or no religion. Article VI, clause 3 of the Constitution says there shall be no religious test for public office. In the First Amendment, the Founders guaranteed religious freedom and opposed the establishment (government endorsement) of any religion. And there is more that demonstrates the secularism of the Founders. In 1787, the U.S. Congress endorsed the Northwest Ordinance, which described how the Northwest Territory (which eventually would become the states of Ohio, Indiana, Illinois, Wisconsin, and Michigan) would be governed. The ordinance divided every town into thirty-six lots and reserved a center lot for public schools that would be paid for by taxes. No lot was set aside for religious schools. It is simply impossible to study American history and conclude that the Founding Fathers wanted the new nation to be a "Christian nation." They did not.

These next few years will surely involve painful episodes, as a bigoted president and a bigoted administration attempt to reverse history. We will push back. They will fail. The Gulf of Mexico will still be the Gulf of Mexico. No matter what Trump says or how many executive orders he releases, he cannot turn back history. He cannot erase reality. A horse will still be a horse even if you order everyone to call it a camel, even if they comply for the moment or for four years. Reality, common sense, decency, and hope for a good society will prevail over ignorance and hatred.

We can restore public education to its role as a key foundation of our democracy. But we can't go back to the schools of a century ago. We must have a more generous, contemporary vision of public schools and what they can be. The movement for community schools points us in a new direction, towards schools that truly serve families and their children, with medical clinics, food pantries, adult education, counseling, summer programs, after-school programs, and connections to other supports that help students and their families to thrive. High schools must broaden their offerings to include career and technical programs for students who want to seek employment directly after obtaining their high school diploma.

If we work with determination, we can drive out the billionaires, the grifters, the heartless libertarians, and the religious zealots who now seek control of our public schools. If we push back hard enough, we can reclaim the public schools that belong to all of us. Any parent who wants their child to have a private or religious education may exercise that choice, but they should not expect the public to pay for it.

Public schools are an essential element of our democracy. If we relinquish them to private interests for private purposes, education will become a consumer good, not a civic responsibility. Should that happen, voters and taxpayers will withdraw their support, as will those who have no children or whose children are no longer of school age. We—all of us—fund public schools just as we pay taxes to support the police, firefighters, public highways, public beaches, and public transportation. We support public services because they serve the public. We support public schools because society benefits by having an educated citizenry. If we lose sight of the common good, our democracy will suffer.

FINAL WORDS

When I set out to write this book, I wanted to give the reader some idea of what it was like to grow up in Houston in the 1940s and 1950s in a very large family that was always struggling to pay the bills and at the same time put up a good front. I wanted to explain how my views changed, rather dramatically. I went from being a prominent neoconservative to a proudly "woke" liberal. For a long time, I embraced the idea of test-based meritocracy. I now think of that period as my time on "the dark side." As a high school student, I had high test scores, despite the fact that my family was neither privileged nor affluent, so I thought that high test scores were the best indicator of talent. It is a supremely selfish point of view. It was good for me, so it must be good for everyone else. Now, having lived a long life, I can say with certainty that I was wrong. Everyone, without regard to their test scores, by virtue of their humanity, deserves to live a good life, with decent housing and food security, medical care, educational opportunity, and the chance to develop their talents, abilities, and interests to the fullest. Although I opposed affirmative action in the past, I believe that it was good for our country and invaluable in helping young people of color break barriers into higher education and into the professions. As a woman, I am now ashamed of my antagonism toward the women's movement in the years when I was married. Again,

I was acting from a place of privilege as well as in deference to my husband. I have changed, and so have the times. When I was in college, my class was all white. Today, graduates of my all-female college are remarkably diverse and are serving in the military and are leaders in science, medicine, the arts, and government, and I am proud of them. As Hillary Clinton said, "Women's rights are human rights." And so are the rights of LGBT people. I support policies that help others to live lives of dignity and purpose.

I have come to understand something very important about the privatization movement that I did not understand at the time when I abandoned it. As I was finishing this book, I heard from my friend and former colleague Joe Viteritti. When we both worked at New York University in the 1990s, Joe and I had written articles and edited books together. We believed that school choice might provide greater opportunities for poor kids. When I later turned against school choice, Joe did not question my motives. We disagreed; he understood. He continued to believe in choice as a means of providing equity. But what was actually happening in one Republican-dominated state after another was the passage of voucher legislation for everyone, rich and poor alike. In reality, vouchers had become welfare for the affluent. Equitable funding was no longer a priority, and the public schools, which were attended by the overwhelming majority of students, were even more underfunded as increasing sums of money were diverted to charters and vouchers.

As I read his latest book in draft form, I suddenly realized that we had been the victims of an elaborate hoax. What we did not understand was that there were dark forces pulling our strings. We were bit actors in a drama that we were not even aware of. While we were out on the public stage making the case for charters and vouchers, reactionary billionaires were watching and cheering us on. They funded a long list of right-wing organizations to promote public disenchantment with all government programs, all government regulations, all efforts to increase equity, and all efforts to make them pay their fair share in taxes. To be sure, there were also centrist billionaires like Bill Gates and Michael Bloomberg who support charters as a free-market, technocratic response to government inefficiency. But they too were bit actors on behalf of right-wing billionaires such as Betsy DeVos, the Walton family, Philip Anschutz, Jeff Yass, Charles Koch and his late brother David, and the evangelical billionaires Tim Dunn and Farris Wilks of Texas. Some of the same people were funding the anti-abortion movement and attacks on LGBT rights. They were the guiding forces behind the privatization movement, and we were unaware that they existed. They must have had a good laugh, watching us make their arguments and believing it was all about "helping poor kids in failing schools." Hahaha! That was never their goal. They wanted to destabilize the public sector, destroy public schools, weaken regulations, and lower their taxes. They wanted to send taxpayer dollars to religious schools, where children could be indoctrinated into their religious faith. Vouchers subsidized wealthy families whose children attended private schools. We didn't expect that. The "equity" talk about "saving poor kids from failing schools" was a hoax. We were fools.

As I have traveled my life's journey, I have had some good fortune and some hard knocks. The worst of all my life's experiences was losing my child to leukemia in 1966 when he was two. That is a blow from which I will never recover. Mary says he is my guardian angel, but I am not sure I believe in such mystical things.

In 2021, I had open heart surgery. The surgery was performed at New York-Presbyterian/Weill Cornell Medical Center, the same hospital where my son Steven died fifty-five years earlier. The surgery was more difficult than I expected. I arrived at the hospital on the evening of April 7. When I regained consciousness, it was almost a week later. During that time, I was sedated in intensive care, and the staff worried about whether I would survive. I was intubated for five days, and according to Mary, they tied down my arms because I was trying to rip the tube out of my throat.

I had curious delusions while I was unconscious. First, I imagined that the nurses were trying to kill me; in one scene, I had a tug of war with them over the surgical tools. Then I believed that I was lying under a clear plastic cover and everyone around me thought I was dead, but I wasn't. When Mary came close, she touched my hand, and she knew I wasn't dead. In my next delusion, I was in fact dead, yet I could see everyone I knew milling around me. I couldn't talk to them, and they couldn't hear me. I was disappointed because I thought I was supposed to go to heaven and get to meet FDR or Lincoln or Jesus, but instead I was just floating around among friends and family. I felt that was unfair.

At one point, when I was semiconscious, I felt certain that there was a framed newspaper on the wall with a headline that said, "RAVITCH DEAD." I vaguely recall a discussion with my son Michael, who insisted I was not dead. He wondered why I thought that the headline was about me and not some other person named Ravitch or why I thought I was important enough to get a banner headline.

I think Steven was my guardian angel after all.

As I mentioned at the beginning of the book, I was the third of eight children. My oldest brother, David, moved to Los Angeles and ran a small printing company until his death a few years ago. My older sister, Adele, went to the University of Alabama to find a husband and married a man from a good family who was subsequently sent to federal prison for drug dealing. They had six children. She stuck by him, and they are now living in a rural town in northwest Florida. My brother Jules worked in the family liquor business, showed off the family's 1927 Rolls-Royce, and raised exotic chickens in Houston until his death in 2025. My brother Robert was a real estate developer in Houston; he committed suicide in 2009, probably because of financial problems. As a friend said at his memorial service, "Suicide is a permanent solution to a temporary problem." My sister Sylvia eloped while she was in high school, had two children, and was a homemaker in Houston; she was often in poor health and lost a lot of weight. Her doctor told her to eat fattening things. One morning in 2014 she made herself a chocolate peanut butter sandwich, and she choked to death. My brother Sandy lives in Florida, where he is happily married and runs a cruise business with his two sons. My brother M. M. lives in Houston; he is a widower and retired from the commercial real estate business. My ex-husband Dick Ravitch remarried happily into a large Irish Catholic family; he adored his wife Kathy, her children and grandchildren. He died in June 2023, two weeks before his ninetieth birthday. His obituary was on the front page of *The New York Times*. Two governors spoke at his funeral, including Phil Murphy, the governor of New Jersey, and Kathy Hochul, the governor of New York, who ordered the flags in New York to be lowered to half-staff to mark his passing. I felt that he was watching and loving every minute of this glorious send-off. Long before his death, we became good friends, and Mary and I shared many family celebrations with Dick and Kathy.

I am very close to my two sons. I consider them dear friends and turn to them frequently for advice and, when needed, for solace or to share good news. After Dick died, they endowed a chair in my name at Wellesley College. It is the Diane Silvers Ravitch '60 Chair in Public Education and the Common Good. That was the fulfillment of a dream.

Mary and I have had a wonderful life together. I have become a part of her wonderful family; we spend Thanksgiving, Christmas, and Easter together. She and I have traveled the world on cruises with two gay male friends—retired elementary school teacher Raymond Rodriguez and his husband, cellist Ted Hoyle—whom we call our "travel husbands." With them, we have explored Bordeaux, Vietnam and Cambodia, the Grand Canyon, and the Danube. Mary and I have also traveled to Argentina, Mexico, the Soviet Union, Ireland, Thailand, Japan, China, and Europe. She has brought me to her church on many occasions. When I had a life-threatening pulmonary embolism in 1998, she baptized me (I am still Jewish). She continues to be my best friend, the person I love and rely on. Through my several health emergencies and in daily life, she was always at my side, protecting me.

I don't have a lot of time left. I will use whatever time I have to fight for the ideals I believe in, to love the people who mean the most to me, to do whatever I can to strengthen democracy in my beloved country, and to advance the common good.

As I watch the sands of time run out, I have a few life lessons to share:

Always tell the truth. As Mark Twain said, "If you tell the truth, you don't have to remember what you said."

If you discover you were wrong, admit it. Don't try to cover up your error. Say you were wrong.

Listen to people with whom you disagree. They might be right.

Keep learning. Never stop learning.

When walking up or down stairs, always hold on to the handrail.

A few years ago, Mary and I bought a plot in Green-Wood Cemetery in Brooklyn. Since she is Catholic and I am Jewish, we wanted to be buried together in a secular cemetery. Our plot faces the gravesite of the family of Boss Tweed. In my first book, *The Great School Wars*, I spent some pages on Boss Tweed's role in the public schools. He began his career as a member of a local school board. As Boss Tweed, he persuaded the state legislature to dissolve the Board of Education and turn the schools into a department of the city, which made it easier for him and his friends to loot the schools' treasury and direct contracts to his cronies. He knew he had to squelch democracy to advance his corrupt schemes.

I see it now: "Excuse me, Boss Tweed, may I interview you?"

ACKNOWLEDGMENTS

In writing a book of memoirs, I accumulated many debts, none of which can be fully repaid. My heartfelt thanks go to my wife Mary. We have been together for 40 years, and she has always exemplified a deep sense of character, faith, and ethics that I strive to emulate. She has been by my side during several life-threatening events, never wavering or faltering. Everyone should have an advocate like her: tenacious, relentless, and loving.

I thank the dear friends who were with me through some of the events described in this book. They include Cecelia Cunningham, Peggy Jayne, Bernadette Hoban, Marianne Kristoff, Carol Burris, Gary Rubinstein, Anthony Cody, Leonie Haimsom, Pasi Sahlberg, Sam Abrams, Ted Hoyle, Ray Rodriguez, Audrey Browne, Maureen Salter, Randi Weingarten, Sharon Kleinbaum, Charles Johnson, and my Wellesley classmates.

Family members have kept me grounded in loving relationships: my surviving siblings Adele, Sandy, and M. M. My ex-husband's close family; Mary's family, who are now my family; my son Joe's wife Sonya and his former wife Lisa; and my son-in-law Daniel Hurewitz.

I want to thank my dear friend Robert Shepherd, who is an editor, author, teacher, and scholar. Although we have never met, we are close virtual friends. Bob offered to edit my books on his own time. He read this book and helped me to sharpen my prose. I thank him for his generosity.

My deep gratitude goes to Gail Hochman, my literary agent, who worked tirelessly to place the book in the right hands. Happily she found Stephen Wesley, senior editor at Columbia University Press, who has given countless hours of his time to making the book a reality. And I thank Gretchen Crary of February Media, who made sure that the book would find its audience.

Diane Ravitch